David Kane is originally from London, and is currently based in Amsterdam where he has lived with his family since 2020. He has written about music and culture since the mid 2000s. His work has been published in *Esquire*, *Dazed*, *CRACK*, *Highsnobiety*, *The Financial Times*, and *Wax Poetics*, among others. David is also the editor-in-chief of the respected streetwear brand Patta's bi-annual magazine.

In 2009, David co-founded *Bonafide Magazine*, where he edited interviews with rappers in the early stages of their careers before they became superstars, including Kendrick Lemar, Tyler, the Creator, and Mac Miller, plus an unexpected encounter with Madvillain.

David has held senior content roles at adidas, Disney, and Microsoft. His work has been recognised with a Webby Award and an Emmy® Award.

WHAT DO YOU CALL IT?

FROM GRASSROOTS TO
THE GOLDEN ERA OF UK RAP

David Kane

First published by Velocity Press 2024

velocitypress.uk

Printed and bound in Great Britain by Clays Ltd, Elcograf S.p.A.

Cover artwork
Trevor Jackson

Typesetting
Paul Baillie-Lane
ingenious-books.com

ISBN: 9781913231613

Contents

Preface

As a teenager growing up on the edge of East London in the mid-late '90s, I was exposed to hip-hop. I'd love to say it started with credible homegrown MCs like London Posse and Tricky, but that wasn't the case. Like most kids at the time, the entry points were bold and obvious US rappers, specifically Tupac and Biggie, and for a while, you either swore allegiance to the East or West Coast, despite being thousands of miles away from either on a playground in South Woodford.

But with time, I broke below the surface. I learned more about the music and its culture through bright and polemical artists like Public Enemy, A Tribe Called Quest, KRS-One, and Mos Def before eventually coming back around to the UK. Another key influence was Soho, the beating heart of London's creative community, which was then a seedy underbelly of peep shows and quirky fashion boutiques, and a mecca for record stores. This was a few years before gentrification swept through the city, particularly Soho. There, mainly through a series of summer odd jobs at my uncle's Daddy Kool Records on Berwick Street—once the oldest reggae shop in Europe—I discovered record shop culture: community-driven, obsessive, and eccentric, mostly in a good way.

A year or two later, my third major musical influence came in the late hours of adolescence: garage music. This was less by choice than design, as all the local clubs played garage, be it smaller raves like Frisky or regional nights like Sidewinder and Garage Nation. But like a musical equivalent to the addictive flavour enhancer MSG, I soon found a taste for the saccharine sound and the scene with its aspirational veneer mixed with a trace of danger. This only accelerated after a 2001 summer holiday with friends in the rowdy Cyprus resort town of Ayia Napa, where MC culture and garage music had truly merged.

The communal aspect of music affected me deeply in those formative teenage years. The rituals, fashion, and, of course, the sound itself crystalised through the vocal timber and imagination of the MC: from the cavernous cadence of Flowdan, then of the underground garage collective Pay As U Go Cartel and a future Grammy Award winner, through to the frenetic flows of a young Dizzee Rascal over a revelatory new sound of staccato beats. Parallel to this, were the likes of Roots Manuva, Jehst and Skinnyman, spearheading a resurgent UK hip-hop scene at the turn of the century. Although stylistically different, they all made rap music—sharing antecedents to rave and sound system culture of the past—steeped in a sense of Britishness. Yet more than two decades later, one crucial question appears through the fog of memory, serving as a catalyst and dialectic riddle: Who are we, and what is it to be seen as belonging to this country?

Like all good art, rap music has the potential to hold a mirror to society, to tell truths, however difficult they might be, and to show the beauty and ugliness that can exist in us all. Undoubtedly, UK rap music, be it hip-hop, grime, or, more recently, drill, is born from the Black experience, and as a white man, I know I'm a guest at this party.

As a Jew I do know how it feels to be the othered. But I've not been stopped and searched for no legitimate reason, nor have I faced statistical evidence of systemic professional obstruction (not beyond the personal, anyway). So, I cannot pretend to have a truly insider perspective, nor will I try. Instead, I'll stick to the facts and strive to keep *What Do You Call It?* aligned with the historical truths as I—together with the help of the dozens of rappers, DJs, producers, writers, and record label folk who have been kind enough to spare their time to the book—see them, but not to speculate any further than the literature and historical record allows.

Initially, the scope of this book was supposed to cover a twenty-year period, beginning in 1999. I wanted to start there because it was the turn of the millennium, a time fraught with tension (remember the 'millennium bug'?), political machinations, and creative possibilities, where technology and culture were changing faster than it had for decades. British rap music, or UK hip-hop as it mainly was known back then, was finding a new identity through a series of blistering EPs, albums, and mixtapes from brilliant but, at best, modestly successful artists. This was also just a few years before the advent of grime, the most influential genre of British music since rave and punk before that. Selfishly, it was also the era I went from being a teenager to standing on the precipice of middle age.

But as I dug deeper, I realised I had to go further back, extending the scope to the start of the 1980s, when rap music landed on our odd little island, imported through the electro-driven hip-hop of Afrika Bambaataa, shaped by sound system culture, inspired by punk and accelerated by rave. This change of direction was mainly thanks to conversations with venerable OGs, particularly Jazzie B, Normski, and Trevor Jackson—who is also responsible for the striking cover art for the book—sending me on new and unexpected rabbit holes. Yet, as I acknowledge, it is a whistlestop tour of the '80s, a time that isn't very well documented in the context of British rap music and deserves greater attention.

The story ends in 2019, the year Stormzy headlined Glastonbury, Dave and Little Simz released landmark albums, UK drill became a surprisingly popular export, and British rap music became big business—and briefly before another bug, the COVID-19 pandemic, arrived and spun the world off its axis. As I finish writing this book, five years later, UK rap is now firmly part of pop music and the greater hip-hop canon, despite how unlikely it looked for decades.

Through the scenes, political machinations, classic albums and mixtapes, anthemic singles, long-forgotten but important labels, and the artists that made the art, *What Do You Call It?* will endeavour to find out how we got there.

Most of all, this is a story about the amazing music that existed in the cracks of culture and went on to take over the world.

Chapter 1

How's Life in London

Every thriving music scene starts somewhere, and that somewhere is usually in the underground. But where and when did the UK rap scene begin? Is it possible to pinpoint a precise location, song, or artist in the same way DJ Kool Herc's block parties in the Bronx are seen as hip-hop's inception made flesh, or how "Rapper's Delight" by The Sugarhill Gang is widely accepted as hip-hop's first commercial hit? The short answer is, no, it is not. The extended answer is far more complex.

A Borrowed Culture: Duck Rock, DJ Newtrament, and Unexpected Beginnings

Let's start with the music. It can't be too difficult to find the first hip-hop track recorded and released in the UK, can it? Malcolm McLaren's *Duck Rock* album is a bouillabaisse of unexpected samples, globalist musicians, and a nursery rhyme freaked fresh to use the day's parlance in the lead single "Buffalo Girls." McLaren—the son of upper-class Jewish parents who was brought up by his grandmother in Stoke

Newington, North London—knew a thing or three about adapting and assimilating to the culture of the day in order not only to survive but thrive.

A proud, card-carrying member of the Situationist International movement, look up "music impresario" in the proverbial dictionary and a photo of McLaren's curly red hair and imperious grin is what you will see. For here is the schmoozer-provocateur who hustled his way to the starting line of three cycles of popular music through the groups he managed (not to mention the influential fashion boutique, Sex, that he opened together with then-wife Vivienne Westwood) in the 1970s and '80s. First, he latched onto the glam rock of New York Dolls second, he launched the incendiary Sex Pistols, turning them into the belligerent mouthpiece of the British punk movement; and finally, he found hip-hop at an Afrika Bambaataa block party in the Bronx. He brought the foetus of an idea back with him to Blighty: "DJs who use record players like instruments."[1] McLaren insisted that this was the new punk rock.

Duck Rock has gone on to become the story of legend, but the fact that the record was even made in the first place is quite a mystery. How McLaren, who had no experience as an actual musician, convinced Charisma, then a major label, to part with £100,000 to fund a solo album speaks to the powers of his yarn-spinning. McLaren is listed as co-producer alongside Trevor Horn, with contributions from Anne Dudley, J. J. Jeczalik, Mahlathini, the Mahotella Queens, and the Boyoyo Boys from South Africa. Session musicians included Peruvian pipe players, Colombian marching bands, Dominican wedding musicians, a family band from rural Tennessee, and New York hip-hop duo The World's Famous Supreme Team.

Much has been made of the fact that none of the South African musicians were credited. As cover art contributor, a then relatively unknown Keith Haring diplomatically put it, "Perhaps it wouldn't be a Malcolm McLaren project if it didn't have a distinctly queasy underside."[2] McLaren responded to accusations of cultural appropriations by saying that the African and South American musicians had been paid very well—"they screwed us" is how Horn recalls it in a 2022 interview with *The Guardian*—and the album helped raise the profile of the musicians in the West.[3]

What is and isn't considered cultural appropriation is murky ground open for debate. Still, there is little dispute that *Duck Rock* helped introduce a generation of British youths to hip-hop and mesmerising music from across the globe. More importantly, it provided a striking visual for hip-hop thanks to the "Buffalo Gals" music video. As soon-to-ascend British MC Rodney P later described it, "In that video, we got to see body popping for the first time, break dancing for the first time, kids putting lino on the pavement, the graffiti writers and the DJs. All the elements were there. Malcolm McLaren was a big part of the UK hip-hop story, though he's often written out of it."[4]

Filmed on New York City streets that flow like a river, its current carrying people along on its inexorable wave driven by the nascent energy of hip-hop, the music video features the Rock Steady Crew popping and locking alongside Vivienne Westwood models performing the Buffalo Gals dance. McLaren prances around emceeing (or speaking?) the chorus in a hat made famous by Pharrell more than thirty years later. A kaleidoscope of vocal samples and yelps, 808 snaps and record scratches by The World's Famous Supreme Team; "Buffalo Gals" was the klaxon call of a new movement.

"Buffalo Gals" is credited to McLaren and The World's Famous Supreme Team, with co-production from Trevor Horn and writing by Anne Dudley. Much like the album, the single demonstrates remarkable prescience for hip-hop's influence and how global pop music is consumed forty years later. In the modern day, the Nigerian artist Burna Boy, UK rapper Dave, and the Spanish-speaking singer-songwriter Rosalía are as likely to appear on the same uber-popular streaming playlists, channelling music from their homelands as they are on each other's tracks. Not for the first time did Malcolm appear to be on to something. For these reasons, "Buffalo Gals," released on 19 November 1982, makes a good argument for the first British rap record. However, to describe what McLaren is saying as rapping would be a severe stretch. Besides, chronologically speaking, it's barely on the podium for the first UK rap song.

One week before "Buffalo Gals" came out, Dizzy Heights' "Christmas Rapping" was released on Polydor (a label that doesn't necessarily cover itself in glory in the history of UK rap music, as we'll discover). Despite its terrible title—a "g" appendage to Kurtis Blow's 1979 track "Christmas Rappin'"—it features a fairly credible, if somewhat derivative rap by the early London-bred MC. The song peaked at number 49 in the charts in the week leading up to Christmas and then pretty much sunk without a trace. Rumour has it that DJ and rapper Newtrament recorded "London Bridge is Falling Down" first, but "Christmas Rapping" was released to maximise Christmas pre-sales and interest in the new electro-driven hip-hop sound proving popular.

Now, "London Bridge is Falling Down" would have been worthy of the mantle of the first UK rap record to be released.

On the track, Newtrament—whose name is a nod to the popular Nutrament drink—revisited the nursery rhyme of the same name, sped up the bassline from Grand Wizard Theodore & the Fantastic Romantic Five's 1980 single "Can I Get a Soul Clap," and rapped in heavy vocoder about the corruption of "the boys in blue" and the pretence of electoral politics. Arguing that the "Election fever on all four (TV) channels... Red or blue?... Either one, it don't really matter," he ends the song with the line, "The truth of the matter, the people at the bottom wish there was a ladder."

"London Bridge is Falling Down" was released by Jive in 1983, the same year Margaret Thatcher gave the Conservative Party its most decisive election victory in half a century. The song contained all the elements of a truly UK rap song: social and local news stories rapped using familiar slang over a nursery rhyme riff every '70s and '80s kid would have grown up with. For bonus points, there's even a version where Newtrament raps sans vocoder in his own voice, a Cockney monotone.

Not much is known about Newtrament. His real name is Bertram Johnson, and his Discogs entry describes a nomadic artist who liked to skate, DJ, and MC, and spent time squatting across London and in Bristol, setting up sound systems with various crews, including The Wild Bunch (more on them later) before moving to the States. Fast forward to 2018, and he appeared in a short documentary, *Newtrament Scapegoat* by Charlie Marbles, where he was living rough on the streets of central London.

There is no explanation of how Bertram got there, but it's a cruel twist of fate to see him at the bottom and nowhere near the "ladder." To quote Oscar Wilde, "Life imitates art far more than art imitates life." Although he had lost none of his drive for social causes, he is seen in the doc trying to attend a *public meeting* on crime and anti-social behaviour at Conway Hall.

Despite his eloquence, he is rudely ejected from the meeting and eventually escorted out by the police before making the astute observation: "It says 'Ethical' and 'Humanity' on the building, and you've not reached either of the standards."

According to Discogs, "London Bridge is Falling Down" was his only official release, but there were at least eleven versions of the song, and it has been featured in various compilations. I hope he saw those royalties. Putting aside his overall contribution to music, to use modern parlance, it is highly problematic to see Bertram—a Black man who has as good a claim as any to have pioneered hip-hop in the UK—in this state, while commentators were surprised that Malcolm McLaren *only* had £169,750 in his estate when he died in 2010, controversially none of which he left to his only child. Yet none of these tracks—"Buffalo Gals," "Christmas Rapping," nor "London Bridge is Falling Down"—were the first hip-hop tracks to be recorded and released in the UK.

After conversations with many ageing B(ritish)-Boys, getting lost down Reddit bunny holes and sketchy 480p YouTube rips of singles, I have found what I believe to be the first recorded and released UK rap song.

Released in early 1980, "Dallas" by The Mexicano was recorded in The Coach House Recording Studio, Stamford Hill, London, just a stone's throw from where Malcolm McLaren grew up in Stoke Newington. The Mexicano was the alias of Rudy Grant, the Guyanese-British reggae deejay and singer who was the younger brother of Eddy "Electric Avenue" Grant. The song was produced and mixed by three brothers from West Bromwich, near Birmingham: Charles, Steve, and Irwin Sylvester, a drummer who achieved modest success in the late '70s/'80s disco soul band J.A.L.N. (Just Another Lonely Night) Band, previously known as Superbad.

"Dallas" sits at the funk, disco, and rap intersection, and you can almost hear the '70s fashion: cosmic afros, swinging bell bottoms, and superfly maxi dresses. In short, it's more Soul Train than Stamford Hill. The song is fun, with spoken-word lyrics bordering on the asinine as two friends debate what discotheque to go to on a Saturday night before deciding to stay home and watch the popular TV show *Dallas* instead. The Mexicano then finds himself rapping in first person as scheming oil baron J.R. Ewing, the show's central protagonist, as the countertenor chorus (possibly courtesy of The Mexicano, there is so little information it's difficult to say otherwise) playfully chirps "JR, the man some people love to hate," making the first rap song recorded and released in the UK an unlikely character-driven concept track.

Rudy released three albums as The Mexicano before bowing out shortly after this single and making music under his own name. If nothing else, "Dallas" demonstrates the work of first-generation immigrants from across the UK, collaborating to create a new variation of Black music through the oversized influence of electro in particular and American popular culture in general. "Dallas" may have been the first UK rap record, but it wasn't where the scene started. However, we must know what happened before in order to better understand what happened next.

* * *

From Social Systems to Sound Systems

Following the travesties of World War II, the British government encouraged mass immigration from the former colonies of the British Empire and Commonwealth to compensate for shortages in the UK labour market.

Attracted by the supposed opportunities of the "mother country," many Afro-Caribbean people emigrated to the UK to look for work. Among the first wave of immigrants were Caribbeans arriving via the former German passenger ship the HMT Empire Windrush on June 22, 1948, thus known as the Windrush Generation.

Despite being granted the right of entry and settlement in the UK thanks to the British Nationality Act 1948—and many of the men had previously served in the British army—the emigrants were met with intolerance, hostility, and racism in their new *home.* Job opportunities were scarce. Either working for British Rail, the NHS, or doing low-grade and poorly paid jobs that few white Britons would do, the promise of "opportunity" was a hollow one.

The social geographer Ceri Peach estimates that the number of people in Britain born in the West Indies grew from 15,000 in 1951 to 172,000 in 1961. In 1962, the UK enacted the Commonwealth Immigrants Act, restricting the entry of immigrants, and by 1972, only holders of work permits or people with parents or grandparents born in the United Kingdom could gain access to the country.[5]

Now, I won't get into the complexities of the Windrush Generation too much here because it's articulated far more expansively and with greater credibility than I could muster elsewhere. Suffice to say, Caribbean people were excluded from much of the social and economic life in Great Britain. Alongside the discrimination, an ideological process was taking place. But through perseverance, they began to adapt and adjust some of the institutions they brought with them—like the church and the "pardner" system, a community-saving plan in place of bank lending or credit—to their new home. By the 1970s, despite the restrictive measures, an entire generation of Britons with Afro-Caribbean heritage now existed, creating a new sense of identity and contributing to British society in virtually every field. And the impact on music was seismic.

For more than forty years, the pulse of Caribbean music has animated the capital's sonic nervous system. from reggae to jungle, through to hip-hop and grime. And one of the first musicians to crystalise the duality of the Black British experience on wax was reggae singer and DJ Smiley Culture, real name David Emmanuel.

In his provocative book, *There Ain't No Black in the Union Jack*, Paul Gilroy—regarded as the UK's preeminent scholar of race, culture, and nationalism—analysed Smiley's 1984 single, "Cockney Translation." Describing the track, which also serves as a Jamaican's guide to cockney rhyming slang, Gilroy writes: "The implicit joke beneath the surface of the record, was that though many of London's working-class Blacks were cockney by birth and experience … their 'race' denied them access to [that] social category."[6] In Gilroy's eyes, "Cockney Translation" was a sign of his generation's emergent, hybrid Britishness.

As Jazzie B explained, beyond showcasing the Black British experience to a broader audience, "'Cockney Translation' provided an insight into what was happening on the underground sound system scene."[7] Whereas in America, jazz music and the funk of James Brown and Sly Stone were extremely influential on hip-hop, in Britain, reggae and punk were highly popular and inspiring genres for youths in the 1970s and 1980s, particularly in Black and working-class communities, so it's no wonder these two genres were so formative to UK rap music.

Released the same year as "Cockney Translation," Smiley Culture's follow-up single, "Police Officer," was a reggae meets proto-rap masterpiece accessible enough to score a UK no. 12 while exposing police harassment to the broader public. And in a tragedy of mimesis, Smiley Culture died in 2011 while in police custody.

Smiley had been charged the previous year with conspiracy to supply cocaine. The incident occurred just one and a half hours after police arrived with a search warrant at his house. The post-mortem revealed he died from a single stab wound to the heart, supposedly in a case of suicide. According to a report at the time, the Independent Police Complaints Commission (IPCC) investigation into Smiley's death condemned the raid as "significantly flawed and compels the MPS (Metropolitan Police Service) to overhaul the way they plan and execute future drug seizures."[8]

Many of the rappers we will discuss in this book owe a great debt to Smiley Culture.

* * *

British hip-hop started as a borrowed culture. Electro was formative to the music, as Roland TR-808 drum machines and simple lyrics sluiced through a vocoder, resulting in 125 beats per mutant funk that compelled kids to the dance floor like flies to a fire. It might seem twee now, but break dancing was a revelation at the time, marked by startling body contortions, shocks of neon adidas and Hummel "jogging suits" (old speak for tracksuits), head spins, locking and popping.

In his rambunctious 1984 report for *The Face* magazine, "Electro: The Beat That Won't be Beaten," journalist Paul Rambali declared: "Rapid and solid, fast and frantic, the Electro beat is the new Sound of the City – as stimulating as the urban jungle that spawned it. Dismissed as a craze, a novelty, denounced as sinister robot music devoid of 'real' emotion, it proved to be a tough seed that took root on England's pavements … No doubt about it though, this is the biggest dance craze to hit the UK since Robotics."[9]

The clubs to go to included Mudd Club, Phillips, and Titanic in West London. Thanks to the convergence of punk, reggae, fashion, magazines like *The Face, i-D, Blues & Soul*, and the diversity of cultures in the capital, London felt like the centre of the universe and ripe for hip-hop when it arrived in the early '80s. Radio DJs like Mastermind Herbie, Mike Allen and his Capital Rap Show, Greg Wilson in Manchester, and Tim Westwood and the then-pirate Kiss FM he co-owned helped the music travel. However, it took a few years before they embraced homegrown acts.

DJs often had their own sound systems; two of the most prominent coming into the decade were Saxon International in South London—the iconic sound system that helped define a British identity for reggae music, and where the likes of Smiley Culture and Tippa Irie sharpened their *deejaying* skills—and Mastermind Roadshow, often cited as one of the forebears of electro-hip-hop.

But distinguishing itself from what was happening in America, the undisputed home and progenitor of hip-hop, one sound system proved most vital in extending the Black British music continuum and—even if it happened indirectly—providing UK rap with the energy and confidence to create its own identity.

"A happy face, a thumpin' bass, for a lovin' race."

At the intersection of reggae, soul, rave, and hip-hop was the inimitable Funki Dred, the sound system belonging to North London music collective Soul II Soul, led by Jazzie B. A teenage tape operator working for the pop star Tommy Steele, Jazzie B was one of the few Black people working in London's recording studios at the time, and, as he tells me, he "was always on this quest sonically, searching for the perfect detailed sound." Jazzie was bitten by the music bug early. Born in London to Antiguan immigrants, the youngest of five brothers, music was central to the household, with three of his brothers having their own sound system.

Yet most sound systems of the late '70s were either centred around reggae or soul. Rarely did the two meet, but there was a fluid music policy in Jazzie's house: "We listened to Joni Mitchell's 'Big Yellow Taxi.' We listened to Englebert Humperdinck because my mum liked him. I found Benny and the Jets, Bowie."

I speak with Jazzie for nearly two hours, calling from his home studio where records and various platinum-selling plaques surrounded him. Elaborating on his eclectic taste, he tells me, "When you have rice and peas and oxtail soup and all them things all the time, fuck me, sometimes you want a cheeseburger. You know what I mean?" (As he explained and exercised during our interview, Jazzie is fond of analogies, and some land better than others.)

Beyond the music, "There was no one thing I was affiliated with. So whether it was being a soul boy, reggae boy, punk, or Seventh Day Adventist, it was a combination of all those things, which I think was a reflection of me growing up in London, the shopping window of the rest of the world." By not fitting in, Jazzie would go on to form and lead a tribe of outsiders, making him a counterculture icon at a time when "the whole world was changing, and we were part of that hurricane."

He cites the deflated climate of the UK following the Falklands War as a pivotal moment. Aged just nineteen, Jazzie saw an opportunity in the free markets of Thactherism, despite the harsh realities facing many young people in Britain's inner cities: "Maggie Thatcher's in power, and we're coming out of fossil fuel and the police were stopping and searching all of us at that point."

Jazzie was a savvy networker, able to collaborate with people from across the capital's ethnic and class spectrum. He also had the vision and fortitude to expand the Soul II Soul sound system from the blues clubs into a mini-universe that encompassed music, clothing (sold across twelve shops in Camden), and warehouse parties by the mid-'80s, where Jazzie "made a lot of money until the whole gang thing started getting out of hand." By this point, his own profile had grown as a DJ. He had a monthly residency at Mars Bar in New York and, as a guest of the Yellow Magic Orchestra, frequently flew to Tokyo, "playing in their clubs, giving them a flavour of what we're doing in London."

These myriad experiences helped him appreciate the growing hip-hop scene, which he observed as "A sound that connected people." Jazzie saw what was happening in hip-hop—"rebellious," young communities expressing their creativity—as being part of and analogous to running the Soul II Soul sound system. "It's the same fucking thing," he says. "Look at people like Smiley Culture and even Rose Windross. She was a singer but also an MC from the scene."

Jazzie B's eclectic, community-focused ethos was crystalised at The Africa Centre in Covent Garden, where Soul II Soul began hosting their legendary club night on Sundays. The Soul II Soul sound was original, new, infectious, and above all a UK thing. Everyone from Prince to Fela Kuti would come through the door, listening to tunes spun by a young Norman Jay and Trevor "Madhatter" Nelson. The venue's capacity was limited to just 300 people, but close to 1,000 kids would turn up every week. Those who didn't get in took to breakdancing outside and graffiti writing nearby, which often caught the unwanted attention of the police. Jazzie laughs at the memory: "All the controversy that went with it only made it more popular."

One of those attendees was the photographer, TV presenter, and DJ Normski. Three years younger than Jazzie, Normski described the Soul II Soul sound system and the nights at The Africa Centre as "Transcending the music for a long time. It was a tribe and felt like being part of a movement." The weekly gathering at The Africa Centre only lasted a few years—it was shut down due to "environmental issues", due to noise complaints from neighbours, which is odd given its location in Covent Garden, central London and Jazzie suspects nefarious play from the police—but it was there that he made connections with executives from Virgin Records, facilitating Soul II Soul's almost inevitable transition to pop stars.

Taking shape as a hip-hop-infused R&B and soul group, Soul II Soul sold tens of millions of albums, topped numerous charts with "Keep On Movin'" and "Back To Life (However Do You Want Me)," and won several Grammy Awards in 1990. Beyond the numbers, Jazzie went on to produce music for the likes of James Brown and Nas, and eventually received an OBE in 2011. Most importantly, he built a legacy as a human router for scenes and sounds—a music community pioneer.

Finally, a hip-hop scene had begun to emerge in the UK, and alongside the Soul II Soul night at The Africa Centre, two other events were vital. The first was UK Fresh at Wembley Arena in the summer of 1986. More than eighty artists performed, and the show featured the cream of the hip-hop crop: Afrika Bambaataa, Mantronix, Roxanne Shanti, and new acts like World Class Wreckin' Cru—the flamboyant, silk suit-wearing electro group that included a very young Dr. Dre and Yella before they formed N.W.A. Seeing all these American artists together—not to mention breakdancers and graffiti artists—must have been a revelation tantamount to a UFO sighting for the 16,000 fans in attendance on that balmy July night in London.

The promotional team behind UK Fresh was a combination of Capital Radio 95.8 FM, DJ Mike Allen—whose influential Allen Army Radio allowed listeners to vote on the weekly chart, an innovation at the time—and the StreetSounds record label. The creation of self-admiring music industry entrepreneur Morgan Khan, StreetSounds specialised in soul, electro, and early hip-hop, combining expensive US import singles into affordable vinyl compilations for b-boys and girls in the UK, often mixed by Allen or Mastermind Herbie.

Khan, the son of an Indian father and Welsh mother, started the label from his parents' garage in Ealing in 1981. Within three years, StreetSounds had relocated to Soho, generating nearly £10 million in annual turnover. Khan seemed quite the contrarian, telling the *NME*[10] that "somedays I get overwhelmed with my own importance," as excited by hip-hop and "specialist music" as he was by the "great" Margaret Thatcher. Khan launched various offshoots of StreetSounds and eventually *Street Scene,* an expensively produced "club music" magazine that suffered significant losses and caused the label to shut down in 1988.

A colossal ego and a fondness for the Iron Lady might be why Morgan Khan and his label are overlooked in the UK's rap story. Yet Khan serves as a helpful reminder of the colourful characters that existed in UK hip-hop at the time and continue to do so, a scene led by Black Britons, with space for the Asian and white working-class youths, left abandoned by neo-liberal politics in the 1980s and beyond.

If UK Fresh 86 was a visceral celebration of hip-hop culture, the 87 Def Jam Tour was an exercise in lyrical dexterity and showmanship. The lineup was more focused, just three acts consisting of LL Cool J (billed as the headliner), Erik B & Rakim, and Public Enemy, whose hype was hotter than hell just a few months after the release of their debut album, *Yo! Bum Rush The Show.*

The 87 Def Jam Tour went across the country, starting at the Hammersmith Odeon in London. It's a show that came up time and again during the research of this book. Public Enemy was effectively the warm-up act, but Chuck D, Flava Flav, Professor Griff, and Terminator X conquered London that night. In grainy videos of the performances on YouTube,

Chuck D's lyrics arrive slowly and with clarity, delivering lines memories can latch onto.

Public Enemy also used the show to test-run a few tracks from their incendiary follow-up album, *It Takes a Nation of Millions to Hold Us Back*, which would include live sounds from the London show in the album opener "Countdown to Armageddon." A dramatic call to arms, it was a warning sign of the potential for hip-hop as a political movement.

In another YouTube clip from the tour, Chuck D teases the audience, "Whistle posse in the house. Check this out: all the people who love the prime minister, be quiettttt." Normski, who had a front-row seat taking pictures from the photographers' pit, recalls to me, "You've never heard anything so loud. We heard the records, but we've never seen it with so much ferocity in the flesh. By the end of the night, everyone was so pumped. That would have inspired everyone to go and do something badass."

"Make something of yourself, have your own story"

I met Normski at his flat in Victoria Park, East London. Well into his sixth decade, some grey hairs sprout around his sideburns and from beneath his navy blue beanie hat. But he's lost none of the youthful energy that made the photographer turned TV broadcaster one of the most recognisable figures from the hip-hop and dance music scenes between the late '80s through to the mid-'90s. He speaks at a million miles per minute, barely finishing one idea before bouncing onto another.

Born Norman Anderson, Normski grew up in Kilburn in a second-generation Jamaican household where freshly immigrated extended family would often come and stay while finding their feet in their new home. There would be "Singing, church, and stuff like that. I was born with music," he reminisces, adding, "The kind of people I've grown up around have all had character, which was very much drummed into you. Make something of yourself, have your own story."

Normski paints a picture of a fairly idyllic existence, comfortable with his dual Jamaican-English existence growing up in the 1970s. As kids do, he tried out a bunch of different hobbies, from building model train sets to riding BMX to learning various instruments, before discovering a camera. He soon graduated from taking photos at "summer fetes" to the jazz clubs of Soho. At one point, he shows me a stunning motion print of the saxophonist Wayne Shorter he took for *Wire* magazine in the early '80s: "I was in the vicinity, being this cool, young Black photographer, wanting to be a photographer for the love of actual photography."

But he fell deep for hip-hop. "Forever, American TV was the fucking *Brady Bunch,* and then we started seeing programmes with Black kids on them," he says, name-checking the ealy hip-hop films *Wild Style* and *Beat Street*, calling the latter "the coolest movie." He also points to "the post-punk people," crediting Vivienne Westwood, Malcolm McLaren, and their connection with Blondie and Fab 5 Freddy in New York, for helping usher in the new: "They're like the rebels of their time who tune into the rebels of the next time."

In hip-hop, Normski found "a new subject that I totally related to." But at the first few live shows, he admits to being shy around artists who would often clam up at the sight of a camera, saying "There was an awful lot of looking and wondering what to take pictures of." With time, his confidence grew along with his camera skills, eventually garnering him the nickname: "The man with the golden shutter."

Fashion played a big part in projecting his louder-than-life persona; a style he described to me as "Rudeboy sort of English-centric clothing, with Italian designer leather." He soon caught the attention of broadcaster and journalist Janet Street-Porter.

From 1988 to 1994, Normski was one of the hosts of *DEF II*, a BBC2 magazine show for Gen X produced by Street-Porter that aired innovative comedies like *Red Dwarf* alongside US imports *Ren & Stimpy, The Fresh Prince Of Bel-Air* and *Wayne's World* sketches.

Normski explains that the concept behind *DEF II* was to "break new ground and boundaries in television broadcasting." It would give the audience "the definitive form of how television, particularly for young people, should look."

But the undisputed jewel in the *DEF II* crown was *Dance Energy*. Filmed in Manchester, the magazine format show would feature "different elements of the scene: the fashion, the club scenes, and people doing cool stuff." The "cool stuff" would be anything from segments on the sneaker brand wars in the US to Frankfurt's gay club scene to legendary live performances from rap and rave acts, including Naughty by Nature and The Prodigy in their first live TV performance, which required an epilepsy warning. The show was a huge success, connecting with as many as one million people per week, going well beyond the intended audience of teenagers.

The show was chaotic and edgy in a natural way. Often, this led to tense, last-minute negotiations between headstrong artists and the show's producers. Normski remembers an appearance by Hijack, a "very controversial UK hip-hop group on the edge of censorship regarding how they went about themselves. Wearing bulletproof vests and the whole balaclava look, the BBC authorities couldn't handle that." Showing violence or sexism was non-negotiable, but at the end of the day everyone dancing in the audience seemed to be having the time of their lives.

At the beating heart of it all was Normski, whether it be his improv raps connecting segments or his cutting Style Police observations from the streets of the UK, Normski was on a mission to bulldoze a space for hip-hop in the mainstream without compromising on the culture. Ultimately, the show's success would prove its undoing, as many musicians wanted to perform on *Dance Energy* rather than the saccharine prime time of BBC1's *Top of the Pops.* His work on the show was highly prescient. While we now live in a world where people "curate" culture with a few thumb taps on Instagram, Normski put in the hard graft to create and foster culture. Thirty years later, he is still stopped by people across the country who fondly remember the show.

Alongside his work on television, Normski photographed some of the biggest names in hip-hop, but he was committed to helping the local scene thrive. He provided many first-generation UK rappers with a distinctive visual identity. Among them were the group Cookie Crew—the duo of MC Remedee (Debbie Pryce) and Susie Q (Susan Banfield)—two vital female voices in the first decade of UK hip-hop. Formed in Clapham, South London in 1983, and winning a national rap championship at the Wag Club, the pair steadily built up their reputation, from recording studio sessions with John Peel to touring with Afrika Bambaattaa. In 1988, they had an unexpected hit with "Rok da House," where they appeared as guest vocalists on the single by production trio the Beatmasters.

The song peaked at number 5 on the UK charts and is often described as the first-ever hip-house track.

Although they never performed the song live, Susie later admits, "We were very adamant that they would not associate us with the track."[11] Cookie Crew felt the song was unfaithful to their hip-hop roots, creating an inaccurate portrayal when rappers in the UK were still finding their identity. However, it didn't stop them from releasing two albums and collaborating on music with Gang Starr and Stetsasonic in the States. Like many of Cookie Crews' peers, their vocal delivery had an American tone, but the content of their message was distinctly Black British, with all three singles from their 1989 debut album *Born This Way* (London Records)—"Born This Way (Let's Dance)," "Black Is the Word," and "From the South" in particular paying homage to their South London home.

They were also passionate about the wider issues facing Black people, regularly performing at anti-apartheid gigs and releasing music alongside other UK rappers like B.R.O.T.H.E.R (Black Rhyme Organisation To Help Equal Rights), where all the artists' royalties were donated to the African National Congress (ANC).

Speaking with the author Aursa Quereshi, in her discerning book *Flip the Script: How Women Came To Rule Hip-Hop,* Susie explains that the Cookie Crew's time in America was often spent educating folk, saying, "A lot of the people we met didn't realise that there were actually Black people in England... We were educating them on who we were, British, but British Caribbean too."[12]

Born This Way was recorded in New York, and Cookie Crew were among the first UK rappers to try and break the US, which didn't go down well with fans or critics back home.

As Susie later explained, "There was a lot of jealousy and bickering on the scene and talk about staying true to the game. But for us, we were officially a business. We'd given up our day jobs and went to New York to learn from them about the whole creative industry."[13]

Cookie Crew released their second and final album, *Fade to Black*, in 1991. The duo cited the pressure from their record label to conform to pop stereotypes as the reason they stopped releasing new music together. Debbie and Susie continue to work in the music industry today, leaning on their experience to educate others, particularly Black female artists, to push through the barriers of misogyny in the music industry. We'll come back to this in more detail later.

Britcore, Music of Life, and the First Generation of UK Rappers

Teaming up with Simon Harris and DJ Froggy's Music of Life label, Normski went beyond photography to creative direction. This included collaborating with the dashing Derek B, who parlayed his DJ residency at the Wag Club (notorious for its selective door policy) into being the first poster-boy of UK rap. After achieving major chart success with "Good Groove" and "Bad Young Brother" (both released in 1988), Derek B became the first English rapper to appear on *Top of the Pops*, an achievement all the more remarkable at a time when the mainstream was dismissing hip-hop (nevermind UK hip-hop) as a passing fad at best.

Bearing the most striking aesthetic of that generation was the baritone-voiced MC Duke, whose music merged murky sci-fi atmospherics and proto-rave synths (he would later release music as I.C.3. on the Shut Up And Dance label) along with old funk and dialogue snippets from film and TV, as he did on the frenetic Britcore classic "Running Man (Kunta Kinte)," which sampled from *Roots,* the American TV mini-series that told the story of the fictional slave character Kunta Kinte." His Afrocentric debut album, *Organised Rhyme,* featured a regal-looking Duke wearing a three-piece tweed suit, flat hat, walking cane, and a vast gold medallion. "African gentleman' is how Normski describes it, adding, "He looked fabulous. A lot of the artists in the early days were very culture-conscious, and that came across in the attire."

When I ask Normski for his most memorable photoshoot, he's unequivocal: "Hijack. Probably because they were dressed in full SAS style, carrying a six-foot samurai sword. We climbed over this wall in a derelict area near Brixton," which is when the police showed up on the scene. With the group members looking like burglars in their matching black balaclavas, Normski's "heart raced," but he convinced the cops that the sword was just a prop for a record cover photo, adding that the end result helped. "The photograph is really powerful."

* * *

Hijack and London Posse emerged around the same time in the late '80s, but their approach to rap and career paths took quite distinct turns, providing a rich allegory of the formal years for British hip-hop.

Hailing from South London, Hijack consisted of DJ Supreme, DJ Undercover, Ulysses, Agent Fritz, Agent Clueso, and Kamanchi Sly, who a decade later reinvented himself as

Unknown MC and scored a hit as part of his brother's garage group, DJ Pied Piper and the Masters of Ceremonies. (More on them later.) The crew announced themselves with the early UK hip-hop classic "Style Wars," released on Music of Life in 1988.

Alongside acts like Caveman, Gunshot, Silver Bullet, The Criminal Minds, Hijack is often credited as being part of the "Britcore" movement—a term reportedly coined by German fans excited by the British hardcore hip-hop sound—a sub-genre that is heavily indebted to the imported sounds of US hip-hop, especially The Bomb Squad, horrorcore, and the nascent breakbeat that could be heard in illegal raves throughout the UK in the late 1980s.

Originally conceived as a trio of turntablists, Hijack climbed quickly from bedroom battles to releasing records, partly thanks to playing live shows with Tim Westwood and the exposure granted on his influential Kiss FM show. Indeed, it was Westwood who introduced DJ Supreme to Ice-T, having played "Hold No Hostage," a demonstration of hyper-aggressive raps over hard-as-nails drums, to him on his radio show in 1989. A meeting was set up the next day between Supreme, Kamanchi Sly, and Ice-T at London's Wag Club. Ice-T was impressed.[14]

"Ice had the rock chain with the pistol on the end of it, the Kangol, looking very confident, and he was basically selling us America," remembers Supreme. "He was like, 'Yo, you guys are going to take over the world.' He saw us as the UK equivalent of Public Enemy. He saw straight away that this could go outside the UK and be bigger and broader.'"

Ice-T offered to sign the group to his Rhyme Syndicate record label. Hijack quickly went to work on their debut album, *The Horns of Jericho,* the most anticipated album in the short history of British hip-hop so far. An ambitious group, they vowed in rhyme to "reign supreme as the British nightmare to America's dream." However, a combination of "Cop Killer" era politics and major record label machinations scuppered the sentiment, repeatedly delaying *The Horns of Jericho* before it was finally released in 1991 via Warner Bros. Records. But crucially and cruelly, the album was only released in Europe.

Like Blak Twang's album, *Dettwork SouthEast* several years later, this chain of events helped later frame *The Horns of Jericho* as a quasi-lost classic and a revered ahead-of-its-time document of UK hip-hop. In these formative years, rap acts in the UK were often the victim of dependencies, music industry politics, and the deeper systemic racism that held Black British youth back when controlling their musical output.

Although there might be another reason why Britcore—something of an alcove within a niche, especially in a historical context—isn't better known, due to the emergence and subsequent popularity of rave music in the UK.

Heavily indebted to the style of Bomb Squad producer Hank Shocklee, were acts like Bomb the Bass, Rebel MC (who later reinvented himself as jungle pioneer Congo Natty), and Shut Up and Dance (who the electronic musician Squarepusher described to me as "one of the most criminally underrated and underexposed acts in the history of dance music").[15] Many of these artists sat at the intersection of rave and hip-hop, before forking off into breakbeat, hardcore, and eventually, jungle. (For further listening, try two compilations: *The British Underground E.P.*, released in 1991 by what was then a rave-focused XL Recordings, and *TCM: The Criminal Minds,* reissued by Aphex Twin's Rephlex label in 2011, an expertly-curated example of the fecund ground that existed between rave and rap in the UK of the late '80s.)

Probably the best-known example of this was The Prodigy, who were once fully committed b-boys until a knife was pulled on Liam Howlett at London club Subterania because he "didn't fit in." This caused him to turn his back on hip-hop, describing it as "an exclusivist, pretentious scene, and to a certain extent, it always excluded white bands."[16]

With Hijack at its vanguard, Britcore was a revelation at the time and, in terms of sonics at least, the first instance of a truly British mutation of hip-hop. The positive tension comes as rap meets the brutal force of hardcore and early rave, with just enough lyrical dexterity to keep the ship asteer—*The Untitled* sessions by Hardnoise and Blade's "Lyrical Maniac" being emphatic examples. Yet it's not without flaws. Listening back to the music, one styling often stands out, jars even: British MCs rapping with an American accent. For example, on "Hold No Hostage," Kamachi Sly shouts out an "Extra special dedication goes out to the people of Brixton, Stockwell, Clapham, Vauxhall..." and most of South London, albeit in an accent that sounds like he's from Long Island. It's no wonder Hijack reminded Ice-T of Public Enemy.

Of course, musicians performing with an American accent was nothing new nor unique to hip-hop. It arguably started with the birth of British rock and roll in the '50s with Cliff Richard and Billy Fury. (I'm fairly certain this will be the first and last time Cliff Richard will be referenced alongside UK hip-hop, never mind Britcore). If a British MC were to rap with an American accent now, it would be considered sacrilege and, worse still, inauthentic. But at the turn of the '80s, it was the reverse; to rap in a British accent was to use a timely

Americanism, *corny.* That was until the intervention of a certain Posse.

"Number one. I do it in my own style. I was a reggae MC before. I still chat reggae lyrics, and I do it in a rap style in a yardie accent and use my own cockney accent. I don't rap in (an) American accent. That's what's keeping English people back," a young and boisterous Bionic tells Tim Westwood in his evocative documentary, *Bad Meaning Good* (1987).[17]

Alongside fellow MC Rodney P (then known as Rodie Rok), beatboxer Sipho, and DJ Bizznizz, Bionic was a member of London Posse, a hip-hop group that came from sound system culture and sounded like it. Their raps were heavy with patois—"youts" and "poon"—and charismatic cockney. Their songs include comical punchlines moored in British life ("I got more flavour than a pack of cheese and onion" from "How's Life In London") alongside aspirational references to high-fashion British brands like Burberry and Aquascutum.

As Rodney P later explained to Red Bull Music Academy, "If you're making music, you should try and be honest about who you are and where you come from. That doesn't mean you have to tell autobiographical stories in every song you write, but you have to have a feeling and an emotion that is true to you, not just something you're trying to copy that you heard on the radio."[18]

The rappers in London Posse weren't just punch-line lyricists but accomplished storytellers. Tracks like "Live Like the Other Half Do," with its easy-going soca production, paint a picture of breezy palm trees and rum cocktails yet contrast powerfully with the song's message. In it, Bionic's character is picked up for a crime he didn't commit. The police rough him up and throw him in the patrol car, calling him "Every name in the book. Except 'crook.'" This happens to him again when he's shopping with his girlfriend and soon finds himself in a prison cell. He casually concedes that it's just another day of racist police brutality and nods to the damning psychological effects of stop-and-search (also known as "sus") policing with "this reality is changed my personality." As of 2022, Black people in the UK are seven times more likely to be targeted by the police than white people. It wouldn't have been better more than thirty years ago.[19]

London Posse released *Gangster Chronicle* on Mango, the reggae-leaning subsidiary of Island Records, in 1990. Although it proved to be the group's only official album, it's a magnetic document of Black British life at the time, blending Jamaican and London street slang in a completely natural and new way.

With the group splintered, Rodney P carved a lane for himself as a successful solo artist and radio personality, Bionic went on to work with trip-hop trailblazer Tricky, another idiosyncratic artist and MC, and Stevie Hyper-D headed in the direction of drum & bass. Why didn't London Posse follow up *Gangster Chronicle* with another album? It could be down to many reasons, although the most likely is pretty mundane, with Rodney explaining, "It became harder and harder just to keep the momentum."

With the group preferring to self-release singles, Rodney says, "Things got hard for London Posse when we started pulling in different directions, just trying to make ends meet," and eventually, "it just wore out." The trouble with being the first to explore new ground, the first footsteps to crack the cool snow on icy new terrain, is that it can be easy to get lost once you get there.

As seen in this whistle-stop tour of the '80s, UK hip-hop was a vibrant culture full of trailblazers, savants, documentarians, and downright oddballs. The preachers, innovators, and grifters were soon to come.

DISCOGRAPHY

Chapter 1: How's Life in London

This chapter is named after the song "How's Life in London", by London Posse.

Albums, E.P.s & Mixtapes

Malcolm McLaren - *Duck Rock*
Public Enemy - *Yo! Bum Rush The Show*
Public Enemy - *It Takes a Nation of Millions to Hold Us Back*
Cookie Crew - *Born This Way*
MC Duke - *Organised Rhyme*
Cookie Crew - *Fade to Black*
Hijack - *The Horns of Jericho*
Various Artists - *The British Underground E.P.*
Hardnoise - *The Untitled*
London Posse - *Gangster Chronicle*
Blak Twang - *Dettwork SouthEast*
The Criminal Minds - *TCM: The Criminal Minds*

Singles

Joni Mitchell - "Big Yellow Taxi"
Kurtis Blow - "Christmas Rappin"

Grand Wizard Theodore & The Fantastic Romantic Five - "Can I Get a Soul Clap"
The Sugar Hill Gang - "Rapper's Delight"
The Mexicano - "Dallas"
Dizzy Heights - "Christmas Rapping"
Eddy Grant - "Electric Avenue"
DJ Newtrament - "London Bridge is Falling Down"
Malcolm McLaren and the World's Famous Supreme Team - "Buffalo Gals"
Smiley Culture - "Cockney Translation"
Smiley Culture - "Police Officer"
Public Enemy - "Countdown to Armageddon"
The Beatmasters Ft. Cookie Crew - "Rok da House"
Derek B - "Good Groove"
Derek B - "Bad Young Brother"
Hijack - "Style Wars"
Blade - "Lyrical Maniac"
Soul II Soul - "Keep On Movin'"
Soul II Soul - "Back To Life (However Do You Want Me)"
Cookie Crew - "Born This Way (Let's Dance)"
Cookie Crew - "Black Is the Word"
Cookie Crew - "From the South"
MC Duke - "Running Man (Kunta Kinte)"
London Posse - "Live Like the Other Half Do"
London Posse - "Gangster Chronicle"
Hijack - "Hold No Hostage"

Chapter 2

Movements

By the early '90s, the excitement and promise of UK hip-hop 1.0 had almost fizzled out. Dismissed by the media and denied by music industry gatekeepers, only the most hardcore fans continued to show interest while the US was evolving from its golden age into the gangsta era, attracting a broader (read, white suburban) rap music fan. Meanwhile, there was friction within UK hip-hop. "Everyone wanted to get a piece of a very small pie," says Trevor Jackson, a.k.a. producer/remixer Underdog and head of Bite It! Recordings, one of the few labels releasing consistently challenging hip-hop at the time.— "Some UK foundational figures felt they owned everything and were entitled to success."[1]

To revitalise the scene, the energy in the UK had to come from somewhere new and sound like something else.

That Bristol Sound and the Troubadour of Darkness: Tricky

Adrian Nicholas Matthews Thaws grew up in Knowle West, a tough, predominantly white working-class area in South

Bristol. Thaws was born to a Jamaican father and a Ghanaian-English mother, a poet named Maxine Quaye, who committed suicide when he was just four years old. His grandmother and various aunties brought him up. It was a happy, if unconventional, childhood despite being surrounded by violence. "Where I come from, a lot of people are either on drugs, in prison, or dead,"[2] he later recalled.

Fortunately, Thaws found solace in music. First, he was known as Tricky Kid, a rapper and sometime member of The Wild Bunch, a loose collective of musicians and artists who were so hip it hurt. They formed in the early 1980s and played at warehouse parties and Bristol institutions like St Paul's Carnival, Special K's cafe, and the dingy Dug Out club. The influence of reggae sound system culture, punk, jazz, soul, and hip-hop were all present, but there was an unhurried melancholy to the music that was unique to a notoriously laid-back and diverse city.

Today, the Bristol music scene is a storied one, but The Wild Bunch—including Miles Johnson (a.k.a. DJ Milo), producer Nelle Hooper, Robert Del Naja (a.k.a. 3D), Grant Marshall (a.k.a. Daddy G), and Andrew Vowles (Mushroom)—were arguably the inception point and rulers of the roost. Confident aesthetes with an uncanny knack for sound, they rolled around town on high-tech mountain bikes decked out in Stüssy and Vivienne Westwood shirts.

When Milo introduced Tricky to the crew, he was a shy and sensitive teenager, but he had a supernatural talent for lyrics, sounding like a troubadour of darkness who had toked his way through a maze of marijuana. When the collective dissolved in 1987, with Hooper joining Soul II Soul and Milo moving to New York, 3D, Daddy G, and Mushroom left to form Massive

Attack. Tricky appeared in three singles—"Daydreaming," "Five Man Army," and "Blue Lines"—from the group's seminal debut album, *Blue Lines* (1991). A broody, epic sounding, and insular feeling masterpiece, it helped redefine dance music and coin an influential new subgenre: trip-hop a name almost every artist associated with it utterly detests, particularly Tricky.

Both Tricky and, to a lesser extent, 3D rap with regional British accents, which was unheard of at the time, but the intention behind *Blue Lines* was to "create dance music for the head, rather than the feet,",[3] according to Daddy G. Yet Tricky was more interested in hip-hop, and tensions within Massive Attack (and The Wild Bunch before that) always seemed to be brimming close to the surface. While working on *Blue Lines,* Tricky produced the demo for "Aftermath," a bluesy, smoky single with esoteric wood pipe samples featuring the dulcet tones of Martina Topley-Bird and Tricky's own haunting vocals. Tricky offered the track to Massive Attack as they were finalising their debut album, but 3D dismissed it, telling Tricky he's "never going to make it as a producer."[4]

The single remained moored to tape, unreleased for a further three years. Shortly after the release of *Blue Lines*, Tricky departed the group and began working on solo material at a stoned snail's pace. "Aftermath" laid the blueprint for what would eventually become his 1995 masterpiece, *Maxinquaye* (named after Thaws' mother), a strikingly original body of work "which acknowledged and accelerated what was new in the '90s, technology, cultural pluralism, and genre innovations." As adroitly proposed by author Mark Fisher, it was a stark counter to the "reactionary pantomime of Britpop,"[5] with its refuge in the past.

That Tricky was even prepared to take centre stage was partly thanks to the mentorship of Mark Stewart, ex-frontman of legendary new-wave outfit The Pop Group and Bristol sound linchpin, who met Tricky via The Wild Bunch and is credited as executive producer for *Maxinquaye*. If Stewart were the mentor, Martina Topley-Bird would often be framed as the muse, with whom Tricky went on to have a romantic relationship with. But in reality, Topley-Bird, who came from a well-off family with experience in the music business, helped actively influence as well as inspire the music for *Maxiquaye,* conceiving the jingle jangle melody of "Ponderosa" and providing an unexpected new take on the lyrics from Public Enemy's "Black Steel in the Hour of Chaos" in "Black Steel."

The legend goes that Tricky met Topley-Bird, then a fifteen-year-old schoolgirl, outside his house, waiting for a bus, and invited her to make a song on an impulse. That impulse continued in the eventual studio sessions, where all the vocals were recorded in the first take. Alongside the expected hip-hop, dub, and soul influences, there is an art-rock weirdness to the sound, a sludgy filter over the percussion and, of course, that famed dark atmosphere with cracks of piercing light courtesy of Topley-Bird's soothing vocal.

"Let me take you down the corridors of my life," Tricky beckons on "Hell Is Round the Corner." Tricky was still in his early twenties when he wrote and recorded *Maxinquaye*, yet he had a pool of life experience to draw from, with no shortage of trauma and complexity, having grown up around gangsters with limited familial affection and often went looking for fights in Bristol's nightclubs while wearing makeup and a dress. Drugs, sex, dysfunctional relationships, and a broader pre-millennium tension are subjects broached in the record. Despite this heaviness, he appears as sensitive as he is street-wise and raw.

Two things stand out on *Maxinquaye*, as well as in much of the music Tricky has made since. The first is how quietly Tricky raps, a silently disciplined zig to everyone else's clamorous zag, which demands the listeners' attention. The second is his androgyny as a lyricist. In "Suffocated Love," a seemingly straightforward track on the inner dialogue of a couple where the man gets the sex and the woman gets the money, things aren't quite what they seem as sexual violence and the man's dread of intimacy play in the background. "I keep her warm, but we never kiss / She cuts my slender wrists," Tricky croons. "I think ahead of you, I think instead of you," Topley-Bird teases in response. It's worth remembering that Tricky is responsible for nearly all the lyrics on *Maxinquaye*, a morass of gender-bending adventure and sonic contortion. In an interview with Mark Fisher for *The Wire*, Tricky admits his "lyrics are written from a female perspective a lot of the time." [6] This takes us to the fourth significant collaborator on the album—there were others, including The Cure producer Mark Stewart and DJ Howie B, who got burned by the experience, but that's another story—in the voodoo homage to the mother he never knew, with Tricky claiming that she channelled his lyrics through him and Martina Topley-Bird.

The album prompted universal and hyperbolic critical acclaim, perhaps the most memorable of which was David Bowie's 2,000-word paean in Q magazine. In typically Bowie-esc glossolalia, the Thin White Duke acknowledged both the arrival of an heir to his shape-shifting crown (or tiara?) and also recognised that his own game might be up. "Here come the horses to drag me to bed," Bowie concluded. "Here comes Tricky to fuck up my head."[7]

Despite the success of *Maxinquaye*—the record proved a completely unexpected commercial triumph, reaching number 3 in the UK album chart, selling over half a million copies since, and regularly appearing in "best of" lists—Tricky's life didn't get any easier. There have been battles with mental health, problems with guns (his cleaner's young son accidentally set off a Uzi in his New Jersey apartment), and a hedonistic lifestyle that almost left him in financial ruin. Most tragically, Mazy, his daughter with Topley-Bird, took her own life in 2019. Like all great minds, Tricky reminds us how noble, tortured, and downright absurd a creature humans can be. And he writes raps as hard as hell.

The Son of a Preacher Man: Roots Manuva

The Angell Town estate in Brixton, South London, was built in the 1970s. Council-run housing estates, offering heavily subsidised rents to low-income individuals and families, began appearing throughout the UK, particularly in London. It was an excellent time to be a government contractor specialising in homogenous property development.

For better or more likely worse—because unkind labels can come with self-fulfilling prophecies—many of these locations became known as "sink estates." The poet Byron Vincent, who grew up in such an estate, described it as "taking a bunch of people with social and fiscal problems and forcing them to live en masse together is an idiotic idea that is destined to create a culture of perpetually spiralling criminality."[8]

Starting in 1990 and finally completed in 2002, there was a government attempt to regenerate Angell Town, which included various improvements to the living conditions: a playground, a cafe, an "enterprise centre," and, most importantly, dear reader, a recording studio. It's 1998, in a room not much bigger than a broom cupboard in Angell Town community studio. A recording desk with a strictly mono set-up takes up most of the space. Toiling away at the desk, finalising his vocal mix, is Rodney Hylton Smith—a.k.a Lord Gosh, Hylton Smythe, and, my personal favourite, Brigadier Smythe—most commonly referred to as Roots Manuva, though he's far from common.

Roots Manuva had already released a few singles earlier in the '90s: "Next Type of Motion" (released on the London-based Sound of Money), "Fever" (which reappeared on *Brand New Second Hand*), and even a remix of Grandmaster Flash. He had created some underground buzz because, at this stage, all the buzz a British rapper could hope for (excluding a genre-defying Bristolian) was rooted underground, but he wanted to put out an album.

More than ten years in the making, *Brand New Second Hand* was originally intended for release on Sound of Money, the UK hip-hop label that helped launch another South London rapper, Blak Twang. Blak Twang's debut album, *Dettwork SouthEast*—a wordplay on the Network Southeast train rail that connected much of South London and the neighbouring suburbs—was slated for release in 1996. It included the single "Queens Head," featuring a guest appearance by young Roots Manuva.

The notion for the track was simple, and the scene was set in the opening line: "It's all about making that wonga in the

'90s," "wonga" being an English-Romany word for "money." The duo had to get the "queen's head" "before they end up lying dead." Bills "coming like a personal vendetta" became a UK hip-hop trope years later, but it was fresh and intrinsically British at the time. Blak Twang (real name Tony Olabode, a.k.a. Tony Rotton) and Roots Manuva's rap style was as much indebted to the toasting of dancehall as it was to hip-hop MCs.

However, *Dettwork SouthEast* didn't make it beyond a limited run of advance press copies.

According to Blak Twang: "It was a situation where we had a verbal agreement. There was a Japanese label called Avex. They said they'd license this album and put it out." Avex promised him a considerable promotional budget,[9] but they went back on their promise and slashed the budget considerably. When Blak Twang refused the new terms, *Dettwork SouthEast* was shelved for eighteen years, when it was finally released by Sony BMG in 2014. If it weren't for this, perhaps Blak Twang would have carried the UK hip-hop baton from the buzz of Britcore, through the barren early years of the decade, and into the mid-'90s.

Instead, we turn to Rodney Smith, an occasionally mystical, eccentric man that his label manager Will Ashon described as "a self-contained, shy individual. Partly why he found all the attention quite painful at times."[10] Smith was once a shy kid with a musical interest in reggae. Moving to the UK in the early '60s and settled in Stockwell, South London, Smith's parents hailed from the rural Jamaican village of Banana Hole, and they held traditional, even Victorian values. By all accounts, the Smith's weren't exactly wallowing in the wonga, hence his mother's use of the term "brand new second hand" to characterise the occasionally pre-used presents he would receive for Christmas and birthdays. And like many first-generation Jamaican emigrants, religion was the glue that held family life together—Rodney's father was a Pentecostal preacher and tailor.

Pentecostalism, a branch of evangelical Protestantism, is based on a critical event in the life of the early Christians: the baptism of twelve disciples by the holy spirit on the day of Pentecost. In popular culture, Pentecostals are best known for speaking in tongues, also known as glossolalia.

William J Samarin is one of the leading linguists to have studied the practice. In his book, *Tongues of Men and Angels: The Religious Language of Pentecostalism* (1975), Samarin concluded that the resemblance to human language was merely on the surface and that glossolalia is "only a facade of language."[11] Reading the book—Samarin adopts dense prose, somewhere between textbook and sermon—I can't help but wonder how Samarin would respond to today's mumble rap.

Lesser known about Pentecostalism is that it is the fastest-growing Christian religion on the planet, with 35,000 people converting to Pentecostal, or "born again," each day. In a contemporary twist, it is a faith that is powerfully experiential, not something that can be found through mere ritual or *thinking*.

Although Rodney himself isn't particularly religious, he was inevitably influenced by Smith Senior. Describing him as "a very great public speaker," he elaborates in an interview with *The Independent*:

"As a grown man, I haven't always agreed with his interpretations of Biblical instances, but he still makes it sound so convincing and uplifting. He always encouraged me and my siblings to speak with the fullness of our voices, but before anything, he has a love for what he is saying – so, yes, memories of my dad's vocal delivery have been a massive influence on how I try to put originality and mystique into my songs."[12]

If religion was the adhesive, providing discipline for the heart and mind, music was food for the soul of the Smith household. While his parents mainly listened to gospel music, young Rodney studied the violin begrudgingly and with limited grace, recalling, "Violin lessons for a 9-year-old the size of a 16-year-old...it wasn't a good look." In contrast, the beat and drum of reggae provided an alluring pull: "Sound systems were always there.. weddings, funerals, parties. I had vivid memories of looking at the sound systems, looking at the various wires."[13]

Growing up in the '80s, alongside dub and reggae, Rodney was inspired by electro, DIY scenes (including surprising sources like synth-pop group The Art of Noise), and of course hip-hop. LL Cool J and Run-DMC were the gateway rappers, but UK hip-hop lit his creative fuse. Seeing fellow South Londoners like Scientists of Sound, London Posse, and Hijack performing live, combined with his fascination for technology as music production tools became more accessible, convinced Rodney Smith to take part and eventually become Roots Manuva.

Sound of Money was run by the wiry and energetic Jeremy "Tuse" Tuson, who was also Roots Manuva's first manager. Something of an unsung hero in UK hip-hop, Tuse introduced Roots to Wayne "Lotek" Bennett, an aspiring producer and face about town selling import mixtapes at Camden Market.

Lotek recalled his first meeting with Roots Manuva: he was at Trinity Studios where Tuse had an office out the back, when Tuse played Lotek a demo of a Roots Manuva song and asked what he thought. "'Vocalist is great, [the] beat isn't,' I told him. 'I'm the vocalist's manager, and I made the beat' he replied. He wasn't upset with my opinion. He seemed more concerned that I didn't like it as I was the target audience."[14]

Tuse asked if Lotek could do any better. "Being a super confident teenager, I obviously said yes, even though I had never finished a song at that time," Lotek remembers. "I had studied sound engineering but didn't have access to the equipment to make beats." Lotek returned to the studio a few days later and made a beat using whatever records he found, "mostly charity shop rejects" and some "drum sounds and then shaped them in the sampler."

Eventually, Lotek recalls how a "weird seeming guy wandered into the studio, nodded his head to the beat in tacit approval, and then wandered off again." Tuse returned a few minutes later and said, Roots Manuva likes the beat. Lotek was familiar with the name as he'd heard "Next Type of Motion" a few months earlier but had no idea what he looked like.

Lotek produced two tracks for the album—"Sinking Sands" and the haunting off-key piano of "Soul Decay"—and, alongside IG Culture, was the only producer to work with Roots Manuva on *Brand New Second Hand*, returning to produce two more tracks for his Mercury Prize nominated follow-up, *Run Come Save Me.*

A conflicted sense of piousness has often seeped its way throughout Roots Manuva's music, emphatically so on his debut and expanded upon in his sophomore release. The fluid vocalising Rodney would have seen in his father's sermons is also evident, although you'll have to check "Kicking the Cack" on *Run Come Save Me* to hear Roots in full glossolalia mode. Rodney is divided by his father's godliness, upbringing, and, perhaps, his own spiritual aspirations. However, the bright lights and "sinny sin sins" of London's nightlife often tempt him.

From the opening chords of "Movements," there is a celestial quality, the sense of a holier presence. This is spelt out literally at times—rapping "I believe in the power of the G.O.D." on "Sinking Sands"—and in more characteristically abstract terms—as heard on "Inna," with its lush and trippy Wurlitzer sound recalling some of the transcendental experiences raving can be capable of. Rodney feels brave, even though his vision is blurred.

If *Brand New Second Hand* had a theme, it would be a dub-infused kitchen-sink realism with a borderline healthy dose of paranoia. Addiction, capitalism, and gentrification are among the concerns: "Soon there'll be no dollars, no yens, no pounds / Just madness, microchips and hi-tech war—but that's not to call it a despairing record.

Quite the opposite, *BNSH* contains moments of freewheeling, transcendent optimism, vulnerability, and lucid confessions from its host. Upon its release, *Pitchfork* described Roots Manua as "the positivity rapper you don't laugh at."[15] Rodney described it as his album for Brixton, "For my next-door neighbours and my mates,"[16] but that was an understatement. A new bar was set for UK hip-hop.

After whittling the album down from fifty to seventeen tracks, *all* they needed to do now was package, release, and sell it. Tuse had secured funding from an East London businessman and had set up a studio in the basement of his gold shop. The original plan was to release *BNSH* through Sound of Money, but, in what was becoming something of a recurring theme, "That investment didn't go well' according to Lotek, and Tuse decided to close Sound of Money as a label and operate as a management company instead.

With his debut album stuck in purgatory, Rodney could have sunk, but, together with Tuse, they determinedly shopped the album around labels, with Lotek drumming up interest at record shops like Dark n Cold and Mr Bongo in Soho. Gilles Peterson's influential Talkin' Loud label was said to be interested in releasing the record. Still, it took a meeting with the music journalist Will Ashon, who had recently launched Big Dada, the hip-hop leaning offshoot of Ninja Tune, to find the right type of record label to release *Brand New Second Hand.*

Over multiple cups of coffee (possibly to stimulate his "terrible memory"), I spoke to Will at a cafe in Shoreditch. He first met Rodney when he interviewed him for *Muzik* magazine, saying "I wrote the 'British rap's moment is coming piece,' one of the many, that would have been 1995." The interview occurred at the Sound of Money studio. "Skinnyman was there rolling a blunt," Will recalls of the charismatic rapper from North London, who we'll return to later, "and Rodney was there barely saying a word."

The avuncular Will Ashon—a politically active middle-class Oxford graduate from Leicester—and Rodney are, on the face of it at least, an unlikely pair. Yet it was the start of a long-lasting and potent relationship. "I asked if he could do us a single," remembers Ashon. "And Rodney said, 'I don't want to do any more singles. I'll do an album for you.'" Familiar with Roots Manuva's music, the powers that be at Ninja Tune gave Will the green light to release Big Dada's first-ever album.

The press reception to *Brand New Second Hand* was overwhelmingly positive, with "Juggle Tings Proper" getting Single of the Week in *Melody Maker* and *NME*. Rodney's expectations were modest: "When I was making the record, I would have been happy to sell five or six hundred copies because, in my head, if you made a challenging record, there were about 400-600 people out there [who] would buy it and support it."[17] But the album did sell well. As Will explained, "We pressed two thousand copies on vinyl and a similar amount of CDs, and it just kept selling."

Complicated Artists and Dreaming of the Future with Big Dada

The surprise success of *Brand New Second Hand* opened new doors for British rap and Big Dada. As Will explained, "The key thing with Big Dada was it wasn't strictly UK hip-hop." He was concerned by the insularity of the local scene and inspired by those at the vanguard of alternative rap. This included American acts like The Roots, Company Flow, Anti-pop Consortium, and Mike Ladd, many of whom Will wrote about for magazines like *Muzik* and *Hip-Hop Connection* and went on to release records by: "I felt at the time it was better to situate British hip-hop within underground hip-hop."

The very idea of underground and overground music scenes has eroded over the years thanks to the relative democracy of the internet. Still, back then at the turn of the millennium, a very thick layer of turf and nettle separated the conceptual rap of Mike Ladd and the shiny veneer of the jiggy era made popular by MCs like Mase and Puff Daddy. Both aesthetically and musically, underground and mainstream hip-hop were heading in two distinctly different paths in the US.

Of course, there was nuance. There usually is. Yet by positioning Big Dada underground, Will Ashon had set the label up to experiment freely, saying, "I didn't think there was anything more true about saying you had to rap in a London accent as it was saying you'd have to rap in an American accent." Just a few years after the mid-'90s era of hip-hop, the "keeping it real" era, as Will put it, had "developed a new set of rules on how you rap to be taken seriously."

But breaking the rules was all part of the fun with Big Dada. The label was inspired as much by the eponymous Dadaism art movement as the lyrical gymnastics of LA's Freestyle Fellowship. "The key thing for me," he says, "was breaking down that sense there was only one way to be a rapper, trying to re-situate what people were doing in a wider context within hip-hop." Unburdened by scene hegemonies, Big Dada soon began welcoming various artists and MCs, unpredictable mavericks at different career stages.

In the early years, this included the beatnik futurism of Mike Ladd, actor-rapper-spoken word savant Saul Williams, and the group New Flesh For Old, who later re-emerged with the snappier name New Flesh. New Flesh, consisting of producer Part 2 and rappers Juice Aleem and Toastie Tailor, made the second album released on Big Dada. *Equilibrium* is an uncompromising sound that the *NME* described, somewhat unfairly, as "a surly, paranoid dirge of an album." Although the music rag was well past its prime at this point, it should be considered some sort of achievement that a group like New Flesh got any mention at all.

A mixture of Afrocentric styling, dense comic book lyricism, sound system culture, and a proto-grime sonic, New

Flesh were influenced by "Sun Ra, Ramellzee, Coltrane and [film director David] Cronenberg. People of that nature," Juice Aleem tells me over a Zoom call from his studio in Birmingham, before rhetorically pondering, "What is reality in regards to your being?"[18]

As Will explained, "The idea with Big Dada was you could be anything. You could be an artist."

* * *

Ben Chijoke was, by his own admission, a complex man. A poet and teacher, he was also a skilled MC, a beatmaker, and most definitely an artist. Better known by his rap moniker Ty, he was born in Brixton to an Igbo family from Nigeria. But like thousands of other young children of West African descent, he was sent to live with various foster families in Essex.

It's a practice that has been going on since the 1950s, and for many migrant families, private foster arrangements have helped them get temporary child care while they find work and establish roots. However, because it happens outside local authorities, regulation officials admit they have no idea how many children are in private foster care, leaving them at greater risk of neglect or worse. In Ty's case, it caused abandonment issues, as he told Channel 4 News in a special report on the subject: "As kids, we had no clue why we were here, and then my parents said 'we're going now, but you're staying.'"[19]

Eventually, Ty returned to live with his sister and parents in Brixton, a strict household where a job as a doctor or lawyer was a preferred career path, but the headstrong kid had other ideas. He began developing his emceeing skills and absorbed a broad range of music through a stint as a sound engineer.

Parallel to this, he was interested in poetry and cut his teeth performing at the Ghetto Grammar spoken word workshops in The Africa Centre in the mid-'90s.

Ty's breakout track was the collaborative joint "I.A.A.D. (I Am A Don)" with Shortee Blitz. A bouncy, jazz-inflected song that wouldn't have sounded out of place among the Native Tongue movement pioneered by the likes of A Tribe Called Quest and De La Soul a few years earlier—and Ty would indeed regularly perform and collaborate with De La and, according to Will, was due to sign to DJ Maseo's aborted label. This song persuaded Big Dada to come in with an album offer. Negotiations were protracted but ultimately fruitful, resulting in the one-two punch of *Awkward* (2001) and the knockout *Upwards* (2003), with the latter receiving a well-deserved Mercury Prize nomination.

Ty's bookish interests—including jazz alongside poetry, less common at the time than it is now—and diasporic experience resulted in a singular artistic vision. In 2011, he told me that "There's no shift for me from being poetic to being musical. It's all part and parcel of the same thing...My focus is on the songs."[20]

In the same interview, he also bristled at the idea of inauthenticity, adding, "I feel like a duty towards making hip-hop *music* again." Ty recognised the commercial benefits of making music for the charts: "It might give me a mortgage or two, but it's not my legacy, and if there's one thing I've done, it's to let other artists know it's possible to do something else other than the bullshit."

His soul patch beard and turtleneck jumpers were deceptive, as he explained to *The Independent*; "I hate the word alternative," and "I'm not a laid-back person."[21] Aside from the lyrical content and styling of his music—confessional, political, witty, and acerbic—credit should go to Ty's production skills and the way he extended the sonic palette of what UK hip-hop could sound like, such as working with Afrobeat pioneer Tony Allen and somehow making good use of a circus sample in "Oh You Want More."

Will Ashon admitted that Ty could be "complicated" and that they "spent a lot of time, particularly on *Upwards*, arguing." He added, "I think when it came to putting an album out, there was always a sense that people had a vision, but a girlfriend or a mum liked a certain track. On that record, it was one of the most painful processes getting to what the finished record would be. But he came to me and said 'You were right about that. I was a pain about it.' And that was Ty really. It was his record, but I wasn't aware of that as I should have been."

Sadly, Ty passed away in May 2020 due to pneumonia after intensive treatment for COVID-19. His death resulted in an outpouring of emotion from the UK hip-hop world, spoken word community, and beyond, with El-P, Ghetts, and Gilles Peterson all paying tribute. And Will thinks Ty "would have been gratified by the outpouring of emotion because I don't think he realised how appreciated he was."

Will continues: "I remember when Big Dada started, there was a sense that UK hip-hop was a bit of a joke. Somehow, the Black American experience was more real and a sense that it [the British Black experience] wasn't as exciting or glamorous." Artists like Roots Manuva, Juice Aleem, and Ty played a massive part in challenging this belief and opening the door for critical dialogue around the music. As society gripped itself for millennium bugs, British rap music gulped down the red pill like the edifying and occasionally sobering truth bomb that it is.

After the critical success of *Upwards* and the first two Roots Manuva albums, Big Dada had a launchpad for an iconic second wave of artists and startlingly imaginative albums by King Geedorah, Diplo, TTC, Spank Rock, and Wiley.

Following two near misses for the Mercury Prize, the label finally succeeded in 2009 with Speech Debelle's *Speech Therapy*, produced by Lotek, who was "just as surprised as everyone else" by the award, and Young Fathers' *Dead* in 2014.

But, according to WIll, one regret remains: "I'm still pissed off all these years later that we didn't get a Mercury [for Roots Manuva's *Run Come Save Me*]. Ms. Dynamite won it, and if she had won it for a garage record, I would have been thrilled, but it was for a neo-soul record [Polydor] made her make. It's a sliding doors moment. If Rodney won that year, would they have given it to Dizzee Rascal the following?"

DISCOGRAPHY

Chapter 2: Movements

This chapter is titled after the song "Movements", by Roots Manuva.

Albums, E.P.s & Mixtapes
Massive Attack - *Blue Lines*
Tricky - *Maxinquaye*
Blak Twang - *Dettwork South East*

Roots Manuva - *Brand New Second Hand*
Speech Debelle - *Speech Therapy*
Young Fathers - *Dead*

Singles
Public Enemy - "Black Steel in the Hour of Chaos"
Massive Attack - "Daydreaming"
Massive Attack - "Five Man Army"
Massive Attack - "Blue Lines"
Tricky - "Aftermath"
Tricky - "Ponderosa"
Tricky - "Black Steel"
Tricky - "Hell Is Round the Corner"
Blak Twang - "Queens Head"
Roots Manuva - "Next Type of Motion"
Roots Manuva - "Sinking Sands"
Roots Manuva - "Soul Decay"
Roots Manuva - "Juggle Tings Proper"
Roots Manuva - "Kicking the Cack"
Mike Ladd - "Blah Blah"
Ty - "I.A.A.D." (I Am A Don)
Ty - "Oh You Want More"

Chapter 3

The Cosmic Gypsies

Braintax was originally a duo consisting of Joe Christie and DJ Test (Tommy Stewart), who founded Low Life Records in 1992. Hailing from Leeds, the pair was part of an emerging local hip-hop scene, including crews like Junkyard Tactics and Kaliphz (who achieved modest pop success after recording the song "Walk Like A Champion" with the professional boxer "Prince" Naseem Hamed in 1996). Braintax also played radio shows on local stations like Dream FM, ran events, and supported US acts like Redman and KRS-One when they played shows in North England. Yet they wanted to get heard, so they started a record label.

Life up North ...

It was an innocent time for hip-hop in the UK, especially in the Yorkshire Pennines. The Britcore explosion had fizzled out. There were no real rules and only modest expectations. It was just a matter of young people having fun, spinning vinyl, having a go with cheap samplers and writing rhymes—a purity of creation that can be difficult to find when you're an adult. Ideas of making money from music must have been a distant thought, if at all.

Low Life's initial releases came from Breaking The Illusion-and Braintax. The *Fat Head E.P.*, released by the latter, is considered a classic by some, with copies selling upwards of £80 on sites like eBay and Discogs. Listening back, it's not obvious to see where the potential is. The production is derivative of the funk breaks and scratches synonymous with US hip-hop at the time, including a sample from Quincy Jones "Summer in the City," which had a reawakening earlier that year via The Pharcyde's "Passin' Me By." Rapping responsibilities are shared by the duo, including a very young Joe, who, barely in his twenties, still seems to be finding his voice. However, there are hints in the subject matter—"People always see race hate as being in another land / Don't kid yourself, and if it happens I'm gonna' talk about it and shout it"—foreshadowing the politically charged messaging that later came to define his music.

Braintax would go on to make music capable of acerbic wit, calling out oil companies, *The Sun*-reading boozed-up Brits abroad, fair-trade coffee-drinking upper classes, and a ticker tape of "politricks" from Thatcher, Bush, Blair, Sharon, and others. Sometimes it worked. Other times, like the sample of a George Galloway speech on "The Grip Again," might cause one to cringe so hard you become a fossil.

For those that were there, Braintax and Low Life were at the heart of the Leeds rap scene. And then they stopped. For reasons unknown, in 1993, the label went on a three-year hiatus and by the time Low Life returned, DJ Test had departed and Braintax was an individual. And for clarity, when I refer to Braintax henceforth, it will be in the singular.

By 1997, Low Life had relocated to a new studio in Shepherds Bush, West London. That same year, Braintax released his *Future Years E.P.*. Handling both the production and lyrics, *Future Years* demonstrates maturity and growing musicality, with considerate jazz samples replacing the funk of *The Fat Head E.P.*. Braintax's move to London is a well-trodden one.

Even at the time of writing, more than two decades into the twenty-first century, there are just a handful of fully functioning record labels—complete with a recording studio, A&R, marketing and publishing functions—releasing rap music outside of London: True Thoughts in Brighton, Manchester's thisisnq, and the Liverpool-based 3 Beat's grime excursions in the early 2010s. In the 1990s, it was like finding a (record) needle in a haystack.

As Brummie Juice Aleem put it, "Every time we wanted to have a meeting, we had to come into London, and that was not fair. No one is necessarily paying your train fare or petrol. And train fares in London are not fair!" Publishing being a key source of income for artists, Juice was clear about the obstacle, "They're not coming to you in Yorkshire or Birmingham. A lot of London artists don't even realise how the label they end up on is probably only two miles from their house."

Universe Building from the Man with the Golden Sound

With a relocation to London, Braintax forged new relationships with artists based in the capital. As heard in *The '98-Series*, a pair of posse cut 12-inch EPs featuring Braintax, the enigmatic Supa T (a.k.a. Sundragon), Lewis "The Man with the Golden Sound" Parker, and scene stalwart DJ MK with the scratches.

Lewis Parker recalled, "I knew Joe through DJ MK, they were flatmates. I would often go around there with Supa-T to check for MK. Braintax used to try to come up in the cypher, [but] I wasn't feeling him." They ended up making some music together, but Parker believes Braintax took advantage of Supa-T's stoned affability to network with the crew, "Knowing I had a big name after I just signed to Massive Attack."[2]

Lewis Parker probably isn't a name familiar to many British rap fans under thirty, but he deserves his flowers. He grew up in Kent, part of a musical family originally from Barbados and recalls hearing hip-hop for the first time saying, "Something just clicked." He tried his hand at various instruments as a teen before focusing on digital samplers, evolving from the AKAI 950 and Cubase software to the complex E-mu SP-1200.

For those in the know, the SP-1200 is as synonymous with the golden age of hip-hop as Kangol hats and shell toes. Unsurprisingly, Lewis Parker's sound is rooted in dusty soul and jazz samples, plus some of the more experimental adventures of horrorcore groups like the Gravediggaz. There is plenty of soul and crunch to even Parker's earliest beats, but more than that, there is technical mastery that was perhaps unparalleled in British hip-hop at the time. These attributes caught the ear of a young Trevor Jackson, the uncompromising music producer and graphic designer, who released Parker's *Rise / Visions of Splendour* and *B-Boy Antiks* E.P.s' on his Bite It! Records label in 1996.

"I would never spend a lot of money on a sample," explains Trevor, "[But] Lewis would buy records for twenty fucking pee.

He bought amazing, easy-listening records and turned them into diamonds before Kanye West did "Diamonds Are From Sierra Leone." Lewis sampled Shirley Bassey ten years before Kanye. Lewis was a genius at finding samples and loops."

Bigger things were to come for Lewis Parker, and in 1998, he released the first of two albums via Massive Attack's Melankolic label. The cover art for *Masquerades & Silhouettes (The Ancient Series One)* features Lewis standing barefoot in shallow waters on a presumably British coastline, captured in silhouette by the photographer Donald Christie.

Although a simple image, it's also one loaded with meaning. A voyage awaits the protagonist and the music and culture he represents. At just eight tracks, it is unusually short for a rap album, and all the better for it. With standout tracks "Songs of the Desert" and "Eye of Dreams" recalling the canon of Marlon James' "African Game of Thrones" *Black Leopard, Red Wolf*, David Lynch's kitsch take on *Dune*, and the psychoactive detective work of Phillip K Dick's mind-bending creations.

Lewis is not "keeping it real" on this record. There are no shoutouts to Catford or other places in South London, and no rap tropes. Lewis is creating a universe on *Masquerades & Silhouettes*. It is a mind-bending trip through a universe twisted to the whims of the author's imagination with lines like, "Thoughts in the shadows / the grey area where angels shoot arrows." Simply put, it's fucking great. Melankolic may have been the creation of Massive Attack and run by their manager Marc Picken, but it was a subsidiary of Virgin, and there was no mistaking who paid the bills. As Lewis recalled, "I was fighting a lot of stuff. They heard I had the potential to go that Bristol kind of route, and I was like, "No, I make hip-hop music, not easy listening.'" Parker wanted to pursue his own path and not become "the next Tricky."

His early singles did have some of the melancholy textures synonymous with trip-hop—Rhodes piano and bass-heavy drums—but these were just trees in a forest of soulful boom-bap beats. "I started to be aware of industry spies when I got signed to Virgin," he recalls. "Strange guys in the office would ask me how I got my drums like that and what machines I used." The new surroundings of his major label and, according to Trevor, a spectacular weed habit made him paranoid: "Seeing how I never had any love for the empire to begin with, it was easy for me to be very cynical about all the industry was doing!"

Neither *Masquerades & Silhouettes (The Ancient Series One)* nor his 2002 follow-up album, *It's All Happening Now (The Ancients Series Three)* made as much of an impact as they probably should have, despite or possibly because of being released on a major label. Confusingly, *Diamond in the Sun's Eye (The Ancient Series Two)* was released more than twenty years later, at the start of 2024, on Dutch label Boom-bap Relickz. But while he may have earned few column inches or large checks, Lewis Parker did something more important: he inspired others.

A High Plains Drifter: The Story of Jehst

The '98-Series E.P.s didn't just raise the profile of Low Life. It helped establish a new "UK hip-hop" sound and galvanise a scene. As William Shields, a.k.a. Jehst, explains, "I don't want to take credit away 'cause there's so much music they did that was wicked. I was a fan before I had any involvement. *The*

'98 *Series 1 & 2* [are] incredible records. It raised the bar for production levels."[3]

I caught up with Jehst over two sprawling two-hour conversations just before Christmas 2021. He is originally from Crowborough, or by his own description, "Between Brighton and Croydon, for lack of a better reference point. I moved up to Huddersfield as a teenager."

Arguably the first important white rapper of this era, Jehst's cultural reference points growing up included Paul Simon records, the original *Star Wars* trilogy, cartoons (he took drawing classes in Ladbroke Grove), and, most passionately, hip-hop. "The first thing I remember [of hip-hop] is Slick Rick and Doug E. Fresh, "The Show" and "La Di Da Di," taking special inspiration from Fresh's beatboxing on the tracks. "There was no technology or thing to construct. Anybody could do it."

As a teenager in Huddersfield, he joined the local graffiti crew, The Chemical Soulz, tagging castle rock and any walls they could find in a town still known for its Victorian architecture and surrounding rolling countryside. He explained, "The graf writers were like local heroes to us, as much if not more so than rappers." Jehst was no slouch in the classroom either. Reading Orwell for English Literature, he began "connecting dots with this worldview and the Chuck Ds and KRS-Ones I grew up with," as well as "looking at science fiction as a vehicle for human existence."

My conversation with Jehst ran the gamut: from Dave Chappelle and cancel culture, Julian Assange, the improbability of reform in social media, the recent passing of the fashion designer Virgil Abloh (Jehst had recently come across an old contract where he agreed to licence the track "City of Industry" for an unreleased vinyl compilation Abloh was making for Louis Vuitton), and of course his two-plus decades spent making and releasing music via his YNR label.

He is an enjoyable conversationalist, often going on wild tangents, throwing up unexpected observations with answers that eventually end up back at the question. To listen to him is to follow arcs like lobbed rocks, landing on the truth. Or his truth, at least. Will has an encyclopaedic knowledge of music, particularly rap. He also has an acute sense of Britishness.

That he spent his teenage years in Huddersfield, a relatively small market town of less than 100,000 people, wasn't as significant a barrier to the music and culture he loved as I would have guessed. Besides, "By the time I moved up to Huddersfield, the window of opportunity for [the first wave of] UK hip-hop closes. You've had your Monie Love, Cookie Crews, Silver Bullets—people who charted."

"This was when Soul II Soul was number one, [with] 'Back To Life,' an anchor for our whole thing. I can't stress enough [the importance] of that song, as that came to you from Black radio. From the clubs or the streets and then in a short space of time, Will Smith is dancing to it on *The Fresh Prince of Bel-Air*. It's that ubiquitous. And arguably that's UK hip-hop. Obviously, there are other influences, but they're rapping over breakbeats."

Jehst had no grand career designs to be a rapper. But through the education system, he saw a route: "it wasn't really about 'making it' as a rapper, or pursuing it as a career. It was really about being immersed in the culture."

He moved to London to study Illustration and English Literature at the University of Westminster. However, he soon became disillusioned with the education system, "not learning anything and paying lots in tuition fees." Barely a year later, in 1999, he released his first record, using his student loan to press up the *Premonitions E.P.* and start the label YNR with C-Wide, "and that's what started the whole thing."

The *Premonitions E.P.* was well received, and live show bookings and invitations to appear on the records of more established MCs soon followed, including the scene anthem "Cosmic Gypsies." The single appeared on Task Force's *Voice of the Great Outdoors E.P.* Task Force, led by brothers Joey and Robin Coombes from Highbury (a.k.a. Chester P and Farma G), had musical chops with their dad, Peet Coombes, the lead singer and guitarist for the new wave pop band The Tourists (the same band in which Annie Lennox and Dave Stewart first met, thus proving that not even six degrees of separation is needed between the Eurythmics and Jehst).

Graffiti obsessed like Jehst, the brothers spent their teenage years listening to punk, smoking weed, bunking off school, and spraying walls around North London. The latchkey kids had a close circle of friends made up of breakers, producers, emcees, and DJs, which eventually became The Bury Crew, so named because the members all came from places ending in "bury"—Canonbury, Highbury, and Finsbury Park—and included the Mud Family group steered by Skinnyman (more on him to come).

However, the Coombes brothers cut an unusual pair on the Highbury Estate, where they grew up. Aside from a musician dad, their mother was an artist. "She was big on punk art," Farma explained, adding, "Kids would come round and see like car doors hanging off the ceiling, paint-splattered on walls, dolls heads, and broken TVs everywhere, and you just knew they were thinking 'what!?!'"[4]

The duo, who originally went by Highbury Hoodlumz, cut their teeth at nights like Cream of the Crop, a rap battle held at WKD in Camden.*[5] Chester P Hackenbush (to use his full moniker) in particular had a fierce reputation as a battle MC. As Jehst explained, "I know Farma won't take it as a disrespect, but Chester had a different type of reputation before Task Force. He was already a bar-setting MC... This was an era where people might not have had any media or radio. The only way you could access them [was if] you were in the cypher or open mic night or in that jam at that community centre."

But for all the vicious punchlines Task Force were capable of, and the fearsome reputation they possessed—rumour had it they once physically threw a journalist out of their estate—they had a lighter, free-spirited side too. "I drink honey from buttercups and sing with the crickets" is a lyric the Poet of Nature himself, William Wordsworth, would be proud of. Instead, Farma G wrote and rapped it one hundred and fifty years later on "Butterfly Concerto", from the group's *Voice of the Great Outdoors E.P.*.

At the turn of the millennium, Task Force was prolific, releasing their Mark B-produced debut album, *New Mic Order* (1999), five annual 'volumes' of *Music From The Corner* starting in 2001, and numerous singles and guest appearances. Yet the *Voice of the Great Outdoors E.P.* captures the Brothers McBane at their best. Tales of urban decay blend effortlessly into fantasy worlds of the natural and the interstellar over Farma G's production, which weaves unlikely samples of classical, folk, and boom-bap beats into an intoxicating bouillabaisse.

Released on Low Life, the *E.P.* was sandwiched in between two cheeky London-centric bootleg singles by Task Force:

"Simon Says" by Pharoahe Monch, morphs into "Grafdabusup" and "Wha Blow!", a reimagination of "Woah" by Black Rob. The vinyl-only releases were limited to 500 and 200 copies respectively and sell for as much as £100 on Discogs if you can find them.

By this point, Low Life had achieved cult status among b-boys and girls in the UK and beyond. In 2001, a sign of the label's growing credibility, Rodney P inked a deal to release records via his own Riddim Killa imprint in collaboration with Low Life.

That same year, as Jehst's star began to ascend in a small scene rooted in the underground, he would inevitably cross lines with another expat from the North: Braintax. The result was the *High Plains Drifter E.P.*, reissued a year later as a CD album with added tracks ("Staircase to the Stage" featuring J-Zone, "People Under the Weather" alongside fellow Huddersfield MC Asaviour, and "The Trilogy (Remix)" with Chester P and Kyza). The E.P. provided a high watermark moment for both Jehst and UK hip-hop, but it was never intended for release as an album, much less a CD.

Given that the first iPod launched that year, Jehst says he sensed a change in the waters for the format becoming increasingly "inaccessible and irrelevant." Besides, "It was still a DJ culture. I was obsessed with having the instrumentals on the vinyl, which were needed to perform. So Joe [Braintax] was like, 'just do shorter versions so we can get more songs on,' things like the 'Bluebell' interlude. It's a very DJ-orientated album, which might sound weird today."

If the previous classic British rap record, *Brand New Second Hand* by Roots Manuva, recognised urban claustrophobia, *High Plains Drifter* was rap through the perspective of post-industrial country living. This feeling is best epitomised by the track "City of Industry." As Jehst explains, "A lot of the imagery comes out of the bleakness of Huddersfield and that part of the country, like referring to dry stone walls." He describes a part of the country with an "uneasy, antiquated contrast of undeveloped rural space which is almost untouched for a hundred years." The Industrial Revolution of the North had long faded by the time Jehst made his first album, and there were layers of history to explore "When you compare to places like America and Australia."

He references Nas as an influence for "putting contrasting images next to each other creates a much bigger world…It's like in painting, where you've got to have a lightness to balance the dark." The "uneasiness" Jehst speaks of is expertly framed by the haunting organ sample from "Sound Chaser" by prog rock band Yes.

Discussing some of the other songs, Jehst has problems with the cowboy imagery unintentionally associated with the title track, "High Plains Anthem": "Growing up in the late '90s, "The Joker" by Steve Miller was an influence, probably via my parents. There was also Sadat X doing *Wild Cowboys*, an underrated record I loved. This cowboy thing wasn't controversial to play off [back then],' Jehst concludes, whereas now cowboys can be seen as, "some white supremacy bullshit."

Writing the lyrics first to "High Plains Anthem," he had a different beat originally: "It was less jazzy and way harder. More like a DITC beat with drums and a minimal sample. But I couldn't quite get it right, and I was happy with the lyrics." He looked to Lewis Parker for approval for the new version: "He loved it. I looked up to Lewis and still really do."

After performing the song so many times live, he concedes, "It doesn't belong to me anymore. It's had a life of its own for twenty years."

Another key track is "Staircase to Stage," from the extended version of the album. It is probably the most traditional "hip-hop" sounding song on *High Plains Drifter*, sampling "Incarcerated Scarfaces" from Raekwon's classic *Only Built 4 Cuban Linx*. Featuring the pranksterish J-Zone, the duo addresses what they see as a sorry state of the union for hip-hop. "J-Zone was ahead of his time. He was Danny Brown, Tyler, the Creator, and Old Droog. He was a very now rapper. He was vulnerable in a very humorous way. That was the era of 'keep it real,' but 'keep it real' meant that you were from the hood [even] when you weren't."

Yet the record also set an unfortunate precedent for Billy Brimstone fans. Recording with J-Zone while staying at producer Harry Love's mum's house "became my gift and my curse, because my whole thing from that point is I've never really done mailed-in verses."

Ever the purist, Jehst believes collaborators make better art by being in the studio together. "If me and another artist kick it for a couple hours, the art makes itself. But if it's an email, I need to make time for it and find an external window." He alludes to a potential opportunity with Pharoahe Monch as one scuppered example.

At the turn of the millennium, the UK hip-hop scene was fertile and productive, particularly from a beat-making perspective. Still, Jehst recognises a common flaw: "The one thing I will stand by—whether it was Harry, LG, or Lewis—is [things would have been better] if there had been more of an infrastructure to get music released and mixed, because there never was and still isn't studio opportunities for proper mixing."

Low Life: "A show like Seinfeld, that's not about anything"

Jehst's first two albums—*The Return of the Drifter* and *Falling Down,* still his best work as far as I'm concerned—were released on Low Life. When I ask him about his experience working with the label, the sigh is very audible, even over the Zoom call, as he sits back, shrugs, and eventually smiles.

"I've lost count of the pitches I've had about making a documentary on Low Life," he says. The label has become known almost as much for its abrupt closure in 2008, leaving a long line of its disgruntled rappers out of pocket, as it has for the occasionally genre-defining music it released.

Jehst has made peace with the situation now, saying, "I try not to give it my energy. I tend to fall on the side of 'this is some super nerdy shit that only the super nerdy would even care about.'" takes a novel view of the episode, comparing it to reality TV or "a show like Seinfeld that's not about anything, but you've got some characters, and that's enough to carry it. Skinnyman is a character. Rodney P is a character. Big characters. Based on this myth, Braintax is becoming a bigger character than he is."

I looked for a counter view on Braintax and the Low Life era. There was no shortage of fans of the music released by the label, but whether on or off the record, no one was willing to provide an alternative characterisation of Braintax, whose disappearance means he isn't around to give a defence. Jehst puts it plainly: "This guy that ripped everybody off, and he's the opposite of who he was trying to be on record. He's very socialist in the politics he puts across, but not in business."

Independent music communities thrive when they are outward-looking and open to shared experiences. And a good record label can be like a magnet for these creative communities. But when they become greedy and insular, they inevitably die. That happened with Low Life when Braintax shuttered the label, affecting the wider UK hip-hop scene for a while.

Owning the Narrative: Mike Skinner, the Liminal Class, and the Problematic Rise of the White Rapper

Between the *Premonitions EP* and *Falling Down*, Jehst had found his voice and a sense of style, but reflecting upon his legacy has caused him a sense of conflict in an art form where identity is so important. Within months of *The Return of the Drifter*, a new sound emerged from the glossy ether of garage music. Youngstar's "Pulse X" may have been produced just a few miles from where Jehst made music, but it may as well have been from another galaxy.

The simple, mutant bassline bears almost no resemblance to a hip-hop beat. And less than a year later, a seventeen-year-old by the name of Dylan Mills took that sound, plus shards of others, and, in a blaze of alchemy, made something so startingly original and un-fuck-with-able that it altered the trajectory of modern music, fashion, culture, and British rap for good. (This is not to say Dizzee Rascal invented grime, but he was its first poster boy.)

Thanks to its co-narrative, conversations around authenticity and identity in the context of Black British music were never the same after *Boy in da Corner*. "There's so much to unpack from that time," Jehst declares, frustrated by the "very narrow definitions that we now have; like 'UK hip-hop…was this, and grime was that.'"

He makes a strong argument that the relationship between UK hip hop and grime was never "divorced" as it seemed. He refers to Dizzee Rascal's "Fix Up, Look Sharp," "which is more old-school hip-hop than anything. None of us ever looped a classic drum break that people knew from Run-D.M.C."

Jehst feels that the media narrative surrounding grime and its relationship to UK hip-hop was intentionally divisive. "It was about ghettoising and segregating the youth," he says, adding, "It felt like one minute the British media were treating Blak Twang like he was the new Johnny Rotten, but then it switched, and it was like 'that's not authentically British, this is…and everything that's not this, is irrelevant.'"

He continues: "There's a reason why Devlin is the only token white rapper in grime. [It's due] to the way grime has been presented to the public by the music industry and media establishment. There's a reason why they drag Dizzee Rascal out on *Newsnight* and try to show him up because it fits a wider narrative that this country has in its very twisted race relations."

Jehst is hesitant to use the word conspiracy, but says "it's the easiest one to apply. You've got political and business interests that are not benefitting from this thing being successful. Let's call it rap music in the UK at that time." Jehst believes that media scrutiny, which has often been negative, resulted from UK rap music becoming "financially threatening when it was developing its cottage industry. This was a new era, after the industry shut it down for the first time in the late '80s and early '90s."

He explains, "Rodney P said something to me: 'You've got to remember, back in that era we were all chasing deals, and none of us had our own businesses or labels. So this time, we've learnt.' Monetising shit outside of the mainstream. MTV Base don't want to play it? Channel U will. And we were all on Channel U. There was no discrimination on what type of rap it was."

For better or worse, rap never stands still. A cynical view could be that the emergence of grime as the dominant form of Black British music, just as Jehst's career was starting to take off, is the sour grapes of a forty-plus-year-old white rapper looking back, but to his credit, he views things more holistically.

'This whole idea that UK hip-hop was white artists, and it was backpackers...how the fuck anyone categorises Skinnyman as a backpacker, I'll never know. It's (a) lazy narrative. Who it harms is all these Black guys (*ed. Never mind the girls - we'll come to this*) who were in the majority.' Jehst listens to Ghetts or D Double E and can't 'Not hear hip-hop, whether it's Gunshot or through to a Skinnyman.' He's adamant that they are part of the same lineage. 'These things have been developed in the same cultures. In the same estates, literally.'

In his seminal book *Rip It Up and Start Again: Postpunk 1978–1984,* and its follow-up, *Totally Wired: Postpunk Interviews and Overviews,* the writer Simon Reynolds explores post-punk and the timing of a unique cultural period, and how Thatcherism was, ironically, beneficial for the arts in Britain. Reynolds has spoken elsewhere about the "liminal class in Britain, this lower-middle class/upper-working-class zone. That area is where a lot of music energy comes from."[6]

Looking at the turn of the millennium and the increasing rancour towards Tony Blair's New Labour, it's easy to find an analogy between post-punk and UK rap music (particularly grime, which we explore further in Chapter 5). Post-punk borrowed liberally from the sound of reggae and dub music. At the same time, British (or mainly English) MCs had enough local inspiration, whether Soul II Soul or London Posse, to recontextualise Black British music and culture into a new identity. It was still largely working-class but also increasingly white. The popular manifestation is Mike Skinner. The genesis of every regular rap guy,his entire schtick has been built on being a very normal, relatable guy. You're listening to The Streets.

Mike Skinner's first two albums—the "post-lad"[7] humour and garage-leaning *Original Pirate Material* and the poppier boy-meets-girl-boy-fucks-it-up concept of A *Grand Don't Come For Free*—are a quasi-biographical approach to everyman stories of solipsism and self-pity. Warbling lyrics like, "She didn't look too bored with what I was saying / Her hair looked much better than the other day," on the chorus of "Could Well Be In", are a tribute to Skinner's ability to reflect and illuminate life's minutiae.

Skinner is perhaps the definition of Simon Reynolds' liminal class. Although by his amusing admission, Skinner is less working and more "Barratt class: suburban estates, not poor but not much money about, really boring."[8]

That *A Grand Don't Come For Free* sold over 1.3 million[9] copies, compared to just over 300,000 copies of Dizzee Rascal's *Boy in da Corner* (granted a very different stylistic execution of

UK rap), nevermind more than ten times Roots Manuva's critically adored *Brand New Second Hand*, might correlate with the country's "twisted race relations" that Jehst mentions.

DISCOGRAPHY

Chapter 3: The Cosmic Gypsies

This chapter is named after the Task Force track of the same name, from the album *Voice of the Great Outdoors.*

Albums, E.P.s & Mixtapes

Braintax - *Fat Head EP*
Braintax - *Future Years EP*
Various Artists - *The '98-Series*
Sadat X - *Wild Cowboys*
Raekwon - *Only Built 4 Cuban Linx*
Lewis Parker - *Rise / Visions of Splendour*
Lewis Parker - *B-Boy Antiks*
Lewis Parker - *Masquerades & Silhouettes (The Ancient Series One)*
Lewis Parker - *It's All Happening Now (The Ancients Series Three)*
Lewis Parker - *Diamond in the Sun's Eye (The Ancient Series Two)*
Jehst - *Premonitions EP*
Task Force - *Voice of the Great Outdoors* EP
Task Force - *New Mic Order*
Jehst - *High Plains Drifter*
Dizee Rascal - *Boy in da Corner*
The Streets - *Original Pirate Material*
The Streets - A *Grand Don't Come For Free*

Singles

Quincy Jones - "Summer in the City"
Steve Miller - "The Joker"
Yes - "Sound Chaser"
Slick Rick Ft. Doug E. Fresh - "La Di Da Di"
Doug E. Fresh Ft.Slick Rick - "The Show"
Soul II Soul - "Back To Life"
The Pharcyde - "Passin' Me By" o-=
Kaliphz Ft. Naseem Hamed - "Walk Like a Champion"
Lewis Parker - "Songs of the Desert"
Lewis Parker - "Eye of Dreams"
Pharoahe Monch - "Simon Says"
Task Force - "Butterfly Concerto"
Task Force - ""Grafdabusup"
Black Rob - "Woah"
Task Force - "Wha Blow!"
Jehst Ft. J-Zone - "Staircase to the Stage"
Jehst Ft. MC Asaviour - "People Under the Weather"
Jehst Ft.Chester P and Kyza -"The Trilogy (Remix)"
Jehst - "High Plains Anthem"
Youngstar - "Pulse X"
Dizzee Rascal - "Fix Up, Look Sharp"
The Streets - "Could Well Be In"
Kanye West - "Diamonds From Sierra Leone"

Chapter 4

Skinnyman

During the research period for the initial chapters of this book, one name kept coming up in conversation. Whether it was stories of him lurking in a studio corner, building a ginormous spliff, or tearing up live shows, Grammy award-winning producers, label managers, and rap raconteurs would namecheck this elusive, political firebrand MC who has only released one album to date.

Skinnyman doesn't have a dedicated PR team or manager, as far as I can tell, but he's fairly active on social media, where I tracked down an email and eventually got a reply. We continued the conversation over a brisk exchange of texts and spoke on the phone a few days after his birthday. I've edited some of the following text for clarity but mostly left it rugged and raw, just like Skinny.

You were born and spent your early childhood in Leeds. What was that like? And how was life different for you when you moved to London?

That was brilliant. It was an eclectic mix of punk rockers, two toners, and people into ska, reggae, dance hall and rock and roll—lots of musical tastes and tribes.

You know when you look at a burger in England and a burger in America, [London] was like that. [Leeds] had everything going on that was in London but on a smaller scale.

How did music come into your life?

My mum was a music lover. We listened to soul, reggae, Motown, and everything on the charts.

Which musicians inspired you when you were growing up? And how did you first get into rap?

Bob Marley and the Wailers. Loads, really. I was influenced by people way before hip-hop came about. We got hip-hop over these shores, but at no time was we ever behind or late as it was emerging from the Lower East Side [of New York].

Hip-hop is a way for poor people to get paid, like a "*Penny for the Guy*." Hold out your hat, and you might get a penny from the Guy. It was an excuse to beg for the money. I'm not a Christian, but we'd do carol singing for the money. Hip-hop was just another hustle.

Can you explain the concept behind Mud Family? What does it stand for?

It stands for Mad Underdog For All of My Individual Living Youth. And it's based on the overstanding that the world's economic elite is now the 1%, leaving 99% of the economically disadvantaged, the underdogs to that situation.

We're all relative to this through the six steps of separation: the whole family, the whole world, the human race.

You were part of the Mud Family, and then there was the Bury Cru and Highbury Hoodlums. What was the relationship between all the crews?

That's regional crews of the Islington area. Highbury, Canonbury, Finsbury, hence the name "bury," so it was a regional thing. We came together from our early days at the Highbury Grove youth centre. Since the age of ten, we'd been hanging around together.

What were the *Mudlumz* nights at Dingwalls[1] like?

We all came together as a collective, wanting to have a platform for everyone to perform, and because there wasn't any such thing, we thought we had to create it ourselves. It was a beautiful time. As a collective, we'd come together to make sure we could acquire venues, design flyers and stickers, and get a street team.

We'd make it free for everyone and anyone could perform: music, poetry, comedy, rapping, or any sort of artistic expression on stage. And we'd have prize money for the winners.

It wasn't just hip-hop. Someone could do a comedy set if they liked or come up and sing a soul song, but it was just promoting local talent that didn't have a platform.

Were they well attended?

Yeah, they were always sold-out occasions. I think the word "free" helped.

Can you talk about the situation with Gilles Peterson's Talkin' Loud label?

The guy who was my A&R, who had faith and belief in me and is still a great friend to this day, is Paul Martin, who worked with Gilles Petterson. A lovely label, full of lovely people doing great things.

The morning we signed with Talkin' Loud at the office was the morning of the 9/11 inside job. So while signing, I think there were some Americans there, and someone said to "put on the news," and there was one plane hanging out of one building, and then we watched as the second plane collided, and it was like, "Right, meeting over."

At the time, I had been reading in Nostradamus that "the man-made mountains of New Jerusalem shall crumble at their peril,"[2] and at the time, we had been playing the song "Like Mountain" by Sizzla, so there were all these mystical connections.

Then the mother label (Mercury Records) decided to axe the label, and all the artists and label workers were axed [too]. I wasn't too bothered about myself, but I was worried about some of the other artists signed at the time, like Roni Size, MJ Cole, and Elizabeth Troy. I didn't want to see anything hinder their success.

I couldn't believe the faith they had in me. I was like, "You lot want to pay me some money to go off and make some music? Ok."

Why were you so surprised by someone else having faith in your music?

Maybe they saw something I didn't see. Or maybe they just thought, "White kid popping up, that's a cash cow."

Being a youth from Britain, surrounded by British culture, when it came to rough jams, there were as many white MCs as Black [MCs] throughout to the present day. There were kids from every nationality. From the early days of break dancing, being white was never a novelty.

Def Jam was the go-to staple for what we considered as hitting. Run-D.M.C., Beastie Boys, Fat Boys. [It was] everything we wanted this new culture to be. There were lots of white youths around the explosion of Run-D.M.C. and Beastie Boys. And when Public Enemy blew up, and a lot of white middle-class kids were hearing the message of empowerment for Black people, maybe they felt excluded.

[After that] I saw the transition of the crowd's demographic when Public Enemy performed in the UK. Where had all the white hip-hop fans gone? Was it because their message may have been pro-Black? But by no means was the message anti-white.

I want to get into the headspace of *Council Estate of Mind*. How long did it take to make the album, and who helped you create it?

Here's what happened. So I went from thinking, *Right, we're gonna' have a big budget, big promotion, big ideas, and people to help me create and achieve my vision* whilst we were at Talkin' Loud. I wanted to reflect on my upbringing and culture, so in the [music] video, I wanted it to be a kind of 1970-'80s blues house party in a terrace house in the back of Leeds, where kids are riding about on choppers—this was before BMX. I wanted someone like Rodigan to be on the decks. So we'd fuse that reggae and punk into my kind of hip-hop.

But I was incarcerated, and I wasn't a whippersnapper anymore. I thought I missed my chance. It was a "I could have been a contender" moment. I felt it might have been time to hang up the mic. But I thought, *What message could I give to the kids coming up?*

And I gave them my honest feelings about how I saw my area. I didn't expect those lyrics to be recorded, it was just me venting through poetry. I got the opportunity to be sent some instrumentals from Baby J and Adam F. Paul Martin was instrumental in getting me the music while I was in custody, and how they had to do that was by buying DMX CDs from HMV and burning the music onto a blank CD, swapping them and sending it to me as an official HMV CD, but really it was pirate with my instrumentals on it.

When I got out there was a guy called DJ Flip, and he was instrumental in making sure that it did happen; he had the studio and the downtime to make it happen. He's equally to be credited for the album as I am.

Samples from Alan Clarke's 1982 TV play *Made in Britain* glue the album together. What was the thinking behind that?

Many messages resonated with me and could have saved me from a lot of mischievous adventures. The film doesn't reflect me. It's about a racist young boy, and I don't relate to the character, but the bits that were said resonated with me. It gelled better than I ever imagined.

Who's the female vocalist, uncredited, on "Loves Gone from the Streets" and "Council Estate of Mind"?

That was my daughter's mother, and when we did the Jazz Cafe[3] performance this year, my daughter did the vocals from the album.

"I'll Be Surprised" is iconic. It's like the soundtrack to a cowboy film set in Finsbury Park. Can you talk us through the themes and the process for that track?

It was a very personal, real-life situation. The lyrics are self-explanatory. He [Baby J] also sent me "No Big Ting" and I had the time to really listen and write lyrical patterns to the song's structure. Until then, I don't think I had the best understanding of the structure of songs.

What makes *Council Estate of Mind* so unique is how it articulates the frustrations of the class system and the resulting inequalities. This country has been obsessed with class for hundreds of years. Do you think that will ever change?

As we sit back and watch this crazy show on planet Earth, we see a divide widening. We're now living in the age of information, where people have access to alternative outlets for information other than what they see through mainstream media.

Some people call this an awakening of society. Some people call this "woke" and then try to mock the word woke. I mean, there's nothing to mock about someone wanting to be enlightened.

Even over this pandemic, the rich have increased their wealth tenfold, and the rest of us have been in despair. I mean, when we see a young, Black footballer feeding the children of the country[4] when the queen fails to do so, and because of his contribution he receives a badge from the queen telling him he has done well, how hypocritical. When the Mud Family formed, the 1% was the 10%.

I'd like to talk about some of the other themes from the record. First up is community. Cuts to youth services in England amounted to £660m over the past decade. There's also research to show a correlation between knife crime and budget cuts to youth services in England.[5] How does that make you feel?

Many a truth said in jest: kids can stab each other all day long around this area, but god forbid you double park your car because the government has no financial return from knife crime or youth violence. Their interest doesn't lie in the safety of the youth from lower working-class environments. Their interests lie in the profits of the corporations they work for.

Let's raise the matter of prison for profits.[6] They are being highly invested by the same people who own the musical industries, radio playlists, and programming lists. And ask ourselves why our music through these outlets [are] so often filled with violent promotion and misogyny. Yet musicians who are speaking an alternative message, other than the agenda of ignorance, get no light by these corporate music masters because it doesn't serve their purpose of increasing crime to go to prison, which they're also interested in.

Many of these musical corporations are invested in playing music that will make the kids behave ignorant[ly]. That will also help them profit when they get sent to prison, which they've also invested in.

On a lighter note, in the years since the album came out, quite a few countries have legalised the recreational use of marijuana (Canada, Georgia, Mexico, South Africa, and Uruguay), plus 24 US states. Should it be legalised in the UK?

Firstly, I am a candidate for medical marijuana and its benefits. For the British government to stop the right for someone to use herbal medicine because it helps a vast range of conditions, and if the British government prevents people from having access, I think it's criminal of them. Recreationally, if a consenting adult decides to use marijuana, who is anybody to say differently?

Just like how alcohol in some Islamic countries is forbidden because it's haram, they mirror the attitude of a country like Britain has toward marijuana. Given the evidence, we know alcohol is highly harmful and intoxicating when marijuana isn't.

Returning to the record, you've got the album, and now you need to find a way to sell it. And then Low Life came about. How did that connection take place?

DJ Flip was renting office space from Joseph...what's that scumbag's name...Christie! He was renting office space from him, and they approached me with a distribution offer, and I thought, *Ok, let it take a natural course. I'll do distribution with this guy.*

Low Life was probably the most successful hip-hop label in the country at the time, and your record is probably the most successful album they released, but you've said that you didn't make a penny from it. Why was that?

Because Joseph Christie is a criminal rat piece of shit.

And he's gone off the radar, right?

No. He's invested in a resort in Goa, I know that much, and there's also an address for him in Australia. The royalties have never been addressed.

How do you see the legacy of *Council Estate of Mind* in the context of British rap music?

It's way beyond British rap music. It's even bigger than hip-hop. It's the encapsulation of social observations within a certain time period. It should go down [in history] just like George Orwell's *1984*.

And when you look at what's going on now—Stormzy headlining Glastonbury, Dave doing arena tours and on the front page of *GQ*, drill songs topping charts—what do you think of that?

My children play them all day, and I'm fully immersed in the current. I've watched the evolution of the UK music industry over the last twenty years since the internet. And now children from the UK, can immediately embrace the artists without any middleman and are allowing these artists to become the pop stars of the modern-day without diluting anything. It's a brilliant time for UK music.

Any final thoughts?

Yeah, for you. About the name of your book, which I like, by the way. Is it from the Heartless Crew track?...

No, it references the Wiley track "Wot Do U Call It?" and our imprecise labelling of rap music in the UK.

Ok. The corporate white devil at the BBC [laughs] decided they didn't want to lose out on the growing Black market in UK music. So they created a music station dedicated to this, 1Xtra, and they introduced it as the "Home of British Black Music."

And it went from being the home of British black music to the home of "urban" music. Now, if I'm a hip-hop rapper from Devon, I'm not even suburban; I'm "rural." So, where do I go in the charts if I live in Devon or Cornwall? Should I be in the countryside or urban?

Because Destiny Child was dominating the urban charts and they are from Texas, Missy Elliott and Timbaland are way rural. But if I'm a country and western singer from London, am I not urban? So much so, it begets "What do you call it?" because they didn't market it as Black music, and they got all confused about what is urban and what isn't.

Do you want to know what it is? Blah, blah, urban sheep have you any wool? 1xtra and the BBC are enemies. I'd prefer it if they never play my music. It seems to me they're conditioning us to use this word ["urban"] instead of "Black."

It's an interesting point because language can be distorted from the truth.

Yeah, it does, blurred lines. And me being a white rapper and you being a [white] journalist writing about Black music. It's our duty now, to champion this cause [because] otherwise Black lives will never matter. And I think our Black audience would appreciate us more for it.

DISCOGRAPHY

Essentials
Skinnyman - “No Big Ting”
Skinnyman - “Fuck the Hook”
Skinnyman - “Council Estate of Mind”
Skinnyman - “I’ll Be Surprised”
Skinnyman - “Love’s Gone From The Streets”
DJ Vadim Ft. Skinnyman - “Life From The Itchy Side”

Deep Cuts
Booty Bouncers Ft. Wiley, Skinnyman, Wunda, Hyperactive - “Hyperactive”
Mark B & Blade, Ft. Lewis Parker and Skinnyman - “Long Awaited”

Chapter 5

Let's Push Things Forward

In the opening chapters of this book, we've looked at the origin stories behind several classic British rap albums leading up to and immediately following the turn of the millennium. The album format remains the most convincing artefact of an individual's sacrifice for their art. However, the currency for getting heard was, and remains to be, singles and mixtapes.

Before the rise of social media, YouTube, and platforms like Napster (which we'll return to), exposure to this "currency" was through three routes: listening to the radio (shows like Tim Westwood's Radio 1 *Rap Show*, pirate stations like Kane FM, and what would become the grime powerhouse Rinse FM), attending club nights and live shows, and buying music. The latter is not nearly as abstract a thought as it is now.

That meant visits to your local record shop or, if you're living in the suburbs, trips "up town"—emporiums like Piccadilly Records in Manchester, and London shops like Deal Real, Mr Bongo and, further East, Rhythm Division, to name but a few. It's become a cliche, but these spaces were more than just stores, often playing the role of a community centre, rehearsal studio, and event space. The positive psychogeographic impact of these places cannot be underestimated.

Deal Real, Kung-Fu, and London's Hip-Hop Community at the Turn of the Millennia

A trip to Deal Real was a particular thrill circa Y2K. The walls were covered floor to ceiling in brightly coloured mixtape CDs, 12-inches from the US, and just as many homegrown acts. Turning up on any given day, you could see impromptu performances by a young Kanye West, Mos Def, or Estelle. The latter was one of several artists who served in an apprenticeship behind the counter.

The first iteration of Deal Real was started by Pete Bond and Tony Vegas of the Scratch Perverts, based on Noel Street in Soho, the epicentre of London record store culture. Former Deal Real employee and DJ Sarah Love picks up the story: "At that time, you could only know what was going on by physically leaving your house and going to the store. You had a lot of snooty stores, but Deal Real was very down to earth. When I started working there, it was normal for Black Twang, Task Force, Rodney P, and Skitz to come and hang out. It was a party in the shop every day. It had a different feel from the other record shops. People would be cyphering, politicking, and even drinking! I feel super privileged to be part of that."[1]

According to Pete Bond, "It was an adventure from start to finish. Record shops have always had this reputation of being intimidating, and I didn't want that [to be the case] with Deal Real. I also always wanted a girl behind the counter to make other girls feel more comfortable."

However, due to Vegas' blossoming DJ career with the Scratch Perverts—they won the DMC World Championships in 1999 and 2001, and toured the world as a result—sinking vinyl sales, an increase in Soho rents, and "drinking heavily and not dealing with the business," Bond closed the shop in

2000, just as UK hip-hop was enjoying its second coming. (Pete tells me he has since been sober for many years.)

Fortunately for London-based b-boys and girls, Deal Real reopened under new management in 2002, in a new location on Marlborough Court, a stone's throw away from the original. Co-manager Vince Olutayo explained, "We just felt like that kind of physical space—that people could connect, develop themselves, meet, and collaborate—was missing." Olutayo believed "a record store would bring some of the community spirit back."[2]

That community spirit Olutayo spoke of was centred around Deal Real's legendary Friday Night Live open mic night. Aside from some of the biggest MCs in the US and UK performing for free, it was also a testing ground for artists on the verge of pop star ubiquity, including the Black Eyed Peas and a very young Amy Winehouse, who played an intimate guitar set and, in a typically candid fashion, took it as an opportunity to throw verbal slugs at the Island Records A&R in attendance. Typical of the neighbourhood, space was at a premium, but what Deal Real lacked in square metres, it made up for in frenetic energy. (The shop's location around the corner from the Shakespeare's Head pub didn't hurt.) One particularly rowdy Friday night, I squeezed in by the door to see Jamaican-American rapper Canibus perched atop the counter performing "Second Round Knockout". The place went wild.

Doc Brown, a young MC who was part of Poisonous Poets and an aspiring comedy writer at the time, cut his teeth at rap battles like Mudlumz before becoming a host for the live sessions at Deal Real. He recalls, "Mos Def and Pharoahe Monch saying that [Deal Real was] hip-hop in that raw form that we were generating, it didn't exist for them in the States because it had become like a pro sport – a way of making a living, seeking millions even, and greed had overtaken. Long after the shop would shut on a Friday night, there'd be 50 of us in a cypher on the corner, just for the hell of it. It's easy to be romantic about it 'cause that's what it was."[3]

For Brown, Deal Real represented a "Feeling of peace and safety. Everyone had their issues at home or on the street or wherever, myself included, but when we were in that shop, there were no postcode wars, there was no poverty, no privilege, it was just beats, rhymes and a togetherness that sounds like it was on some cheesy shit but it wasn't."[4] And for Brown, real name Ben Smith, Deal Real changed his life. It was there he met superproducer Mark Ronson, who took him on tour supporting his album *Versions*. This opened more doors and, albeit indirectly, provided a platform for a career as an actor and writer in television. Some might call it social networking.

Interestingly, Deal Real had an open-door policy when it came to what type of MCs could perform, and more than a few grime rappers made their way down that infamous side road from Carnaby Street, through the baying crowds, and into the bright lights of the shop on a Friday night. Tinchy Stryder recalls being invited to Deal Real, "Performing a couple of tracks with Ruff Sqwad and my track 'Not Like Me,' I was proper happy. It was a good day."[5]

Eventually, Deal Real shut its doors in 2007, with Olutayo citing marketplace forces: "Ultimately, vinyl had stopped selling as much. Most people had gone online by that stage, even DJs."

For both iterations of the store, Deal Real's place at the heart of the UK hip-hop community can't be disputed; it was a living, breathing testament to the passion for the culture. Yet, hip-hop is a hustle, whether you're starting out or an established star. It may sound like a stereotype, but be prepared to hustle hard or get hustled (as we saw in the case of Low Life). As Will Ashon put it to me in the context of record labels, "Everyone [was] scrambling around for pennies, which creates a certain amount of competitive rivalry."

In my own experience self-publishing a hip-hop magazine, I'll probably always shudder at the acronym "SOR" (sale or return) given the number of times in the early days that distributors or shop assistants would "need to check with my boss where the copies are."

In the case of Deal Real, there appears to be a case of *the hustle* in effect over the naming rights of the new store. Sarah Love was keen to stress that the second iteration of Deal Real "wanted to continue what the shop was known for, but they ripped off Pete's store and name."

According to Pete, Vince stopped answering his calls despite agreeing to buy the Deal Real name and stock: "They took the stock, and they never paid me a penny." He believes that they must have contacted the landlord of the building and taken all the leftover stock, including "my signed Big L record, who died before they opened that shop...I saw a picture of it on the wall in their shop, and it was stolen from me. That guts me."

It's a painful memory for Pete, who "wished they changed the name" because of the confusion it has caused people and the perceived damage to his legacy.

* * *

Sarah Love was also one of the resident DJs at Kung Fu, a fabled UK hip-hop club night that started in 2000 in a tiny bar on Upper Street in Islington. Alongside fellow residents DJ Harry Love (Sarah's boyfriend at the time) and motormouth host Mystro, Kung Fu played host to "anyone of note from hip-hop in the UK," according to Sarah, adding, "It was important for us, regardless of who was on the flyer, [that] we made it £5 to get in. And we'd always end the night with an open mic."

It was a simple but effective formula for a community that wasn't being taken seriously. As Sarah explains, "It was such a special atmosphere with regular faces dedicated to UK hip-hop. And at that time, no one gave a shit. It was just us. The industry shunned it."

Kung Fu soon outgrew its original venue and moved to the bigger WKD in Camden, eventually settling nearby at Underworld. The night also had a brief residency at Fabric Nightclub, a testament to its crowd-pulling credentials, even if the wider industry was taking little notice of the music.

Sarah grins broadly as she recalls her favourite performances: "When Klash[nekoff] and Terra Firma performed, it was insane. We had the sort of origins of road rap with Klash and…then someone like Ty, [who] did a really special party with a live band."

The Body Horror of Klashnekoff, Ms. Dynamite Goes "A Little Deeper"

Terra Firma founder Klashnekoff's description of the group as "The closest thing you can get to the British Wu-Tang"[6] was wide of the mark for several reasons, particularly given the productivity of Staten Island's finest, while Terra Firma only released one album together in 2006. That said, their impact on UK hip-hop and what would later become road rap remains highly significant.

I interviewed Klashnekoff and fellow Terra Firma founding member Kyza (alongside Skriblah) several times throughout the noughties. Musically, they were part of the UK hip-hop lineage, but their lyrics possessed a fierce urgency that set them apart, particularly Klashnekoff.

There was an authenticity to Klash, real name Darren Kandler from Stoke Newington, that would have been an A&R's dream had he timed his entry into music a decade later. But in the early noughties, it would have sent major label executives running into the hills as fast as their skintight jeans would permit them.

When I first met Kandler, he was a late-twenty-something single dad living in a Hackney high-rise. He was a boisterous, charismatic chap who possessed little internal filter—in our first interview, he called Tim Westwood a "silly cunt"—yet both the talent and passion to be a genuine success. His first-ever release was the "Daggo Mentality"/"Jankrowville" double single, produced by Lewis Parker and released by YNR label in 2002. It was a million miles away from the spacey "backpacker rap" that Jehst mocked in Chapter 3 and very different to the sound Lewis Parker is best known for.

Sparse West Indian drums, flutes, and banjos juxtaposed with boom-bap beats laid the groundwork for Klash to tell apocalyptic stories of city life. "I live amongst the murderers...The east maze metropolis, filled to the brim with metro police officers," he spits in his fiery, cockney patios cadence on "Daggo Mentality." "Jankrowville" starts with a rowdy live skit with Klash singing ragga style "just liiiive your life" before getting into the track proper, where, over a simple Leon Thomas soul-jazz piano loop, Klash raps as if his life depends on it.

He crams thirty-two bars into the first verse and at least twenty-four into the second verse, before hitting the final line, impassioned and vexed, "Ah them nah like we and we nah like them!" The strain in Klash's voice is so audible it sounds like he's inhaling all the oxygen left in the mic booth. Yet this is not youthful verbosity. Lyrics like, "You know the status, players hate us, the coppers chase us...'Cause I've worked for the worst wages," might rhyme nice but they also paint a vivid picture. And when combined with,"The East Maze where the lifts are full of piss / And pitch black skies and clouds of red mist / I wrote this shit, fury flying through my fist," Klash conjures up imagery of a war zone and, simultaneously, his own reality where "Negroes stay negative, I guess that's relative...It all relates to the life that where we live."

There's a quality to the music that recalls the film theory of body horror, a concept that began with the first cinema adaptation of *Frankenstein,* directed by J. Searle Dawley in 1910, and peaked in the 1980s with films like *An American Werewolf in London* (dir. John Landis) and *The Fly,* by body horror auteur David Cronenberg. It's a demonstration of the graphic destruction and mutilation of the physical human body to entertain audiences through shock.

It's the same impact Klash's lyrics cause, with rhymes like, "Get dropped on your doorstep like Dando" (for all you noughties babies, this is a reference to Jill Dando, the television presenter and journalist who was murdered on her doorstep in 1999) and the almost comical, "I'll split you in half like a gun blast from Lennox," a nod to the likely shellacking Canadian British heavyweight boxing champion Lennox Lewis would give his competitors. Your eyes and ears are threatened and disgusted, but you can't pull away.

Whereas the human body is a medium for representing terror and fear, "Transformed by mutations and deformations for the imagination,"[7] in *The Fly*, et cetera, in the case of Klash, it's the city. Specifically, Hackney's "east maze" and a society that leaves him constantly on edge, oscillating between fight and flight.

It's an anxiety that becomes all the more potent in the years that followed as Hackney became swept up in gentrification, with two distinct worldviews emerging in the busy East London borough. The "Daggo Mentality"/"Jankrowville" singles laid the foundations for K-lash's excellent full-length debut, *The Sagas of Klashnekoff*, and provided a roadmap for road rap. The mixtape-come-album sold more than 30,000 copies thanks to its nearly perfect mix of rawness and technical lyricism.

Rap dynamics aside, other qualities marked Klashnekoff out from his peers during the noughties and the roadmen rappers he influenced in more recent years. Namely, his crooning, where he freely channels his inner Sizzler on tracks like "B4 U Die", his willingness to experiment with producers—he was one of the few "hip-hop" MCs of the era to welcome grime, working with Terror Danjah, jumping on Kano's "Sometimes" remix, and telling me that JME "was a genuine artist, talking about real stuff"—and his use of Soviet-era militant imagery throughout his musical narrative.

The "Black Russian" isn't just a prop but a conceptual backdrop that provides Klash with enough creative juice to envelope his world into what experts on Russia have described as a "besieged fortress" narrative, helped by reading "books written by forbidden government authors." ("It's Murda") Finally, and most importantly, his vulnerability on wax distinguishes him when contrasted with some of the violence in his lyrics. Klash often laments the loss of his father, but, as in the case of "Black Rose," he combines it with the drama a surprise pregnancy causes.

This tension made Klash such an exciting and contrarian artist. "Sometimes I stutter and get things wrong and contradict myself, and that's because I'm not always 100% certain of what I'm saying. But there are no regrets. That's what makes me me, and when the passion goes, the music does, too," he explained to me when we last spoke in 2010. The interview was a cover feature for *Bonafide*, timed for the release of *Back to the Sagas*, a patchy sequel to his astounding debut, although the magazine feature nearly didn't happen after he skipped the photoshoot, reasoning that he accidentally shaved off his moustache. When the photoshoot finally took place, Klash declined all the latest clothes the stylist offered and instead chose a vintage army jacket provided by photographer Yev Kazannik to wear for his cover image.

* * *

The same year that Klashnekoff blew the doors of British rap music wide open with his "Daggo Mentality"/"Jankrowville" singles, a debut album arrived from another determined MC eager to make her mark, albeit to a far broader audience. Ms. Dynamite's *A Little Deeper* isn't exactly a hip-hop album or a garage record, but it's not precisely a neo-soul album, either (sorry, Will Ashon).

Released in September 2002, probably timed with a view toward the awards season, the album was helmed by American producer Salaam Remi. By then the New Yorker had more than fifteen years of studio experience, starting his career with Kurtis Blow and Biz Markie, and was coming off a hot streak, having produced records for Nas, Lisa Lopes, and The Fugees. Just a year later he co-wrote and produced Amy Winehouse's first charting single, "Stronger Than Me," and subsequently worked on both of her albums.

Jehst admitted to me that he was "influenced by [Remi's] sound" and envious of the beat for Ms. Dynamite's "Dy-Na-Mi-Tee," a track that reached number 5 in the charts and is the album's undoubted earworm: "I don't think anyone would describe what she did as underground boom bap rap, but pop hook aside, the beat is."

Remi's rich production, highlighted by bright reggae-tinged percussion and drums, provided *A Little Deeper* with a big sound that was synonymous with American R&B and hip-hop, but Ms. Dynamite's lyrical content was moored in British life while simultaneously dealing with universal themes and concerns: being a teenager, domestic abuse, death, violence, and ultimately, owning the line between love and hate. When woven with her own personal experience and ragga singer-MC style, some of the songs develop an impressive depth of character. "Afraid 2 Fly" was inspired by the infancy death of five siblings, while "It Takes More" aims at plastic gangsters with razor-sharp lines like, "Now, who gives a damn about the ice on your hand, If it's not too complex, Tell me how many Africans died for the baguettes on your Rolex." It's heady stuff that is deceptive on initial listens because of the general mood of the sound.

Salaam Remi's association with the record may have helped raise it and Ms. Dynamite's profile in the US, with *Rolling Stone, Spin* and *The New Yorker* all gushing in its praise of the album, even if the attention didn't convert to sales in the country. Remi remained ambivalent, saying, "I'm just happy that there's a market for good music somewhere, whereas, in America, it's just been a repetition of what's hot." Although *A Little Deeper* has since gone on to sell more than half a million copies worldwide.

The album's reception was a culture shock for Ms. Dynamite, whose real name is Niomi Daley. "One day, I was living in a hostel, going to college and on Jobseeker's Allowance," she told *The Guardian*. "The next, I was walking into my local newsagent and seeing my name and face splashed all over the papers. It was as quick as that."[8]

Ms. Dynamite's origins were in UK garage, with a critical moment being her appearance on the infectious bounce of DJ Sticky's "Booo!" released in 2001. The UKG sound had just about enough influence on her debut album to demonstrate the potent alchemy that can occur when British dance music fuses with rap. And this provided a roadmap for how British MCs could experience chart success if they wanted it.

* * *

Although I was essentially hip-hop obsessive by the time I was old enough to get into nightclubs (OK, maybe I wasn't quite as old as my birth certificate stated), I mainly went to garage raves, as there just weren't many hip-hop nights in the suburbs of East London and Essex during the late '90s. There was often an "R&B and hip-hop" room at the bigger garage events, although they were invariably an afterthought, where DJs mainly played the chart fillers of the day.

As a result, nights like Frisky, Pure Silk, and Garage Nation are etched in my memory. Dancefloors were awash with gaudy Moschino and Iceberg shirts, heavy silver bangles bouncing, boldly buckled Patrick Cox shoes, and girls in cowboy hats with champagne flutes and glasses of 'JD' swishing to the sound of sped-up R&B vocals over two-step beats. As Maxwell D, of garage crew Pay As U Go Cartel, put it "That was the garage-style: dress to impress."[9] UK garage is known for its "two-step" rhythm, which deviates from the traditional four-on-the-floor beat of house music where it evolved from, particularly the more soulful and vocal-heavy subgenres like New York garage and Chicago house. It also drew influence from Jamaican dub and reggae, as well as hip-hop and R&B.

Given its divisiveness within dance music and lack of acknowledgement as a cultural movement at the time, UK garage has enjoyed an outsized influence on popular culture in the years that have followed. Hip fashion labels like Palace have mined the Croydon bling aesthetic, documentaries by *Boiler Room*, reverential articles in *The Wire* and *Guardian* newspaper, and lux £100 photography books like *UKG* by the photographer Ewen Spencer, all providing gushing retrospectives.

UK garage has enjoyed a renaissance musically, too, through electronic producers like Joy Orbison and Mount Kimbie and labels like Kiwi Records. Yet, at the time, it was criticised for lacking substance and often treated like the bastard little brother of more rhythmically complex forms of UK dance music like jungle or drum & bass.

In both sound and style, garage was a world away from UK hip-hop, but by the turn of the millennium, UKG was metamorphosising into a darker, MC-driven sound. And without it, I don't believe grime would have come to exist. Even in 2006, four years after what is broadly acknowledged as the inception point of grime, the distinction was unclear, with Lethal Bizzle telling me, "To me it's still garage, I'm not really sure where this grime thing comes from, I think the media came out with it."

A Daily Mail Reader's Worst Nightmare: So Solid Crew

Three singles were critical to this development. The first was "Do You Really Like It?" by DJ Pied Piper and the Masters of Ceremonies, released just in time for summer. With its two-step, by-the-numbers approach to production and nursery rhyme chorus—"We're lovin' it, lovin' it, lovin' it / We're lovin' it Like this"—it was hardly "Butterfly Concerto," but that was probably the point. The song was immediate, infectious, and undeniably feel-good, the soundtrack to a thousand sloshed barbecues and balmy Ayia Napa nights. Talking of metamorphosis, the MC-in-chief was Kamachi Sly, once of Hijack, now the Unknown MC.

Perhaps unsurprisingly, the song was a hit and topped the charts in May 2001. It wasn't the first garage song to achieve this, it wasn't even the first MC-led tune to reach number 1 in the UK, but it proved a moment of mainstream ubiquity, a song your gran could hum along to, or one used to close out children's TV show *Dick & Dom in da Bungalow*. In other words, it was the death knell of garage's credibility.

Fortunately, other forces were pushing the UKG sound into new and adventurous territory. Pay As U Go Cartel didn't exist for too long, although their discography is extensive compared to DJ Pied Piper and the Masters of Ceremonies. The crew had a rolling cast of members, the most notable of which included Maxwell D, Wiley, God's Gift, DJ Target and DJ Slimzee. Target, Wiley and Maxwell D were mates from Limehouse and Bow in east London. They had a popular garage show on Rinse FM called *Ladies Hit Squad*, which led right into a show that featured Rinse FM founders Slimzee and Geeneus together with the MCs Plague, Major Ace, and God's Gift.

And as Target recalls, "For some reason, every Sunday afternoon when their show was on, the Pay As You Go [mobile phone] network used to go down, and everyone could call into the studio for free. It kept happening so after the fourth week they was calling it the *Pay As You Go show.*"[10] From those innocuous Telo network failures, a name was spawned for a crew that made music that would morph into something else—Roll Deep—developing a sound that would radically alter 21st century music, popular culture, and even British politics.

But first, that critical garage track from Pay As U Go. "Champagne Dance" was released in 2001 and charted the following April. The track is more informed by hip-hop than the saccharine two-step that had begun to spread through the airwaves. It wasn't as weird as their first single, "Know We," with its icy synth proto-eski sound and dancehall-meets-garage MC raps, but for a track that charted at number 13, it was very weird. This was epitomised by the accompanying music video for "Champagne Dance," where the group flipped the cliche, performing outside a boxing ring where two two female sparrers try to knock the living daylights out of each other. It's a proper posse cut with each MC delivering: God's

Gift as the lover man, triple time from Maxwell D, and Wiley, who already sounded completely unique.

Pay As U Go Cartel came up through pirate radio and raves. First and foremost, they were friends, mucking around, having fun, and making music. Between the commercial success of "Do You Really Like It?" and the innovation of "Champagne Dance," there was "21 Seconds" by So Solid Crew, all released in the same year.

So Solid Crew were an altogether different beast. The South London collective, which included thirty members at its peak, was literally the *biggest thing* to happen in UK garage. And, for much of 2001, pop music. The group was founded by Megaman, who was previously remanded and released after four months in prison for attempted murder at the age of sixteen.

Brought up by his grandparents in a religious household, his experience in jail and the glamour of mid-'90s hip-hop motivated him to start So Solid Crew, saying, "Diddy, Biggie and Tupac hit the screens, I was like 'woah, mans got to do something.' Otherwise we'd have been R&B singers."[11] Megaman, real name Dwanyne Vincent, possessed an RZA-esque vision for So Solid Crew, and in the Channel 4 documentary *This Is So Solid*, he explained that his objective was to create a brand strong enough that different So Solid members could be sent out to ten different raves to do ten So Solid PAs on a single night.

Such savvy marketing found a perfect fit in Relentless Records, the nascent indie with major label connections founded by Shabir "Shabs" Jobanputra. Shabs had already experienced success in the music industry, first in PR, with Media Village, where he adapted the US "Street Team" grassroots approach to promotions to the UK landscape, and then Outcaste Records.

Established as a joint adventure with Tommy Boy Records in New York, Outcaste's objective was to provide visibility and amplification of British Asian culture in music.

Relentless started by releasing mainly garage singles. So Solid's debut album, *They Don't Know*, was the first full-length release on the label. Shabs and Megaman had an inherent understanding that by merging garage and hip-hop with a gangster veneer, the group would appeal to a young audience well beyond London and the major urban centres in the UK.

Through a combination of the group narrative and Shabs' marketing skills, So Solid was a *Daily Mail* reader's worst nightmare, a media-managed anxiety. Their introduction to the wider world, "21 Seconds"—so named for the designated time each MC was given to get their lyrics out—was built over a minimal two-step production and showcased the various personalities within the crew. The single topped the charts and sold almost 120,000 copies in its first week. It was the first of four So Solid Crew singles to appear in the top 20, but violence and controversy were never far from the group, many of whom came "from struggle," MC Harvey explained in an interview with *The Independent*. Everything we've done, we've had to struggle."[12]

The group was often tarred with inciting a culture of violence by the media, as was the case in the after-hours of a New Year's Day party in Birmingham in 2003, when teenagers Letisha Shakespeare and Charlene Ellis were shot dead in the crossfire between rival gangs. Mid- and senior-level Labour ministers were quick to lay the blame on So Solid, even though they didn't perform at that event, held more than 120 miles from their home. It was as if, in the eyes of politicians, their music caused murder by proxy.

"Idiots like the So Solid Crew are glorifying gun culture and violence," declared culture minister Kim Howells. While Ms. Dynamite, a regular collaborator with the group, dismissed Howells' claim, responding that, "The media have blown it out of all proportion. Garage is a young London scene. That's why people in power are afraid of us and try everything to shut us down."[13]

Yet even after success, So Solid Crew often found themselves in the middle of mayhem. Skat D was fined, having admitted to breaking a fifteen-year-old school girl's jaw after she rejected his advances, both G-Man and Asher D were arrested for possession of a firearm, and producer Carl Morgan is currently serving a thirty-year sentence for murder.

The latter saw Megaman stand trial on three separate occasions for encouraging his friend Carl Morgan to shoot dead twenty-four-year-old Colin Scarlett, the partner of Morgan's ex-girlfriend. Megaman spent two years in jail before the case was rejected due to lack of evidence, and he asserts that the police tried to use his lyrics as evidence against him.

Of course, this is only a snapshot of the So Solid Crew story, which has become a tale of genuine stardom and reality TV ennui, of fortitude and improbable drive, of murder charges and shootings, of beef with everyone from Dizzee Rascal to then Home Secretary David Blunkett. The sensationalist narrative surrounding the group, like some sort of tabloid mimesis, often obscures the occasionally great and deceptively influential music So Solid Crew made. This is all the more significant when you consider the various individual's music careers post-So Solid; the whole was greater than the sum of its parts.

Whether it's Stormzy's all-conquering headline appearance at Glastonbury, Boy Better Know selling out their own festival at the O2, or Russ Millions and Tion Wayne topping the charts with the first UK drill track, So Solid walked the long yards so others could run.

Somehow, they made the underground sound of pirate radio and roadman lifestyle into pop music, while retaining a sharp edge. At least for a year. Through a combination of being banned from performing live through to their own implosion, So Solid never had the chance to lead a 60,000-strong festival call-and-response chant of "21 seconds, t-t-t."

As Simon Reynolds put it, "Out went two-step's high pitched diva vocals, sensual swing, and sexed-up amorousness; in came gruff rapping, stiff electro-influenced beats, and raucous aggression."[14] Through So Solid Crew, and Pay As U Go and Heartless Crew before them, this was ground zero for grime. And it was most definitely rap, only garage-style.

DISCOGRAPHY

Chapter 5: Let's Push Things Forward

This chapter is named after The Streets song, "Let's Push Things Forward".

Albums, E.P.s & Mixtapes

Mark Ronson - *Versions*
Klashnekoff - *The Sagas of Klashnekoff*
Klashnekoff - *Back to the Sagas*
Ms. Dynamite - *A Little Deeper*

Singles

Canibus - "Second Round K.O."

DJ Pied Piper and the Masters of Ceremonies - "Do You Really Like It?"

So Solid Crew - "21 Seconds"

Pay As U Go Cartel - "Champagne Dance"

Klashnekoff - "Daggo Mentality"/"Jankrowville"

Amy Winehouse - "Stronger Than Me"

Klashnekoff - "B4 U Die"

Kano Ft. Klashnekoff - "Sometimes (Remix)"

Klashnekoff - "Black Rose"

Ms. Dynamite - "Dy-Na-Mi-Tee"

Ms. Dynamite - "Afraid 2 Fly"

Ms. Dynamite - "It Takes More"

Ms. Dynamite - "Booo!"

Tinchy Stryder - "Not Like Me"

Chapter 6

Wot Do U Call It?

As grime began to emerge from the ethers of garage, the world was changing rapidly and shaping music in response. The impact of 9/11 was seismic. Fear and confusion soon gave way to anger and demonstration over George W. Bush's retaliation, together with Tony Blair's support, of the War in Afghanistan, followed by the War in Iraq. Weeks after Al-Qaeda decimated the World Trade Center, I began studying at a university in Manchester.

There were large demonstrations against the war throughout that first year, with locals and students from all backgrounds joining them, including myself. However, university was also a timely reminder of the UK's entrenched attitudes around social class. This was partly due to the combination of three institutions in the country's biggest university city: Manchester University, Manchester Business School, and Manchester Metropolitan, or "the Met," where I studied. I recall drunken (Manchester) "Uni" rugby players chanting songs about "Met dads working for my dad" and being called a "dirty Commie" (at best, I dabbled).

It was an exciting time and has often been the case for me; music provided a backdrop and a catalyst. Aside from hip-hop and garage music—which, contrary to popular belief at the time, did have some following in the North—I was attending drum & bass, house, and jungle raves, which provided a new perspective, opening my eyes to powerful shared experiences. But music was changing from the inside, too.

Disrupting the Industry with Napster, the iPod, and Music 2000

Napster, the peer-to-peer file-sharing service, was shut down that same year by a court order. It was founded by Shawn Fanning and Sean Parker and had only been around for two years. Still, its disruption to the music industry was epic. Available to anyone with a computer and internet connection, it allowed users to download tracks sometimes months before an album release date for free (and free of royalties). Perhaps most importantly, it allowed them to cherry-pick the songs they wanted.

Napster provided the foundation for a worldwide black market that traded MP3s. Without the legal rights to songs, bands, and records, Napster—and the many similar platforms that sprouted up after its demise—severely damaged music sales. To put it in perspective, "In 2000 alone, total recording sales decreased by 33%. And by the end of the year, it had an estimated '75 million users.'"[1]

It wasn't all bad—just as the music industry it disrupted wasn't all good—and it did help promote emerging artists and foster a new internet community of music fans. It could even be considered an early example of social media centred around the purity of one thing: music as MP3. The age of streaming that dominates the music industry today started with Napster. A year later, Apple effectively legitimised what Napster had started with the glitzy launch of the iPod, introduced in October with the slogan "1,000 songs in your pocket." The iPod wasn't the first MP3 player, but it was among the smallest and easiest to use, with its distinctive scroll wheel function. And since Apple didn't release the iTunes Store until 2003, users had to add music to their iPod from ripped CDs or other "online sources."

Parallel to consumption, the tools for making music were rapidly changing too (there were also significant changes afoot in the music media, but we'll return to that). Not unrelated to the rise of Napster, DAW (digital audio workstation) music production software, such as Music 2000, allowed users to record audio on a personal computer cheaply.

In the case of Music 2000, the software was a game for the original Sony PlayStation 1. Aside from its affordability—the game would have cost around £30 upon its release—it was straightforward to use, with players navigating a grid of sound channels, effects, and even a video sequencer. It was hardly cutting-edge technology back then, and now it's viewed with a kitschy charm.

Music 2000 included MIDI support and even basic sampling. Users could replace the game's PS1 CD with an audio CD and rip, chop, and edit samples to their heart's content, or even record their own sounds from scratch by connecting up a microphone. Its simplicity and speed made it an ideal tool for an emerging generation of grime and rap producers, who were less concerned with high fidelity and more interested in making simple eight-bar loops for an MC to spit over that could be blasted from a cell phone.

Early supporters of the software included brothers Skepta and JME, dubstep pioneers Benga and Skream, and So Solid Crew, who managed to squeeze a bona fide hit out of Music 2000 with "Oh No." In an interview with *VICE*, JME reminisced about the formative technology: "People at school used to come up to me and ask me to make them ringtones on their phones." He took to Music 2000 after graduating from the game Mario Paint to make music. "Our music was born into a digital age. Grime is a lot to do with that digital sound," he added. JME admitted in the same interview that before he knew what Spotify was, he considered removing his music from the platform, having heard that it was "like a legal Napster, mainly intended for casual listeners."[2] Perhaps he did know after all.

New Labour's Urban Renaissance Strategy, Pirate Radio, and the Birth of Grime

Not long after I graduated from Manchester, wide-eyed and heavily in debt, the 7/7 bombings took place, when, on 7 July 2005, four coordinated attacks were carried out on London's public transport system by Islamist terrorists. Apart from the bombers, fifty-two UK residents of eighteen different nationalities were killed and more than 700 people were injured in the attacks.

I recall the day well: panic-stricken phone calls with loved ones, eyeballs glued to BBC and Sky News with such intensity that blood might curdle with tears. It was a tragic event that—for better or worse—felt all the more real living in the city. Without CCTV cameras, the attacks could have been more deadly, even though they ultimately failed to prevent them.

Between the 9/11 attacks in 2001, the 7/7 bombings in 2005, and New Labour's Urban Renaissance strategy, the Labour government doubled down on installing CCTV cameras throughout the country. The Urban Renaissance strategy was essentially an attempt to bring the middle classes back to the inner cities by promoting new development in central areas rather than the suburbs through a mixture of retail, leisure, and housing. However, critics said it was viewed from and primarily benefited a middle-class perspective and was a catalyst for gentrification. The strategy was intimately linked to the increase in the use of CCTV cameras in the capital, and "Research has shown that CCTV control is characterised by a 'selective gaze' onto specific categories of people (teenagers, ethnic minorities) considered 'suspicious.'"[3] (As of 2022, London has the most CCTV cameras outside of China and India, with an estimated 942,000 units installed, or one for every fourteen residents. Big brother really is watching you.)

Simultaneously, inner-city playgrounds and youth clubs began to shut across London. At the turn of the millennium, this shutting off of social opportunities created a challenging and increasingly paranoid environment for those already living on the breadlines of society.

But from pressure comes diamonds, and these conditions helped birth grime music.

Grime is a sound born from the working-class communities based in and around East London, and yet another result of the musical ingenuity of Black Britain. With its spiritual home in Newham and Tower Hamlets, two of the poorest boroughs not just in London but the whole of the UK, beyond the music, grime enabled young people to create a sense of belonging.

As Dr. Joy White puts it in *Terraformed: Young Black Lives in the Inner City*, young people made "music that allowed them to narrate the conditions of their being, and to articulate their struggles, their joys, and their losses."[4]

As mentioned in the previous chapter, physical spaces, such as record shops, raves, youth clubs, and radio stations, were crucial to grime. This was particularly true as it was the last significant music scene to emerge in the UK before the internet and smartphones took over. "People don't really talk about the ecosystem enough. It's like in garage music, [record shops] sold tickets and they sold vinyl, thousands of people used to rave to it every week," DJ and Butterz label co-founder Elijah explains to me over FaceTime, whilst walking through London's Liverpool Street on a sunny autumn day in 2021. Continuing the observation of how grime built on the foundations of garage music, Elijah says, "There was already a system in place. There were already crowds for the music. The same venue, same promoters, everything. It was just a natural continuation of that. And then it gradually became something else."[5]

Due to its timing, before advanced smartphones and social media, grime could build and flourish at its own pace, with many of the first-era MCs taking five to ten years to perfect their craft. Ghetts, Kano, and, most significantly, Skepta are good examples. This timing also meant its history was rich in archival material—from *Run The Road* compilations and *Lord of the Mics* DVDs to *RWD* magazine—and entirely of its moment. The punk analogy to grime is well-worn, but it's for a good reason; Jammer even made the track "Dagenham Dave," possibly in homage to punk rockers The Stranglers' song of the same name.

Due to the accessibility of music technology, DIY media and—for those in cities and much to the authority's chagrin—pirate radio, encouraged a mentality that if something didn't exist, create it. Similar to other independent music scenes, the early foundations of grime were built on passion, and people made their own jobs: photographers, marketers, promoters, journalists, PR, A&R, and label owners. In those early years, grime was less a disruption to the music industry and more a xerox of it, with its own set of rules and gatekeepers.

There was even good money to be made. In a 2010 interview at the BBC Radio office, DJ Target told me Wiley "made well into six figures just off white labels. He would sell the shit ones for £3 each, which went entirely to him. I remember once we had 3,000 white labels, and my Punto was doing wheelies; it was so heavy. We took it to Ammunition [a distribution plant], and Danny Weed came out with £10,000 in cash. We were still really young at the time, we were like 'shit!'"[6] (A white label is a vinyl record produced in small quantities. It is often used for promotional purposes, test pressings, or by DJs to play unreleased or exclusive music. White labels are typically distributed to select individuals before the official release to generate buzz and feedback.)

Pirate radio was significant. Outside of raves and the trickle of mixtapes, it was the best way to keep up with the latest grime releases. Invariably makeshift, transient, and usually hidden away in a highrise estate in East London, these broadcast spaces also acted as a hub for MCs and DJs to practice and master their skills and for mates to hang out. However, pirate radio wasn't immune to institutionalised racism. In 2000, there were 1,300 Department for Trade and Industry raids on unlicensed stations in London. Many stations with legitimate intentions were "made pirate" due to the difficulty of obtaining a licence.

Founded in 1994, Rinse FM began its bid to become a legal station in 2006, but it wasn't until 2010 that it was finally granted an FM broadcasting licence. DJ Logan Sama, one of genre's most loyal advocates, described Rinse as "the petri dish in which the sound of grime grew. The culture of grime might be more linked to Deja because that was very crew-based. It was so chaotic, and where lots of the clashes happened."[7]

Building on Target's point, "There's a certain amount of money and fame that could be made via pirate radio" says'[8] Martin Clark when I talked to him in the late summer of 2021. The writer, label boss, and producer, also known as Blackdown, was an early supporter of grime, covering the fledgling scene for magazines like *FACT*, *Pitchfork*, and *The Guardian*. Or, as he puts it, "I was an observer of grime."

Dizzee or Wiley. Hip-hop or Grime, Who Holds the Mic?

"I was honoured to help write a bio, but it was so easy because Dizzee was so inspiring," Martin says of writing the XL promo material for *Boy in da Corner*, which he wrote after connecting with Nic Detnon, a.k.a. Cage, Dizzee Rascal's manager and A&R for the record. Influenced by jungle, garage, and southern US hip-hop, Dizzee's first forays into music production were via Music 2000 on the PlayStation before he graduated to using Cubase at Langdon Park secondary school, thanks to the encouragement of an influential music teacher, Mr. Smith. DJ Target lived in the estate next to Dizzee's and was another early influence, recommending records and introducing him to Wiley.

Dizzee Rascal recorded his first song,"'Bounce" with Roll Deep, at a pirate radio session in Battersea. He met Cage there, who was managing Roll Deep at the time. Cage was a techno DJ, and had a studio set-up that allowed Dizzee to "experiment like a madman" whenever it suited him. Martin and Cage periodically kept in touch. His interest was piqued by the teenage MC and producer responsible for a startling new sound. His debut single for XL Recordings, "I Luv U", is a track that "blew the doors off" according to Martin, and reportedly took Dizzee only twenty minutes to write.

Around that time, New York rapper Memphis Bleek's song "Is That Your Chick," featuring Jay-Z and Missy Elliott, had recently been released. Dizzee was a big fan of the track's producer, Timbaland, and the call-and-response song structure had hit a chord. "I was like, 'What's this?' Most things at a mainstream level aren't that brave. But that was different,"[9] recalls Dizzee. In turn he found the female vocalist, Jeanine, at his youth club. Admitting he "wanted a mouthy girl, a troublesome one to sing, but someone said to ask her." Given the song's misogyny, on a surface level at least, Dizzee didn't provide much of a brief, quite the opposite, in fact: "I lied to her. I didn't think she'd understand."

Instead, he provided lots of guidance in the studio, playing her "Is That Your Chick" and "Love to Make a Stang" by Three 6 Mafia, which repeated the latter title in a woozy, Tennessee drawl on the chorus. This improvisation all contributed to the track's impulsive and urgent energy. Dizzee had gotten a girl pregnant around the time he made "I Luv U," and he was rapping about the world around him. A single mum brought him up on a council estate in Bow, and by the time he made the song, he had been expelled from four schools. By his own admission, "I was dealing with straight rage."[10]

Grime, with its sonic antecedents in dance hall, drum & bass, and jungle, tore up the tentative blueprint provided by Britcore to make a startlingly new sound and a rap scene truly unique to the UK. It is neither part of UK hip-hop nor has it ever been completely disconnected, and *Boy in Da Corner* was its first testament.

It's difficult to overstate the importance of *Boy in da Corner.* Not just to grime, Black British music, or British culture in general. Its cultural impact is comparable to what Nas' *Illmatic* did for advancing hip-hop as an artform, or what Mathieu Kassovitz did in *La Haine* for its euro-centric take on hip-hop as a visceral vista. In a musical context, as impactful as Aphex Twin's *Selected Ambient Works 85-92* was for IDM, which is all the more remarkable given *Boy in da Corner* is widely recognised as the first grime album. Its societal impact is more significant than that of both of those albums—a Damascus moment for young, marginalised Black British kids like Dylan Mills to be seen and, more importantly, heard.

Sadly, this album's all-important legacy is soured for some by the artist's off-stage behaviour. At the time of writing, Dizzee Rascal has recently been charged with physically assaulting his former fiancee in relation to custody issues. He isn't the first rapper to appear on these pages with a criminal charge, and he won't be the last. Like Pablo Picasso, Roman Polanski, and James Brown before him, the music historian must distinguish between Dizzee Rascal, the artist, and Dylan Mills, the man.

Back to *Boy in da Corner*. After the success of "I Luv U," a major label signing frenzy ensued for a generational talent about to release a genre-defining album. Dizzee agreed to a recording deal with influential indie label XL Recordings. After hearing the song, label manager Richard Russell said, "I can't really think of one record that had quite as much impact on me as that did...I just thought, 'that's a whole movement.'"[11]

The album was released on 21 July 2003 in the UK. Speaking to Martin Clark about making the album almost twenty years later, he's understandably wistful given his proximity, even as an acknowledged outsider. "It has this emotional and sonic breadth that other producers didn't have. I'm not saying Dizzee was off making free jazz, but he was expanding the mood and the emotional template of what is possible. In that world, it's pretty macho, and it can be a violent, difficult environment, so showing vulnerability is not in their DNA. They form crews to protect themselves." Dizzee's willingness to "show vulnerability was brave," Martin adds.

The critical praise for *BIDC* was adoring—"A vision of the future of hip-hop and techno," declared *Rolling Stone,* and "One of the most assured debut albums from the last five years," according to the *NME*—and something that would prove problematic over time.

Like others before him, but to newfound levels, Dizzee Rascal became the poster boy for British rap music and, even more enticingly for a music press obsessed by the new and the mainstream, majority white media, a figurehead for grime and young "urban" Britain. He was very young, and besides, who wants to bear the responsibility for an entire scene?

* * *

No Dizzee Rascal origin story, even one as abridged as this, would be complete without Wiley. Hip-hop has long mined *Star Wars* for inspiration, literally and laterally, but the Dizzee-Wiley relationship has to be the closest rap music has ever come to the Darth Vader-Luke Skywalker analogy.

Wiley, the local hero and mentor of Dizzee, would become "the godfather of grime"* in the wake of Dizzee's success.[12] The pair became embroiled in a long-running, accusational, and often asinine beef that played out through bars and went on to take place mainly on Twitter (the rich man's plaything now known as X). Most people familiar with the story know where it started: at the Ice Club in Ayia Napa, the spiritual home of UK garage. It was the summer of 2003 when Dizzee, partying with Wiley and other members of Roll Deep, pinched Lisa Maffia's bottom. A fight with So Solid Crew members and affiliates ensued.

Wiley picks up the story in an interview with *Time Out*: "Me and Dizzee went out one night [in Ayia Napa], and there was some fighting with another crew – I won't say who, but basically everyone knows. Then I decided to carry it on the next day – I didn't pull out a knife. I was just fighting. After we started it up again, those guys came looking for us. But the person they found was Dizzee. The thing we done (sic) the next morning led them to go looking for us, but see him and stab him."[13]

Dizzee Rascal has never been so forthcoming with his version of events, but relations between the two appear to have thawed, although any new collaborations seem unlikely. What the falling-out, and sometimes soap opera-like reaction surrounding it, masks is the music at the start of this story. Wiley signed to XL first and was all set to be the breakout star of the new and increasingly MC-driven strain of garage music. However, the label decided to schedule the release of his debut album, *Treddin' on Thin Ice* (April 2004), between *Boy in da Corner* (July 2003) and Dizzee's sophomore LP, *Showtime* (September 2004, which ended up charting at number 8), effectively flooding the market with a new and tempestuous sound.

Boy in da Corner bubbled with boisterous energy, with stories of troubled teenagehood told at propulsive speed. *Treddin' on Thin Ice* is occupied with more mature concerns like money-making and mental health. The sound and aesthetic of *Treddin'* is glacial by comparison—and by design. Hence the "eski-beat" genre naming Wiley played with at the time, the snow-drenched album cover—a striking contrast to the yellow heat that dominates the image in *BITC,* both designed by Ben Drury—and the sparse alien-wave synths, seemingly made by a mad scientist of chionophile spawn, but in reality the invention of a bloke called Richard from Bow.

On 26 April, 2004, the twenty-five-year-old not-yet-godfather of grime—original, funny, contrarian, and on the cusp of becoming a "'name brand"—had to deliver a full-length project to satisfy his underground fanbase, his label's expectations, and a music press eager to anoint grime music as England's answer to millennial hip-hop. The comparisons between the records and artists were inevitable and unhelpful, initially at least. Fans were confounded by the softening of Wiley's underground sound on singles such as "Special Girl" and "Got Somebody," XL was probably confused by songs about "Pies," and not many people bought the album.

Treddin' on Thin Ice was also frequently brilliant, combining aspiration, aggression, humour, and grim reality, while the sound is still so futuristic—it could have been made tomorrow. As one Son Raw wrote for *Complex*, "The album expressed uncut Black angst but also packaged it in a way Radiohead fans could understand–a feat not even Dizzee himself would be able to repeat."[14] The album laid the blueprint for Wiley's career only in so much as it was utterly unpredictable.

* * *

It's easy to get bogged down by how grime has been politicised as a music and youth culture movement—especially when tied with personal history. Yet politics has rarely been central to its narrative, especially in those early years. More interesting is the transformative effect grime had on UK rap and beyond, through the performative aspect, the timbre of voice, and, of course, the music itself.

Grime expanded the language of rap music in the UK. It also forms a direct lineage to the sound system culture of the Windrush generation via jungle, drum & bass, and garage music while being adjacent to hip-hop.

An early experience of the sometimes awkward relationship that existed between (UK) hip-hop and grime came when I interviewed the husky-voiced MC Bruza, whose "Get me, Get me!" catchphrase was a signature of the first generation of grime MCs, in a car outside his local McDonalds in Walthamstow, sometime in the mid-'00s. I asked about his musical influences.

"Drum & bass was, and in a way, still really is my thing. People like Skibbadee, MC Det, Shabba, Navigator, all these sorts of MCs, Randall, Mickey Finn, DJ Brockie. All those tape hustlers. Man, I used to love it! Proper, I used to listen to nothing else. I wasn't too bothered about hip-hop to be honest. Lyrically there was more to it but if you wanted to go out it was all about going to jungle and drum & bass rave, ya' get me, that's where it really went off."[15]

Bruza's point of view wasn't necessarily reflective of all the MCs of the time—Durrty Goodz being a notable exception who could switch between hip-hop and grime bars seamlessly and with fanboyish enthusiasm—but it wasn't unusual either.

Although it does make me ponder, what is the difference between rapper and MC, analogous to grime and hip-hop? Both sounds are born from sound system culture, and grime continued a hip-hop fixation of local pride—swapping postcodes for boroughs.Structurally, eight and sixteen bars of lyrics worked across both, even if the style and patterns within the bars could be very different.

Yet there are pronounced differences, too. Hip-hop tends to run at 80-100 BPM, certainly in the UK, while grime is more consistently around 140 BPM, and true to Bruza's intimation, grime has always prioritised *vibe*—difficult to define, but all important—over the message, especially in those formative years.

In the mid-noughties, I began writing for magazines such as *Touch, Big Smoke, Trace,* and nascent blogs with vociferous forums pages like *UKHH.com*. These titles specialised in what was then known as urban music. I tended to write about hip-hop and grime, convinced there was a connection between the two.

I interviewed a few UK hip-hop MCs at the time who were not receptive to this and saw grime as a passing fad, while fans were often less kind. Speaking to Juice Aleem about the relationship many years later—his group New Flesh has frequently been described as "proto-grime"—he made a wise point: "There was a disconnect, [it was like] 'Hey, young man, come off the mic,' 'Hey, fuck off, old man.' And that's the nature of be-bop to fusion, blues to jazz."[16]

DISCOGRAPHY

Chapter 6: Wot Do U Call It?

This chapter is named after Wiley's "Wot Do U Call It?"

Albums, E.P.s & Mixtapes

Aphex Twin - *Selected Ambient Works 85-92*
Nas - *Illmatic*
Dizzee Rascal - *Boy In Da Corner*
Wiley *Treddin' on Thin Ice*
Various Artists - *Run The Road*

Singles

Memphis Bleek Ft. Jay-Z, Missy Elliott, and Twista - "Is That Your Chick (The Lost Verses)"
Three Six Mafia - "Love to Make a Stang"
So Solid Crew - "Oh No"
Roll Deep - ""Bounce"
Dizzee Rascal - "I Luv U"
Wiley - "Special Girl"
Wiley - "Got Somebody"
Wiley - "Pies"
Jammer - "Dagenham Dave"

Chapter 7

The Revolution (Will Not Be Televised On Channel U)

Aside from radio, magazines were the most prominent form of media representation for UK hip-hop and grime in the early-mid '00s. Compared to pirate radio, they were legitimate channels for artists to receive mainstream attention, be it on the shelves of corner shops, WH Smith or the counters at Urban Outfitters.

Read All About It: Hip-Hop Connection and RWD Magazine

In the history of UK hip-hop and grime rags, there are two key titles: *Hip-Hop Connection* (often abbreviated to *HHC*) and, much later, *RWD Magazine. Hip-Hop Connection* published its first issue in 1988 in the unlikely surroundings of Cambridge, making it one of the first music magazines dedicated to covering hip-hop. The magazine boasted cover interviews with some of the world's most important and (pre-internet) visible rappers, including A Tribe Called Quest, NWA, Jay-Z, Nas, and Outkast. It also published the lists of anticipated and hotly debated Album of the Year and Readers Album of the Year.

Given the magazine's 30-plus-year life span, publishing an impressive 232 issues, *HHC* covered the blossoming of hip-hop, following its growth from music genre to culture to its commodification, albeit 3,500 miles away from the source of the action. The magazine was founded by publishing veteran Chris Hunt, who had enjoyed a successful career as a journalist in the '80s and had edited the influential heavy metal magazine *Solid Rock.* The commercial success of groups like Run-D.M.C. and the Beastie Boys inspired him to create a hip-hop version of *Smash Hits* to find a place in the sweaty palms of teenagers across the UK. Fortunately for him, a year after starting the magazine he met Andy Cowan, an aspiring music journalist and avid b-boy who helped define the magazine's identity.

It also covered the homegrown scene. "*Hip-Hop Connection* was important," remembers Rodney P. "It was a magazine that felt 'for us by us'. It was a time when hip-hop was seen as a bit of a fad, and UK hip-hop was seen as a copy of the American thing. This magazine actually took us seriously."[1] That said, the relationship between *HHC* and the UK scene could be fractious, particularly in the latter years. I spoke with the long-time editor, Andy Cowan, to learn more.

"We discovered through trial and error that putting UK acts on the cover was a no-no. It was a pattern that continued throughout *HHCs*' existence, even when it came to bigger names like Roots Manuva, Rodney P, and Skinnyman. From a business point of view, we knew we'd take a sales hit by putting a UK act on the cover. I had numerous conversations with UK rappers that 'if we put Ja Rule on the cover and if you have a feature inside it, you'll get 4,000 more people (who) would read it, and you'd get more exposure', but obviously, everyone wanted to be on the cover."[2]

Andy, with his wispy goatee, softly spoken voice, and a PhD in nutritional studies, appears less like the editor of what was once the longest-running hip-hop magazine and more like a yogi fresh from an expedition to India. Fittingly, he tends to offer sage-like advice in our correspondence over the years. He summarises the magazine's relationship with readers and UK hip-hop around the turn of the millennium neatly with this point: "As much as [readers] paid lip service to British rap, [they] didn't necessarily support it, or in record shops, they didn't buy it to the same extent that they would buy American hip-hop. It was seen for a long time as the lesser version, apart from a very die-hard crowd."

Andy referred to two peaks for *HHC:* "Commercially, the early '90s, because of all the Golden Age rappers, there was *The Source* and us. Every month there was just a fantastic album, it was just a wonderful time to be working on a magazine." The second peak came after being sold by the Ministry of Sound in the early '00s. "I had this dream editorial team [although] that beautiful moment coincided with the hardest time business-wise as we were so reliant on advertising." *HHC* couldn't make subscriptions work as an alternative revenue stream and Andy "was coming up to a dilemma of not paying contributors, and I don't think you can get that expertise for free."

The magazine changed owners multiple times, including the ill-fated pairing with Ministry, leading to the "notorious Mariah Carey cover." And when it did experiment with garage and early grime, it didn't go down well with fans, coinciding with what Andy calls the "lowest moment in my editorial career...putting Oxide and Neutrino on the cover of the magazine." Andy believes they lost a few hardcore fans due to antipathy towards garage and proto-grime.

Although there were exceptions that made the crossover onto *HHC's* page without disgruntling too many readers, like The Streets with *Original Pirate Material*, which Andy describes as a "bridging record" that "did what British rap hadn't done for many years, which was success in a native accent with native concerns and very British things." As for Dizzee Rascal, he muses that the "ironic thing with Dizzee was he went more pop than anyone."

Hip-Hop Connection represented the old world of print, a glossy paid-for monthly magazine with a vociferous readership which, according to Andy, included Louis Theroux, regularly writing into the letters page under the alias King Louis. In a time before the internet and social media, *HHC* and the magazines it inspired—the satirical *Fat Lace, Big Smoke, Undercover* and others—were vital to hip-hop in the UK. However, in the end, the magazine couldn't hold out against or operate within the digital revolution. Andy recalls, "We didn't treat it seriously enough then. We hadn't conceptualised a way of running it complementarity to the magazine."

RWD Magazine was a different proposition. Launched in 2001, the free monthly magazine was smaller in format than *HHC,* somewhere between a zine and a magazine in presentation and tone. It covered the tail end of garage and the emerging grime scene. In keeping with the glitzy aspirations of UK garage, the first issue even had a bootleg Versace advert on the back cover.

RWD made money through advertising and artists paying to appear in the magazine. Although the practice had been happening in the publishing, radio, and music industry for years (the euphonious 'payola') it was unusual to see it done so transparently, even if it suited the DIY nature of the grime scene. "Everything about *RWD* was crass…text speak and all"[3] recalled founding editor Matt Mason. Unlike HHC, *RWD* often ran cover interviews with homegrown rappers—Skepta, Giggs, Dizzee Rascal, and Kano, memorably stylised in a *Scarface*-style black and white visual, and others all received early coverage.

And the scrappy magazine went from 5,000 to 100,000 copies distributed monthly in less than ten years, making it the biggest music magazine in the country. Although *RWD* had drifted from its original editorial focus of grime by that point, covering pop music and mainstream interests had alienated its core readers.

Both *HHC* and *RWD* came from cottage industries supporting music outside of the mainstream, but *RWD* was born of the era and in the locality of grime. Alongside radio, record shops, raves, and DVDs, *RWD* was part of the thriving ecosystem that Elijah spoke of previously.

Whereas *HHC* had its letters page, the RWD Forum continued the publisher-audience discourse into the 21st century—an extension to the website where fans, producers and ebullient MCs could meet, test out bars, and debate. The forum proved even more popular than the main website.

The Founding of 1Xtra and the Strange Signals It Sent

As a new British (or mostly English) rap identity began to take shape, a national institution took notice.

"I got a phone call out of the blue from a guy called William Wilberforce, who says he's setting up a new radio station at BBC," theatre director Matthew Xia explains to me, "And the pitch was, 'We want to be the legit pirate. Where we're going to be the home of new Black music.'"[4] It was the late '90s in East London, and Xia wasn't enjoying college, so he agreed with his mum that he would drop out and make it as a "superstar DJ." She gave him two years to make good on his promise. Back then, Xia was known as DJ Excalibah, and he ran an open mic night and radio show called *Tales from the Legend* on the pirate station Juice FM.

DJ Excalibah grew up in a "white household as a mixed-race kid," explaining, "I was searching for something, and I think I found that in hip-hop music that reflected a version of my existence, albeit on the other side of the pond." His *Tales from the Legend* show had been getting some traction, but the call from Wilberforce had come as a surprise. He describes it as "mind-blowing," saying, "I was 18 when I signed my contract, I think 19 by the time I did my first show."

According to *The Guardian*, BBC 1Xtra had a launch budget of £6 million, more than double any other digital station the BBC was launching at the time. The launch of 1Xtra was announced with a slick promo video that looked like something between a John Singleton film and an episode of *EastEnders*, and ended with a tagline dedicated to "STREET MUSIC."

The ambition, talent and resources were in place to make 1Xtra a huge success and push the envelope for Black British music, but those early years were bumpy for several reasons. The station's commitment to 'Urban' music (much to Skinnyman's chagrin) included hip-hop, R&B, garage, dancehall, drum & bass, and more. Alongside DJ Excalibah, the founding hip-hop shows were *Original Fever* with Rodney P & Skitz—the latter being fresh from his well-received *Countryman* album and the preeminent DJ/producer in UK hip-hop—every Monday night and the *Saturday Mixtape* with DJ Semtex every Saturday evening.

For those with digital radio, the station was a blessing, particularly in rural parts of the UK, but the clarity of the signal came at the cost of the reach. There were also editorial concerns over the music. No swearing was permitted, so clean versions of the songs had to be used or they wouldn't get played.

And as Sarah Love, who later joined the DJ roster to host two shows, explained, "The remit was quite strict when I first started. You couldn't have guests on the show and could only speak three times an hour." Most restrictively, 1Xtra DJs were only permitted to play music less than eight weeks old. These rules contrasted starkly with pirate radio. "That's kind of the nature of a big broadcaster," Love explains, admitting she found the representation of UK hip-hop on the daytime shows "minuscule." There may have been Estelle, and lesser still, the likes of Black Twang and Roots Manuva, but at that time, "there was very much a focus on grime 'is about to blow up.'"

As Excalibah put it, "Weirdly, the emergence of grime was part of the end of my time at 1Xtra. I remember playing 'Signs in Life' by Kano and having a huge editorial conversation with Wilbur and the senior producers and executive producers at

1Xtra about where the remit stopped. Klashnekoff was straight UK hip-hop for me, but now and then I'd play a remix of one of his tracks and maybe it's a Terror Danjah beat...you started to get this kind of bleed-through into what is now road rap, out of which came drill."

At the time, grime and UK hip-hop seemed to be heading down separate paths. After a few years at 1Xtra, Excalibah admits that he felt "UK hip-hop probably didn't quite deserve its two-hour slot on a national broadcaster."

The industry needed to figure out where to place UK hip-hop and grime. "I was at Radio 1 when dance music passed it by,"[5] said Ian Parkinson, the head of specialist music at Radio 1 at the time of 1Xtra's launch. He added, "Black music was nowhere to be heard on the network, so I understand the initial suspicions, but I say give it a chance." At the time, every one of BBC's 18 Executive Committee members—the group responsible for the day-to-day management of the BBC—was white, as was still the case more than 15 years later.

Many MCs and those working in the industry at the time shared frustrations with me about 1Xtra. The gist of these complaints was that it emulated American radio (e.g. Hot 97), rather than pirate radio, a little too closely and failed to develop a unique take on what a Black British music station should be.

I put this view to Excalibah, who sees both sides of the argument. "I think 1Xtra did support Black artists. If a song were commercial enough, it would go into the daytime playlists," he says, while conceding, "There was no African-influenced music, which I think is interesting. It had this two-hour slot with DJ Etta in what was deemed a 'world music' special. And now the Afrobeats sound is ubiquitous."

He goes on to say that something "complex" was going on with UK hip-hop at the time, where the "dominant MCs were mainly white working-class lads from across the country."

To him it seemed like "everyone was working with everyone, so Harry Love would produce 'Murder,' which would be wrecked by Klashnekoff." There was no question of the "ethnicity of those artists" and what the song represented.

However, there was "an interesting dichotomy in the ethnicity of who was celebrated and who people hold up as the champions of UK hip hip-hop." As Jehst spoke of in Chapter 2, a distinction emerged in the narrative. As Excalibah put it, you "had UK hip-hop, a predominantly white art form, and then you had UK rap, a predominantly Black art form."

The Pirate Radio of TV: Channel U

It is ironic that one of the world's best-known broadcasters attempted to imitate pirate radio when British rap music, and grime in particular, was crying out for a visual identity. A few homemade DVD boxsets were circulating—*Lord of the Mics, Practice Hours, Risky Roadz*—but very few copies were available nationwide.

"It was the pirate radio of TV"[6] is how Jammer described Channel U, the scrappy digital TV channel launched on Valentine's Day 2003 by Darren Platt and his business partner Stewart Lund. Platt had been running a modestly successful ringtone business when he had the idea to develop a cooler version of the BOX, a poppy music video channel mainly dedicated to viewer's requests. Neither Platt nor Lund had any music or television industry experience, but they saw an opportunity to do something audience-focused (hence the 'U').

Channel U had problems from the beginning: Ofcom fines, payola, royalty issues, and controversy over artists signing a waiver to get their videos on the channel. Yet its impact on grime and UK hip-hop cannot be overstated. However, this wasn't the case initially, with its early rotation dominated by videos from 50 Cent and Eminem, alongside the usual pop fare.

It took an intervention by music and promotions manager Riki Bleu to provide a UK focus. He was an aspiring rapper who had "shot a video with my group that we spent six grand on, and there was nowhere to play it."[7] Riki had relationships with Blak Twang and Estelle and dozens more hungry MCs whose content finally had a place to go.

"21 Seconds" and "Champagne Dance" may have had their quirks, with So Solid Crew performing at what looked like the gates of Armageddon and Pay As U Go flipping the gender paradigm with female boxers. However, both music videos had more than a hint of Hollywood and involved high-end productions, which helped them get exposure on MTV Base playlists.

A big budget wasn't necessary to get onto Channel U, with many of the popular playlists decided by the audience through an SMS vote. With a visual offering, MCs and artists could explore new creative possibilities through comedy, idiosyncrasy, and nuance. More importantly, it provided a visual platform for Black British music beyond the capital and into the homes of 7.5 million Sky TV subscribers nationwide. As a result, Channel U helped launch the careers of numerous artists, even if it struggled badly as a business.

One of those artists was the affable Sway. His music video for "Flo Fashion" featured a proto-meme card-swishing dance with a girl on each arm, as Sway gets himself into a mountain of credit card debt over an earworm beat and cocky verse decrying consumerism.

The music video was clever, funny, and cheap to make. It also provided a memorable visual of an MC embracing his Ghanaian roots and Britishness by accessorising both flags into a bandana. Sway followed this up with "Little Dereck," the meditative and almost entirely black-and-white video, save for the colours of his Union Jack scarf.

The song's producer was Al Shux, who went on to make the track "Empire State of Mind" by Jay-Z. Nipsey Hustle later described "Little Dereck" as one of his favourite records, "not (just) his favourite UK track," as Sway qualifies it. "It travelled so far," explained Sway in a documentary on Channel U made by Link Up, "it was that Channel U era that gave it the spark and enabled it to grow."

Because of Channel U's dedication to UK music and indiscriminate approach to programming, there was a fantastic range of music videos from artists across the spectrum. This included slickly produced visuals like "Memory Lane" by Choong Family that sat at the intersection of US-inspired hip-hop and R&B, the militant "Murda" by Klashnekoff, through to the proto-hip-pop of N-Dubz, and a slew of grimy posse cuts that began to flood the channel in the second half of the '00s.

Some of the latter would be remembered as "Channel U classics," two of the most notable being "Pow! (Forward)" fronted by Lethal Bizzle, of course, and "Orchestral Boroughs" by Mr Wong, featuring grime 1.0 superstar Crazy Titch, JME, and Flirta D. As Jeffrey Boayke describes it in *Hold Tight*, Mr Wong "epitomised how idiosyncratic grime was in its earliest phase." Mr Wong used his "racial identity as a gimmick," and the video for "Orchestral Boroughs" captured the early, hyperactive energy of grime before it even had a name and long before it was "honed into a marketable commodity."

"Pow! (Forward)" has gone on to create a story of its own. It was the first grime track to chart (blasting in at no.11 in 2004), got banned from clubs and radio due to supposedly inciting violence, pissed off former prime minister and all-around "doughnut"—as Bizzle memorably called him in an op-ed for *The Guardian*—David Cameron, and was the unofficial soundtrack to the student protests of 2011. And that's not to mention the two reincarnations of the song since: "Forward Riddim 2" in 2005 and "Pow! 2011."

Across the three songs, the great and the good of grime MCs have featured, including D Double E, Flow Dan, Kano, Ghetts, long-time collaborator Ozzie B, and one-time foe Wiley. Yet, like most things, the first ride around the rodeo was the best. Its success was down to the formula of a catchy chorus, bombastic baseline, hungry MCs, dissident energy and, as Mr Bizzle put it to me, the desire "to try new stuff."

"That's something I've always maintained throughout my career and always will," says Bizzle. "Like 'Oi', when that came out, there was nothing else like it, the same with 'Pow'. It was just completely out of the blue, combining all sorts of musical elements."[8] We'll never know if it would have done as well without the visual—each MC performing in the claustrophobic confines of an estate corridor, with Napper holding a skull. While "Pow! (Forward)" leant into macho stereotypes, "Orchestra Boroughs" subverted them using humour.

The music featured on Channel U was largely London-centric, much like grime itself. Still, there were videos from artists across the country, along with content like Devlin's "London City," which explores the capital from a nearby outsider's perspective through a night out in "the best city in the world when everybody not shanking and blasting."

In short, nuance allowed artists and MCs to truly represent who they are and where they are from, rather than finding meaning in America. It also meant a generation of fans could finally put faces to names from pirate radio.

Despite its growing popularity and influence, "no one wanted to invest [in Channel U]. It was way too grimy", and even the authorities were watching, according to the former channel manager, Cat Park. As Stewart Lund put it, "the business side was much more difficult," with Channel U experiencing a "legal battle through its whole life with the royalty collection society and major labels. We were paying a lot more royalties than MTV was paying. We spent hundreds of thousands in legal fees."[9]

The royalty fees and the solvency of its advertising agency partner, leaving hundreds of thousands of pounds in unpaid debt, eventually brought Channel U down. In 2009, Darren Platt rebranded it to Channel AKA (Lund had left the business by this point), before dying of heart complications in 2016. At the time, Lethal Bizzle called Darren a "visionary", while Tinchy Stryder said the channel was "key to his career," and Ghetts described Channel U as "the biggest platform for us at the time."

Channel AKA eventually shut down in 2018. The channel often drew comparisons to MTV, but they weren't the "glossy hip-hop videos" of MTV Base, as Kat put it, and sometimes, those comparisons were unkind. Some of the stripped-down productions featured on Channel U could be "terrible quality," even if they attracted millions of loyal viewers in their prime.

I worked at MTV towards the end of the '00s, and it was mostly a positive experience. Yet its influence on music was declining, as was its interest in music. Inside the business, there was indifference towards the longevity of YouTube, let alone Channel U. The head office was in the heart of Camden, the centre of the indie rawk universe and the dominant music at the time. Many people who worked there were passionate about all sorts of music, but only a few were at the top—a group that was exclusively white, middle-aged, and male. Every other year, there was a 're-org', corporate-speak for redundancies, which led to unexplainable decisions, and a Game of Thrones between various self-interested directors and V.P.s.

Although MTV acted as an incubator for behind-the-scenes talent—people who would go on to do good work representing UK rap music, like Alex Hoffman, who would make grime documentaries for *VICE*, JP Patterson, who went on to found *TRENCH*, and the journalist Laura 'Hyerfrank' Brosnan—it didn't seem particularly interested as an institution in advocating for the full spectrum of British music. Whereas BBC 1Xtra's contribution to the culture may have been misguided at its inception, overall, it has been largely positive. Conversely, MTV UK has not, a contributing factor to its irrelevancy today.

Aside from its impact on music, Channel U's legacy was its trojan horse-like presence among establishment gatekeepers—a genuine media disrupter. Channel U opened the door and created a space for GRM Daily, SBTV, LinkUp, and others.

As Post, the CEO and founder of GRM Daily, explained, "It made me fall more in love with UK music. {And} in a way, it did inspire me to start GRM Daily because I grew up on it." Channel U shook up the industry, allowing anyone with passion and access to a decent camera to get involved and support the music they love.

DISCOGRAPHY

Chapter 6: The Revolution (Will Not Be Televised On Channel U)

This chapter is named after the track by Klashnekoff.

Albums, E.P.s & Mixtapes
The Streets - *Original Pirate Material*

Singles
Klashnekoff - "Murda"
So Solid Crew - "21 Seconds"
Pay As U Go - "Champagne Dance"
Mr Wong. Ft. JME, Crazy Titch, and Flirta D - "Orchestral Boroughs"
Lethal Bizzle - "Pow! (Forward)"
Choong Family - "Memory Lane"
Sway - "Flo Fashion"
Sway - "Little Dereck"
Jay-Z - "Empire State of Mind"

Chapter 8

Too Many Men

Schrödinger's Cat is a 1935 thought experiment in quantum mechanics proposed by Austrian physicist Erwin Schrödinger. The experiment involves a hypothetical cat placed in a sealed box and a radioactive atom with a 50/50 chance of decaying and releasing a deadly poison that would kill the cat. I'm no expert, but according to quantum mechanics, the state of the atom is described by a mathematical formula called a wave function, which represents a combination of both the decayed and undecayed states.

Until the box is opened and the cat is observed, the wave function is said to be in a "superposition state," meaning that the cat is simultaneously alive and dead. This paradoxical situation illustrates the strange and counterintuitive nature of quantum mechanics. It's also a pretty good summation of the state of grime music by 2007.

It was only two years earlier that grime had its first peak, with breakout stars like Tinchy Stryder, Shystie, and Kano, an MC with style as smooth as a silk glove on a velvet carpet. Some artists were greeted with big cheques from record label execs eager to sign the Next Big Thing®.

Confusing Fans and Confounding Critics: Kano and Roll Deep

On the surface, concessions of artistry were made to reach a broader fan base. Kano and Roll Deep's debut albums, *Home Sweet Home* and *In At The Deep End*, sold reasonably well but confounded fans with incongruous music production—such as the nu-metal riffs, courtesy of producer Paul Epworth, on Kano's "I Don't Know Why" and "Typical Me"—and saccharine pop songs like the bizarre and brazenly commercial doo-wop of Roll Deep's "The Avenue." These were released alongside absolute scene heaters like "Ps & Qs" and "When I'm Ere."

With time, these albums have aged better than the initial listen and can be acknowledged for broadening the horizons of grime. Still, back when the music was released in 2005, critics were keen to keep it in its box, with *The Guardian's* Alex Petridis describing the debut album of then 19-year-old Kane Robinson as "the last roll of the major-label dice for grime,"[1] adding in the same review that grime was "too sonically harsh for mainstream acceptance."

What these records did in hindsight—with remarkable prescience in the case of *In At The Deep End*—was expand the musical palette of grime and UK rap, and broaden the aperture of possibilities, even if it meant pissing off a few fans and confusing critics at the time.

As DJ Target explained to me, "When we made our first album in 2005 coming from grime— underground, dark music, it said what it did on the tin—we said, 'Let's try some other stuff, a bit of pop, a bit of this and that.' And we went and did it. At first, people from the scene turned their noses up at it, but if you look at that scene now, a lot of the main artists have crossed over."[2] And without Roll Deep's intervention, Target thinks "it might have taken longer to do so."

But this didn't stop detractors from declaring the death of grime, even in its infancy. Logan Sama, whose Kiss FM DJ residency reigned for ten years as the country's preeminent grime show, (in)famously wrote a "Grime is dead. Didn't you know?" op-ed for *RWD*. In it, he called out artists and execs "looking to rinse out the scene for money and then fuck off without ever investing in grass roots (sic)."[3]

"If you don't love it, don't try and make it. Don't try and get into it. There's no money for you here," Sama added with a siege mentality. Sama later explained, "I'm very protective of things," adding, "I hate people being exploited. And seeing a lot of opportunism, which I know isn't geared towards the sustainable success of the people who are the creative powers behind the revenue being generated, was frustrating. And then obviously to see people moving off of it because, 'Oh, it's not cool this week.'"[4]

Although darker clouds were brewing. More ominously than grime MCs selling out, legislation was passed in 2005 that would have a significantly detrimental impact on rap music in the UK—legislation that is so wrapped up in prejudice that it may as well wear black shirts, read the *Daily Mail*, and pledge allegiance to Oswald Mosley. Form 696 was a risk assessment legislation aimed at events featuring music from DJs and MCs. Introduced by the Metropolitan Police and adopted across all 21 London boroughs, it required music promoters and club venues to submit information on the ethnicity of the performers and the likely ethnicity of the audience.

Double Standards and Form 696

Although filling out the form was described as 'voluntary' when applying for a licence for an event, promoters who did not submit the form 14 days before their event found that their application for a licence was refused. Those who went ahead and put on events could face six-month jail terms and £20,000 fines. Even promoters who filled out the form often found that the Met shut down their night or refused a licence for inadequate or unexplained reasons.

The form consisted of loaded questions such as "Music style to be played/performed (e.g. bashment, R&B, garage)," while another asks for examples of types of musical artists such as "DJs, MCs, etc."[5] Most concerning was, "Is there a particular ethnic group attending? If 'yes', please state group." This is yet another example of the Met's talent for racial profiling.

Dan Hancox, the journalist and author of *Inner City Pressure: The Story of Grime,* led the charge against Form 696, writing for *The Guardian* that the form was designed so that the "Met are lone arbiters of what kind of music is (a) high risk." [6]

In the same article, Hancox spoke to David Moynihan, promoter of the club night Dirty Canvas: "[I was at] a meeting with council officials and the Met, when I was involved in putting on a community festival on the Hackney/Tower Hamlets border. The police told us categorically that we weren't allowed to put on music that was 'grime, garage, rap, reggae or R&B.'" I can tell you from first-hand experience the most likely threat at a Dirty Canvas night was an evolved Hoxton Fin haircut in the eye or being nudged by over-enthusiastic skanking.

For all the Met's attempts to silence grime and rap with Form 696, there was some basis for their policing. As we saw in Chapters 4 and 5, the So Solid Crew era of garage and proto-grime came with some violence at live shows, even if it was a "generalised racist folk memory"[7] as Hancox described it, rather than a specific and consistent trail of intelligence.

In 2008, Feargal Sharkey, the UK Music chief and former lead singer of punk group The Undertones, told a House of Commons select committee—the Department of Culture, Media and Sport—that the Met issued the policy to shut down a charity concert of school bands in a public park organised by a local councillor.

Sharkey explained, "No alcohol would be sold. Tickets were limited to three maximum, and the councillor offered to supply eight registered doormen." Yet Police objected because "the performers' names, addresses and dates of birth could not be provided," added Sharkey, before concluding: "Live music is now a threat to the prevention of terrorism."[8]

But as far as the Metropolitan police were concerned, critics of Form 696 were "naive" as David Isles, a Detective Superintendent with the Clubs and Vice unit, insisted in a rare and unguarded response from the police. "This is about Black kids being shot, stabbed and targeted...you have particular gangs aligned to particular types of music." According to Isles, this "created an environment where rival gangs would target them. It wasn't about the music, it wasn't about the venue, it was about the promotion."[9]

It's a contrary and misleading defence because what's also curious and so central to Form 696 was its targeting of artists. It's not like grime MCs had the propensity to attack the audience, like the time Axl Rose jumped a fan in the crowd for recording at a Guns N' Roses show or when Josh Homme of Queens Of The Stone Age threw a bottle at a teenage fan— or "12-year-old dickless turd" as he bawled—at a festival in Norway. Then there's the time when Keith Richards, of rhythm and blues tribute group The Rolling Stones, walloped a fan who jumped on stage with his guitar at the Hampton Coliseum. You get the gist.

Veteran grime MC P Money has lost count of the times he has been removed from gig lineups because of information passed on via the form. He summarised the form's intentions as a "race thing," saying, "It's been happening for so many years that now we know it's just our scene. They [police] target grime a lot. They just blame a lot of things on grime... We know they're just trying to shut down grime because if it were anything else, they wouldn't have this issue.[10]

P Money goes on: "If, for example, Ed Sheeran had a show and a fight broke out, he's not going to do a 696 on his next arena tour. A fight might have broken out, but they don't look at it like that. They just think, 'Oh, it's different for them.'"

On a warm summer's day I met with Logan Sama at a cafe in Dalston. His career has shifted somewhat into Esports in recent years, but his passion for grime music remains the same. "Grime was a cultural phenomenon. It was getting unbelievable traction in an era (that) Myspace and YouTube had just launched," he recalls, while musing how "Grime was viewed as too much culturally, but also not bringing in enough."

Sama contrasts grime with the gangsta rap of 50 Cent, which crossed over to substantial financial success (his first three albums have sold over 22 million copies): "It doesn't matter if 50 Cent gets shot because it made so much money that you can forgive almost anything. Grime wasn't making that much money. Whereas now drill as a sound, you can completely offset the horrific elements of what's going on with what it brings in."

It wasn't just grime MCs that suffered, either. Giggs, a pioneer of UK road rap, had a golden opportunity to support Lil Wayne, one of the biggest rappers in the world at the time, in concert at a London show in 2006. Yet the offer was revoked for unknown reasons. Giggs recalled the incident; "I just felt sad because I was trying to get myself off the street and do something positive, and then that [opportunity] was just taken away."

"They never issued one of them 696s. It was more subtle than that," Giggs explained. "I think they must have called the venues and threatened them with taking away their licences if they ignored their 'friendly' advice, should something happen."[11] The Metropolitan Police also wrote to XL Recordings, advising the label not to sign him. The label declined the Met's advice and released Giggs' first full studio album, *Let Em Ave It,* in 2009.

A year later, thanks to the police's guidance, Giggs' entire UK tour was cancelled. He has been plagued by Form 696 for most of his career. Granted, Giggs was arrested in 2003 for firearm possession and sentenced to two years and eight months in prison (he was later arrested and acquitted for a similar charge in 2012), but aren't people allowed a chance at redemption, or is that limited to white rock acts?

As Leroy Logan—former Metropolitan Police Superintendent, founding member of the Black Police Association, and a handy trumpet player (reportedly)—put it in 2020: "Over the decades, it's been impossible for me to ignore the stark contrast between the way the police have approached Black and white anti-establishment music. Some heavy metal over the decades has had a strong narrative of violence, but it has never had the same trouble with the law that grime and drill have had to contend with."[12]

It took 17 years and three London mayors before Sadiq Khan finally abolished Form 696 in 2017. However, for many aspiring artists, the damage had been done. Thanks to the Metropolitan Police, infinite shows were cancelled, hundreds of thousands—possibly millions—of pounds were lost, and potential fan bases were stunted just when artists needed them the most. It's difficult to calculate the cultural damage of Form 696—the number of MCs, DJs, and producers whose careers were cut short due to the oxygen of live music being suffocated from their dreams.

If the first half of this book reads like a story of a music scene hindered by record label shenanigans, either ignored or misconstrued by the media and, worse still, blocked by the institutional racism that held UK rap music back—be it hip-hop, MC-driven garage, or grime—well, that's because it was.

Seven-figure advances for moderately promising indie acts weren't uncommon in the noughties. The music industry was thriving for most of the decade by contemporary standards. Global recorded music industry revenues topped $18.4 billion in 2007, and it wasn't until 2018 that figure was exceeded, at $19.1 billion, primarily thanks to ad-supported and subscription music-streaming services.[13]

But all this was a long way from the endangered youth clubs, community centres, and pirate radio stations that provided the fertile training ground for young MCs and DJs. Yet despite—or possibly because of—this resistance, UK rap was becoming successful.

This raises an important question: how do we define 'success' in this context? I believe it comes down to two attributes; the first is autonomy. From Smiley Culture to the various Britcore incarnations, London Posse, Hijack, and Blak Twang, even a sniff of success depended on publishing and promotional infrastructures of the music industry, which the artist had very little control over.

The groundwork laid by labels Big Dada, Low Life, and YNR in the late '90s and early '00s was supercharged by close-knit grime crews like Boy Better Know just a few years later. Independence became a necessity for UK hip-hop artists to get their music heard, but by the mid-noughties, it was often a rapper's preference.

The rapper Sway built a whole narrative around it for his unofficial debut album, *This Is My Demo,* where he leveraged his autonomy and a point-blank refusal to work with major labels as a marketing device. "No record label can buy you respect," he later said. "They could take your credibility and respect and package it in a way to make you a household name, but [earning respect] that's something that has to be done organically."[14]

Autonomy comes in all shapes and sizes. It can be big and obvious, subtle or obtuse. Yet invariably, it invites something else: range. Where there's the confidence to live by one's own rules, disregard the hegemony, to drown out the din of how you're supposed to create, provide and live, there's the range to experiment freely, make mistakes (often many) and learn from them.

A Tale of Two Styles from Boy Better Know and The Movement

Two collectives provided a pertinent example of autonomy and range. The first was Boy Better Know, led by the ever-inventive and entrepreneurial brothers Chief Joseph Olaitan Adenuga Jr. and Jamie Adenuga, better known as Skepta and JME, alongside Frisco, Jammer, Shorty, and DJ Maximum, with various associates and former members, most notably Wiley.

Long before the co-sign from Drake, Sotheby's selling Skepta's artwork for close to six figures, the eponymous Boy Better Know T-shirts, the "Rolex Sweep" dance, a slew of game-changing mixtapes, a short-lived mobile phone network, and a vast discography of independently released music, it's essential to recognise the role of Meridian Crew.

Back when Skepta was a DJ/producer known as DJ Moschino Joe, a nod to the garage brand *de rigueur,* he played garage music and made beats with his mates as part of Meridian Crew, a homage to Meridien Estate in Tottenham, North London. The crew included talented spitters like brothers President T and Big H and their cousin Bossman Birdie, who would later form Bloodline. But they also had at least one foot on the road.

On the 30th May 2004, there was a sliding doors moment for Skepta. An altercation occurred on Meridian Walk, where a local man named Douglas Mullins was shot in the head at the doorstep of his home after an argument with local youths, including members of Meridian Crew. There was a pirate radio station reportedly broadcasting at a house nearby. Mullins survived the attack after having a bullet removed from his brain.

Somewhat surprisingly, the investigation into the case, just days after the shooting occurred, was filmed for a documentary titled *London Gang Culture*, which can be seen on YouTube.

The user comments speculate that a man who comes forward with details is Skepta, with his face blurred out.[15] Big H can be seen sheepishly providing evidence later in the same episode.

What isn't up for debate, if you follow the various breadcrumbs left in early interviews[16] and songs like "That's Not Me," is the event's significance to Skepta. The shooting also led to Skepta and his family being evicted from the estate despite receiving no criminal charge.

Around 2005, Meridian Crew disbanded, and with Wiley's encouragement to develop his skills as an MC, Skepta and JME formed Boy Better Know.

JME was a different character to his older brother and the company he kept at the time. He was studying for a degree in 3D Digital Design at the University of Greenwich, an experience he credits for developing both his creative and technical skills.[17]

Like his brother, interviews with JME have become increasingly rare, as unusual a sighting as two moons. Slightly bookish, teetotal, famously vegan, and a proud Pokémon collector, he contrasts the hard-as-nails Skepta. But he is also a very savvy marketer and fiercely independent—for a long time, his Twitter bio read, "No label, No PR, no publisher, no manager, no pa, no stylist, No Instagram, no meat."

Between the two of them, Boy Better Know has grown from a grime mainstay to a force of culture, proving that making music without compromise is possible and fairly lucrative—if you check the BBK records on Companies House, the company had well into six figures in net assets in 2021[18]—if you have the talent and are willing to put in the effort.

As Skepta's star has shot into orbit, it's easy to forget how good a spitter his younger brother is. In 2005, a 20-year-old JME blew the doors wide open in terms of what grime was supposed to sound like in the self-produced single "Serious." There were many in UK hip-hop that turned their nose up at grime MCs, thinking they lacked true lyricism, but in that one song, JME shows the kind of razor-sharp, self-awareness that belies his years:

"Just 'cause we come from the gutter
We know about scraping the bottom of the butter
Don't mean we have to be sinners
Major labels don't want killers"

Shouting out Kano and Buzz Lightyear while showing a softer side to grime, JME demonstrated the potential range of grime. His wordplay became more intricate as he developed his craft, and what he may have lacked (but improved) in style was made up for by his older brother, Skepta.

Skepta's emceeing style is heavily influenced by drum & bass MCs like Skibadee and Shabba D, as well as dancehall. "That's where grime got a lot of its persona from, the whole emceeing, reloads, everyone shouting when you say a good lyric,"[19] he says, elaborating in the same Red Bull Music Academy interview, "Grime is England. In Europe, we have a real dance vibe in our lifestyle. America is hip-hop, proper hip-hop, but I've been everywhere. That is all grime is. It's MCs, but we're rapping on beats of any speed. Whether it's garage, house, grimy, funky house, electro, everything, and that's what grime is."[20] In short, Skepta saw rap as a way to complement a beat, a vibe setter typical of the drum & bass MCs that filled his tapedecks as a kid, texture over text. And this takes us to the second collective.

The Movement emerged around the same time as Boy Better Know. Its members included Ghetts, Mercston, Wretch 32, Scorcher, Devlin, Lightning, and DJ Unique. They weren't area-specific like many grime crews at the time, coming from different parts of East and North London. In a sign of what was to come, The Movement made their names with their *F**k Radio* sets. Frustrated by a lack of airplay, they worked with like-minded MCs to bypass radio and distribute their music straight to the internet. Despite appearing on multiple projects together, The Movement only dropped one official mixtape, *Tempo Specialists.* They don't have anything like the legacy of Boy Better Know, yet they are an essential part of the story, a kind of Galácticos of MCs from the time.

First and foremost is Ghetts—formerly of N.A.S.T.Y Crew and then known as Ghetto—a dynamic and versatile MC who once described "music as a pain relief,"[21] which is helpful given that he can go from sounding like a punch in the face to succour for wounded souls within a verse. For the first half of his career, he always seemed to be in someone else's shadow—Kano, Wiley, Skepta, or whoever else was next up in the grime scene—but this didn't deter him.

Ghetts' artistic evolution has been fascinating to watch, from the frenzied grime flag bearer that marked the first third of his career, with standout mixtapes *2000 & Life* and *Ghetto Gospel* (as Ghetto), through to the battle-hardened rap-ready version of Ghetts, pugnacious and ready to take on all comers, and finally J. Clarke, with a slower, steadier tempo that showed an artist ready to be vulnerable with his listeners.

That he can zig-zag between these personas, from hip-hop, occasional forays into UK funky and even R&B, and back to his grimy origins without concession or compromise, speaks volumes of Ghetts' artistry. This was realised to stunning effect with his third album and major label debut, *Conflict of Interest*, in 2021. The best album of the year, according to review aggregator Metacritic, from a year that included albums by Dave, Tyler, the Creator, pop behemoths Adele and Taylor Swift, and critic favourites Self Esteem and Nick Cave, says it all.

But let's not jump ahead of ourselves. Back to The Movement, Ghetts was first introduced to Scorcher and then Wretch. Mercston was the glue[22] who had experience making songs like the Channel U-favourite, "Good Old Days." Ghetts knew Devlin separately, having met him as a 13-year-old, later recalling, "He could rap when no one could rap."[23] Devlin is unapologetically white and working class, with a voice like a blunt instrument that he knows exactly how to use. Unlike his peers, his superpower is his stark realism and dexterous lyricism painted with stretched-out cockeyed vowels.

Between the vibe-setting grime purists in Boy Better Know and the hip-hop-inspired lyricism of The Movement, a collision course was set. "Musical stylistic differences and then personality clashes" is how Logan Sama described it. At first, these differences played out in live clashes. It almost inevitably started with Wiley—who had just released *Da 2nd Phase*, his second album and the first from Boy Better Know—who turned up unannounced to clash with Ghetts and Scorcher at 93 Feet East in Shoreditch.

The back and forth soon intensified with Jammer, Frisco and God's Gift joining Wiley in representing Boy Better Know, with all members of The Movement joining in through a series of 'war dubs' on Sama's Kiss 100 show named, appropriately enough, *The War Report.*

Some of the dubs were funny, like Ghetts asking Wiley, after much taunting by the latter, "Why you [still] no bigger than the kid's Air Max?" Others were downright scandalous, with a fierce Devlin accusing Wiley of having an addiction to cocaine and being a "nonce" (British slang for being a child molester). Sama picks up the story: "Everyone's showing off the very best of what they could do artistically. Obviously, dubs, recordings, and sets were made, but very real physical altercations also happened."

Except for Wretch32, all of the other rappers in The Movement came from and considered themselves grime MCs. Wiley teased them for imitating the sound and fashion of Dipset and other big-name American rappers. "Please don't watch *Smack* DVDs 'cos it clouds your judgement…What is all this Biggie and Pac business?" he asked on the *Nightbus Dubplate.*

Many in the grime scene agreed with Wiley and wondered why their own were turning to hip-hop. But the reality was that rap music was evolving in the UK, and *The War Report* acted as a microcosm of what was happening—a patchwork with friction that creates cultural energy rather than a bland soup of sameness. To paraphrase Juice Aleem, grime may have been the young man to challenge (UK) hip-hop who deserved to be on the mic, but UK rap music has been the beneficiary.

Stretching the Sound with Akala, Foreign Beggars, and The Bug

This range and autonomy also helped the sound spread across the country. Devil Man in Birmingham (who took part in a legendary *Lord of the Mics* clash with Skepta) and Virus Syndicate in Manchester represented regional takes on grime. Aside from what was happening regionally, organic changes took place, with traditional UK hip-hoppers Foreign Beggars adapting their sound to include the wobble bass that had become a signature of dubstep, the instrumental genre adjacent to grime in mood and texture.

Foreign Beggars have proved to be something of an outlier in UK rap, diversifying their sound with collaborations from indie rappers like the Stones Throw-affiliated Wildchild, through to Jehst, Devlin, and Riko Dan, and Dutch drum & bass collective Noisia. Noisia and the Beggars' 2009 single "CONTACT" was a noisy, face-melting stomper of a drum & bass-UK hip-hop mashup that proved popular on the festival circuit at the time (and stands at 15 million plays on YouTube today). The two collectives later came together as I Am Legion, releasing a self-titled album on Skrillex's Owsla label in 2012.

Further to the left of the field was Kevin Martin's The Bug. Martin had already been writing about and making music professionally for the best part of two decades—exploring the outer limits of sound with the industrial hip-hop of Techno Animal— but it was as The Bug where Martin's bass, space, and unaligned sonic trajectories were left to go wild. *London Zoo,* released on Ninja Tune in 2008, saw The Bug achieve wide critical acclaim, with *The Wire* naming *London Zoo* its record of the year. While not a rap project, per se, Martin enlisted the support of Roll Deep's husky-voiced Flowdan and Ricky Ranking, from Roots Manuva's Banana Clan.

For the UK hip-hop purists, there was Akala, the rapper, writer, and activist from North West London. (In another example of the familial interconnectivity within UK rap, Akala is also the younger brother of Ms. Dynamite.) With a mixture of writerly craft and tireless stamina, Akala released three full-length albums, two mixtapes (including *A Little Darker,* in collaboration with his big sister), an *E.P.* and a slew of singles on his own Illa State Records in just five years. Some of those releases included tracks that grazed the mainstream, like the single "Roll Wid Us," which charted at no.72, from his debut album *It's Not A Rumour.*

Like Kano's debut, *Home Sweet Home,* Akala looked at the popular music of the moment—mainly indie rock—and attempted to marry that sound with his perspective as a hip-hop polemicist (although producer Dexplicit does a pretty good job of a grime-flavoured remix of "Roll Wid Us" featuring Baby Blue, Jammer, and Riko). *It's Not A Rumour,* with its biting critiques of the establishment and analysis of racism, drew plaudits, including the Best Hip-Hop Act at the 2006 MOBO Awards. Still, it's unclear how many copies of the album sold, and that's probably because it didn't receive much in the way of airplay.

Responsible for creating cerebral art that deals with critical social issues, Akala didn't get the size of the audience his ideas deserved, later commenting, "You can make songs about how you love killing people or how much drugs you take. Certain things are considered 'radio-friendly,' and critiquing power isn't one of them."[24] And by the end of the noughties, he had all but given up what the popular sound to leverage was and furrowed his own lane, culminating in the conceptual album *Doublethink,* based on George Orwell's dystopian concept from the book *1984,* which is "To know and not to know, to be conscious of complete truthfulness while telling carefully constructed lies"[25]

Doublethink was released in 2010, not long after Akala founded The Hip-hop Shakespeare Company ('THSC'), a music theatre production company that explores the social, cultural, and linguistic parallels between William Shakespeare's works and those of modern-day hip-hop artists.

* * *

But outside of the cat in the box, there's the elephant in the room. Rap has a complex relationship with gender. Factor gender into a relationship between capitalism and hip-hop that had truly gone global by the start of the 21st century, and it borders on the Byzantine.

"Why does it always have to do with my gender?" commented Little Simz in an interview with *VICE.* "Why can't I just do what I want to do freely without feeling like people are trying to put me in a box all the time? Do you know how annoying that is? When you feel like you're doing something greater than life, but you're always just a 'female rapper'?"[26]

DISCOGRAPHY

Chapter 8: Too Many Men

This chapter is named after the song by Skepta.

Albums, E.P.s & Mixtapes

Roll Deep - *In At The Deep End*
Kano - *Home Sweet Home*
Sway - *This Is My Demo*
The Movement - *Tempo Specialists*
Ghetto - *2000 & Life*
Akala - *It's Not A Rumour*
Akala and Ms. Dynamite - *A Little Darker*
Ghetts - *Ghetto Gospel*
The Bug - *London Zoo*
Akala - *Doublethink*
Giggs - *Let Em Ave It*
Ghetts - *Conflict of Interest*

Singles

Kano - "Ps & Qs"
Kano - "I Don't Know Why"
Kano - "Typical Me"
Roll Deep - "When I'm Ere"
Mercston - "Good Old Days"
Akala - "Roll Wid Us"
JME - "Serious"
Skepta - "Rolex Sweep"
Foreign Beggars and Noisia - "CONTACT"
Akala - "Roll Wid Us"
Skepta - "That's Not Me"

Chapter 9

Shystie

Chanelle Scot Calica, aka Shystie, is widely recognised as among the first female grime MCs, and certainly the first to break through from the underground. An East Londoner of West Indies heritage, Shystie, or Shy as she is often known, grew up alongside grime music as it emanated from her Hackney home and the nearby boroughs of Bow, Newham, and Tottenham.

Shy explains that she didn't start listening to rap music until her late teens and was raised on a musical diet of soca and dancehall, thanks to her parents, but she soon found a love for writing rhymes through an interest in garage music, *The Slim Shady LP*, and Bone Thugs-N-Harmony. The latter was a particularly strong influence; her triple-time rhyming technique, combined with charisma, a fierce determination and yes—that she wasn't an unattractive female in a male-dominated scene—marked her out from the crowd of first-generation grime MCs.

This might explain the name of her first and only album, *Diamond in the Dirt.* The album was released on Polydor in summer 2004, after a major label bidding war following the buzz around a few white-label releases, including her "I Luv U" response to the classic Dizzee Rascal track of the same name, where Shy shows grace and rapier-sharp wit through her lyrics. Grime had its first and all-too-fleeting moment of gender politics.

Diamond in the Dirt isn't without its flaws, like many albums I've explored here, but there are more than a few good tracks. Looking back at the reviews, which included many music magazines and a surprising amount of newspapers, there were the same recurring themes also found in the critiques of debut records by Kano and Roll Deep: grime was "too aggressive" for the mainstream, while contrarily being criticised for trying out new sounds. You were damned if you do and denied if you don't, especially as a woman of colour.

Another, more concerning element of nastiness was reserved for Shystie's music. Andy Gill, the chief music critic for *The Independent*, wrote a snarky 220-word review of *Diamond in the Dirt* where he referred to Shystie as "babbling" and referenced the very icky "assumptions of repressions." Yet Mr Gill spared just one word for an actual song from the album, "Questions," a skit. His view of how a woman should or shouldn't make grime music wasn't isolated, and Shy shares her frustrations over radio and MTV playlisting, or lack of it, in our conversation.

Looking further back, the 1980s represented a fruitful period for women in rap music. Alongside Cookie Crew were hip-house pioneers She Rockers, Wee Papa Girl Rappers, and perhaps best-known, Monie Love. These names are a fundamental piece of the broader UK rap puzzle while simultaneously being relegated to the footnotes of history.

The well of opportunity seemed to dry up for women MCs in the UK during the 1990s. Although things improved at the turn of the century, it still seemed to be a case of one-in and one-out for women in rap when it came to gatekeepers in music. Even Speech Debelle, who won the Mercury Award in 2009, seemed to surprise everyone around her by the success.

Alongside Estelle and Ms. Dynamite, Shystie was one of the era's three most prominent women MCs. And it's a damning reflection of the music industry and the UK rap ecosystem that Estelle felt the need to relocate to the USA to 'make it', just like Monie Love a decade before and M.I.A. a few years later.

According to a 2021 UK Music Diversity Taskforce report, women in the UK music industry hold just 30% of senior executive roles. It's an even worse story in creative roles, as women make up less than 22% of artists and 12% of songwriters on the UK charts.[1] As the author, Arusa Qureshi puts it in her insightful book *Flip the Script*, "In terms of talent, gender isn't relevant – in terms of treatment, visible legacy and structural issues, it is."[2]

Following *Diamond in the Dirt,* Shystie released a few more singles and was featured as a guest on others, including a troublesome collaboration with Azealia Banks on "Control It." However, she became disillusioned with making music and found success as an actor.

Aside from the initial encouragement of agreeing to do this interview, I wasn't sure how rose-tinted Shystie's sunglasses would be when looking back over the past. Yet she proved to be a candid and engaging interviewee with plenty of gratitude for her journey and optimism for a future in acting and her newest venture, launching boxing gyms.

How did you first discover grime music?

I was maybe 17, because I didn't grow up on hip-hop and rap. My parents are from Barbados and Grenada, so I grew up on soca, reggae, and dancehall. My mum would have our front door open, and the speakers would play music throughout the entire estate. So that's all I grew up on.

When I moved from Hackney and went to school in North London, a lot of boys that I used to hang around with were really into grime. And they were like, "Oh, there's this thing called grime," and "There's no girls that do grime in North London." Obviously, you've got [women rappers] in South London, Lioness, NoLay, and people like Baby Blue and Estelle, but there weren't any girls doing grime in North London.

The boys taught me how to put some bars together during lunchtime. And I kind of got addicted to it. I would go home, and I wouldn't even eat dinner. I'd be missing my dinner because I'd just be writing lyrics. I didn't even start writing to grime. I would write to what I would listen to; I would rinse Eminem's album, and then I started listening to Foxy Brown. She's my favourite female rapper because she's a dark-skinned girl from Trinidad, from the West Indies, like me.

And I really liked Bone Thugs-N-Harmony. Because they used to spit so fast, and no girls were spitting fast. So I was like, "Oh, that's how can I stand out." And eventually, I began rapping over grime beats.

Many people were introduced to you via the "I Luv U" reply. Did you sense an opportunity? Were you genuinely upset by the original song? What was the thinking, and how did the track come together?

I got signed to 679 Recordings, and I was at the studio with the guys, and Lumidee was really big then. We spoke about jumping on the instrumental to "Never Leave You." And then someone else is like, "Dizzee Rascal has a song out, 'I Luv U.' And no one's done female replies." So I just went home, listened to the instrumental, wrote the song within a few hours, and returned to the studio and recorded it. And 679 loved it.

They got it pressed up [onto white label promotional vinyl], and I remember we dropped it off to Rhythm Division at the time and to a few other places. I am trying to remember what DJ played it first, but it took off. [Dizzee Rascal's original version of the] song would get played. And mine would get mixed into it. And because his song was just everywhere, I guess it was riding the wave. Radio stations would contact my manager asking, "Where can we get the song? Where can we pick up the vinyl from?" And from there, it just snowballed.

[To some people] it felt like it happened overnight but didn't because I had started at 17. I was doing like local clubs, not even getting paid. People were saying, "Yeah, I'll pay you like £50." And they're paying me nothing. So I'm having to do things for free. I'm getting bumped and everything. But because I just loved it so much, I didn't care.

Did you ever speak with Dizzee about the track?

I spoke to him over Myspace. And I was just like, "Oh, thank you for letting it run." And he messaged back like, "Nah, it's all good. So love" type of thing.

That track was a white label. Can you talk about the importance of dubplate culture?

Yeah, because that's basically what started my career. When I did "I Luv U" loads of DJs would be like, "Can you do me a dub?" So I'd have to go to the studio and do separate dubs for all the DJs. Then I started understanding that when you do those jobs for the DJs, they're more likely to play it. So I remember I had a list so long because my manager at the time was so meticulous. He was like, "Right, we've got to get every DJ, even the DJs that you might not even think are big; they might be up in Manchester, Liverpool, Glasgow and whatever. Whoever is emailing us asking for a dub, we've got to get you in the studio and do it."

That helped the song spread. In and out of London, DJs were playing the song everywhere. So now, when I'm getting booked to do shows and perform "I Luv U" in the middle of a set because their favourite DJs have been playing it on the radio. So it's quite strategic but really good, man.

It sounds like you had a really solid relationship with your manager. It's interesting because I've spoken to quite a few people from grime and UK hip-hop from that period, and many people have decried the lack of infrastructure at the time.

So it was always different for me because it was so male-dominated. But when I came as a woman, it must have been refreshing to hear. The only thing I didn't like came a bit later on, when I got signed, and the radio wouldn't play two Black females at one time. It was out of me and Estelle, and they went with Estelle. When my video for "One Wish" got released, I wasn't getting played on MTV Base, only on Channel U. So that kind of deterred me from making more music because I was not supported. I was getting supported loads on pirate radio stations and the underground scene, but crossing over was so hard. We didn't have YouTube, Twitter, Facebook, and all these things.

In 2004, you released *Diamond in the Dirt* on Polydor, had a deal with Puma, and appeared in a computer game. Only a few months before that, you worked on the checkout at Tesco. Big things happened very quickly to you. How did you adapt to being in those different spaces?

I worked at Maccy D's, various leisure centres, and then Tesco. But I never lasted longer than three to four months doing a 9-to-5. I hated it so much because I was distracted by wanting to pursue music.

I'd get paid every two weeks, and it was such small money, but I would buy a pair of trainers because I was addicted to trainers. I only travelled to Grenada and Barbados because my parents would fly us there. And then I got signed for all this money, and I'm getting flown out to these countries to perform. I was like, "What is going on?" It happened so fast that some people came to my Instagram and said, "Shystie is an industry plant because how did all this stuff just happen to you so quickly?" I'm flattered they think that, but people who know about me know I've been around since I was 17 doing pirate radio stations in North London. I was in the same heat of fame with Skepta and all those types.

I had a good manager at the time. It was [MC] Keflon from Genius Cru[3]. Because he was still performing, he would take me as an understudy. Showing me how to perform on stage.

And then occasionally, he'd bring me out on stage, and I'd do a freestyle. So I was around him a lot. And because he was in big situations, on big stages and in big meetings, he would just take me, and I adapted to it.

And you're in the eye of the storm.

Yeah, you can't grasp how big the situation is and all these things happening to you. It's only like when everything starts settling down, and you're doing other things, you're like, "Shit, I have been to over how many countries and got so many deals" and all these things which I'm grateful for.

Let's talk about *Diamond in the Dirt*, because it has a few different sounds. I like "Step Back," which sounds like grime, and then there's "This Woman's World," which is like this old-school Mantronix electro-style. Did you have a specific vision for it, or was it quite organic how things came together?

It was organic. After I put out "I Luv U," there was a bidding war from many labels wanting to sign me. I ended up signing with Polydor. They said, "We'll buy you a studio, buy your equipment, get your advance, and we'll put you in and let's just cook." There were two producers, I can't remember their names. That's so bad of me. But they said, "We've got something that's a bit different. Let us know what you kind of think of it." And then they played the instrumental to "Woman's World." I thought, "This is sick."

It was around the same time I had been performing as a support act for Basement Jaxx. I looked down at the crowd at one show, and everyone was going insane. And then, when I saw that, I had an epiphany. So, when I returned to the studio, I wanted to tap into the crowd's energy through my album.

That's why my music is not always rap or grime. If you listen to some of my mixtapes, there are loads of different genres on there because I'm an energy person. On stage, I like the crowd to have a good time and move.

Interestingly, you talk about this fusion of music. Around the time your album came out, we had the first albums by Kano and Roll Deep, which both experimented with different sounds, but there was quite a lot of criticism in the press for trying different things out, which you also got. Some of it was even quite nasty.

I was so young. I was like 21. And remember, I've grown up in Hackney, so I'm around some proper characters and stuff. So when I'm reading these things, I don't give a fuck what they think. It was very much like that attitude. And then you meet like these journalists, and they're just some little neek.

Everyone's entitled to their opinion, and I'm always open to constructive criticism because sometimes you can take something really good from it. They might be like, "I like this album from Shystie. But I can't understand anything she's saying." That's constructive. So the next project I'll do might have more clarity when I'm spitting, maybe slow some of the songs down. For some people, the album is not for them. It's fine. There are a million other artists. Go listen to them.

I think there may have been some sexism going on there. We're going back 20-odd years ago it's a very different world. Do you think we're past this time of being referred to as a 'female rapper' to just being a rapper? If you will, you had to sort of break down the door for those who followed.

One hundred percent. Because, again, only a few female rappers were signed. The only ones I can think of that were signed were me, Estelle and Ms. Dynamite. So those are the ones that mainstream people will be like, "Oh, these girls, get back in the kitchen." Yeah, shit like that. But now, because there's so much more crossing over and you've got social media, you don't need to be signed to get recognised.

Coming into this, I wasn't sure if you would speak positively or negatively about your experience with Polydor, but it sounds like you're quite relaxed about it.

I don't think they gave me a big enough push. A lot of what was happening wasn't really related to Polydor. It was often down to me and my manager. When "One Wish" was meant to get playlists on radio, it was like, "MTV is not taking it. So that's kind of it. The radio will only play one Black female, and it's out of you and Estelle." And because Estelle sang, she was more palatable, I guess. It was as if my music was an angry Black girl type of thing. Do you know what I'm saying?

None of my songs got playlisted on commercial radio. So my manager and I had to do all the groundwork. Polydor thought they had done enough because I had an album out in shops, but they didn't back me how I would have liked to be backed if that makes sense. I don't hold a grudge, but it was disheartening at the time because I worked so hard to make the album, only to be told, "Oh, you can't get playlisted, your video can't get playlisted. So you're capped."

For pretty shitty reasons, by the sounds of it.

Yeah, very shitty reasons. How can you say you can only play one Black female? That's mad. It's sexism and racism both straightaway. So when my next songs come out, we make it easy. It's more singing and it's not, as they would say, aggressive. But then it wasn't grimey enough. You can't win.

That's why, when I speak to artists now, I'm like, "Just do you. Don't try to please these people on radio or whoever." So that's why I never made another album.

Do you regret that?

Not really. Sometimes, I say, "Oh, if I was a bit more consistent, my name would be more solid." If you look at Skepta and Kano, they get mentioned in all these things, but it's because they were more consistent. I got a bit deterred and disheartened, so I didn't keep my foot on the gas. And I'm like, "Man, I was the first fucking female MC." I should still be getting mentioned in certain things, but like I said, I'm very laid back. I'm a Capricorn.

You played the lead role in the Channel 4 show *Dubplate Drama*. How did that come about?

My manager was friends with Luke Hyams, the writer and director of *Dubplate*. He set up a meeting between us at Luke's house. Luke was like, "Just tell me how it is to be an artist. Tell me what your journey has been like as Shystie?" So I told him everything. He wrote the character Dionne, and we developed her together— we're going to see what it's like from a woman's perspective coming up in the grime world. It was based on my story, but things were exaggerated to make it work for TV.

Luke knew some people in the television industry and asked me to reach out to artists I liked. I reached out to a few people. I'm not going to say the person's name, but I reached out to one artist and was like, "I'm doing a TV show. I'd love to get you in it." They tried to little girl me. He was like, "Good luck with your little TV show." Then *Dubplate Drama* came out, and it was a huge success. Then the second series came out. That same person messaged me, saying, "Oh, I'd love to get in it." I didn't even respond.

The show was a who's who of MCs from the time. You had everybody from Goodz, Crazy Titch, Rodney P, and Skepta either playing parts or performing as themselves. What was the energy like on set?

Everyone, it was crazy. I remember the day we got Channel 4 on board. It was me, Luke, and [my manager] Justin in the car after, and we were so gassed. I turned to them and said, "Guys, I haven't had any acting experience. How can you have a flipping lead actress who hasn't even acted before!?" They just said to think of it as a music video. It was very DIY.

I was used to memorising lyrics, which helped me with the scripts. Being on set with Big Narstie, Dappy, and the rest of the MCs was funny because we had no acting experience. Sometimes, Luke got stressed out dealing with all these crazy kids from grime. He is a proper film director who's used to working with professional actors who know what the golden hour[4] is. We shot so many episodes people just ended up smoking [weed] on set. I think that also played a part in why there were no more *Dubplates*, because it's tough to work with people who haven't come from that world.

It was well received, though, right?

It was amazing. We were expected to get 60,000 viewers, but we got 3.3 million. It was one of the best experiences of my life. It was innovative because it was the first show ever that was interactive. Obviously, Netflix later did it with *Black Mirror*. But we were the first ones to do it. That set me up to do more acting, such as in films like *Adulthood*. We opened the door for shows like *Top Boy*. Big up, Luke Hyams.

Is acting your focus now?

Kind of. I'm in the process of pitching my own show. I've signed a deal with [television company] Fremantle. It's similar to *Dubplate* but an older version and more based around a crime element. The pitching process can take two to seven years. So while they're doing that, I'm just cracking on with other things, and if and when it happens, it happens.

DISCOGRAPHY

Essentials

Shystie - "Step Back"
Shystie -"This Woman's World"
Shystie- "I Luv U" (Dizzee Rascal Reply)
Shystie - "Heat Fm 96.6"
Shystie - "Wake Up"
Shystie - "Stop"

Deep Cuts

Fireworkz Ft. Shystie, Durrty Goodz, L.Man, and J2K -"Hold It Down"
Black The Ripper Ft. Shystie - "Home Sweet Home"

Chapter 10

Terrorist?

Heading into the late noughties, it was an exciting time for UK rap, even if the rest of the world didn't know it yet. As always, location was vital, and something, in particular, was happening in South London.

Hollow Man Meetz Blade, Moral Nihilism, and the Global Financial Crisis

Three young men are creeping out of the darkness, avoiding the glare of the camera in the corridor of an anonymous housing estate. The first to come forward looks suspiciously over his shoulder. Dressed in a baby-blue adidas tracksuit and navy New York Yankees hat, his boyish features belie a dead-eye stare, "stuck in the rat race," he lists off a string of offences: strap, food (drugs), and robbery with violence. Before concluding, with cold intention, "I ain't in it for the fame, I'm in it for the papers / I've been moving peng since 3210." The man is known as Blade Brown.

The next rapper to appear is Fem Fel. A mischievous grin stretches across his face, he knows this is a music video. He warns the viewer, "We got guns that'll sink a boat, and we got funds, so we don't think we won't." Finally, up steps a hooded figure. It's Giggs, or Gigs as he's incorrectly credited; he is imperturbable. He looks much younger than the superstar we know today but sounds the same. Compared to Blade and Fem, Giggs' delivery is slower and delivered with greater clarity. With lines memories can latch onto, each vowel and word is stretched precisely through that hollow voice, the signature grunts and 'cheech' ad-libs are there, as is the mandatory SN1 shout-out. This is road rap, and it absorbed grime's road energy into hip-hop's lyrical traditions.

The scene is from the music video for "Sink a Boat" from *Hollow Man Meetz Blade,* a collaborative mixtape from Giggs and Blade Brown. The beats are forgettable, but there's something new about the bars. Hearing English MCs rap about selling drugs wasn't new, but it was unusual to hear it done with such a deadeye commitment. "N***as saying hip-hop is dead? I don't give a fuck. I'll just go flip rock instead," Blade Brown asserts.

This was 2007, not long after Clipse had released their sophomore album, *Hell Hath No Fury*, the magnum opus of crack rap. So perhaps it's no surprise that some of the influence was seeping into our own rap scene—but the language had adapted to include UK slang, with the duo ready to provide customers with "food" but never on "tick" (credit).

Giggs and Blade Brown didn't invent road rap. Like many rap origin stories, its precise starting point is contested, but its South London home, specifically Brixton and Peckham, is generally accepted. The likes of PDC, the gang-turned-rap collective known as Poverty Driven Children, from Brixton (based in the same Angell Town Estate where Roots Manuva recorded *Brand New Second Hand*) were pivotal pre-cursors thanks to their nihilistic gangster rap take on UK hip-hop. But *Hollow Man Meetz Blade* was significant in evolving the sound, and "Sink a Boat" arguably gave road rap its first anthem. And in 2007, road rap was blowing up.

A year later, the global financial crisis began, starting with a collapse in the housing market bubble, accelerated by credit freezes and regulatory failures. The interconnectedness of the global financial system meant that the crisis quickly spread beyond the United States, causing severe economic contraction globally.

This led to a sharp rise in unemployment in the UK, particularly among young people. During the height of the financial crisis in late 2008 and early 2009, the youth unemployment rate peaked at around 20%, the highest it had been since the bleakness of Thatcherism in 1984.[1] Even in the aftermath of the recession, youth unemployment remained persistently high. In 2010 and 2011, the youth unemployment rate in the UK hovered around 18% to 20%, and it wasn't until 2016 that the numbers declined steadily and the economy began to recover. Multiple sectors were impacted—from finance to the arts and the building trade.

I was devastated to lose my entry-level job at MTV in 2009, mostly because I was convinced it would be difficult to find a new one; some of my friends spent years out of work.

This is a roundabout way of explaining the reasons behind the moral nihilism that was beginning to take over rap music in the UK, from Blade Brown's trap excursions to *Redrum*, the debut mixtape by Krept & Konan. Yet it's important to note that nihilism isn't inherently negative; it can be a starting point for important introspection and philosophical inquiry.

In *Ethics: Inventing Right and Wrong*, the atheist philosopher J. L. Mackie argued that objective morals are relative, writing, "Moral scepticism must therefore take the form of error theory, admitting that a belief in objective values is built into ordinary moral thought and language, but holding that this belief is false."[2] This leads to Mackie's renowned "error theory," built on three principles;

1. There are no moral features in this world; nothing is right or wrong.
2. Therefore, no moral judgments are true.
3. However, our sincere moral judgments try but always fail, to describe the moral features of things.

A modern response from error theorist Richard Garner is especially relevant when discussing road rap, an antecedent of trap—focused on the trap house and the acquisition of material wealth through slinging both drugs and compelling rhymes—on to its evolution in UK drill. In *A World Without Values: Essays on John Mackie's Moral Error Theory*, Garner advocates for the idea of "moral abolitionism." He argues that if one were to believe that there are no objective morals, then engaging in moralism is a deceptive behaviour. Furthermore, by refusing to make moral judgements generally, people would be more likely to engage with others more genuinely.

The social benefit, Garner writes, is that "We will find that there will be less to argue about, and that our conflicts and disagreements with others, at last seen for what they are, can be addressed and resolved."[3] And it's here that Blade Brown's "Sorry for the Fiends" becomes a compelling case study. Blade "feels sorry for the fiends," he repeats three times in the chorus before skillfully weaving a narrative of multiple characters and customers over a simple, melancholic piano loop. Even though Blade is making income off their addiction, "It don't mean that we ain't got a conscience." He recognises the people beyond their commercial value to him—"Sally's only 22, said she's tryna kick it...Garry's kinda safe, Ian's kinda strange"—but the vice-like grip of heroin and crack addiction is too strong for one less dealer to make any difference because Blade raps, "They're still gonna smoke. So I might as well get my paper.".

It's like passing individual moral judgement on the unfortunately named Dick Luld, the CEO of Lehman Brothers when it collapsed in 2008, for the global financial crisis although it was ultimately a systemic failure involving multiple interconnected factors—just like the UK's drug epidemic.

Hollow Man Meetz Blade is not the high point of rap mixtapes some social media critics would claim it to be. Giggs' claim that "Man ain't making mixtapes like this where you have to skip shit" is wrong; the first third is very skippable, primarily because of the lack of imagination to the beats. Yet there are some stand-out tracks, including "Freestyle" (the second of three songs with the same title), "Pecknarm Freestyle," and "Sink A Boat," which contain serious bars and will have the most pious of nuns pulling screw faces.

But *Hollowman Meetz Blade* did serve as an inflection point for UK rap, a precursor to the new direction the scene was taking.

Talking Cross-Pollination and Commercial Crossover with 1Xtra DJs

In the summer 2010, I went to the offices of BBC Radio in Central London to meet with Benji B, Mista Jam, and DJ Target (also of Roll Deep), who were all key DJs on 1Xtra at the time. I was editing *Bonafide*, an independent (marketing speak for 'small') music magazine that was still releasing a print edition, and was there for a round table discussion on the state of British music. It was the closest I ever really got to the music industry establishment. I was bullish in not providing the BBC PR my questions in advance, but compromised by providing some of the subjects I intended to ask about, and was politely asked to refrain from asking questions about the reported closure of BBC 6 Music (the station survived thanks to a high profile online campaign fronted by the musician and station DJ, Jarvis Cocker). But really, we were there to cast a new complexion on an old subject: Was UK rap finally stepping out of the shadow of its American cousins and gaining respect for its MCs?

"We always felt as a [rap] music scene in the UK we were inferior to America. No one thinks that anymore,"[4] explained Target.

"On a skill level, we always have respect from people in the States," responded Mista Jam, adding, "What we haven't had is numbers; we never had a number one record. Now we've got that, which is why they're paying more attention."

He was referring to "Pass Out" by Tinie Tempah, a sugar-rush hybrid of hip-pop, grime, reggae, and drum & bass wobbles. Labyrinth's genre-busting production—built around one bass note, a Korg Polysix synth, and a layered, jittering Nintendo-style 8-bit sound—somehow contains enough thunderous logic, as if an equation has been solved and a number one record has equated. "Pass Out" spent a few weeks at the top of the charts earlier that February.

After the chart success of "Bonkers" by Dizzee Rascal in 2009, and "Wearing My Rolex" by Wiley the following year, "Pass Out" marked a new moment in British pop music as the pendulum traced a new path from indie rock ubiquity to "urban" music that was suddenly in the ascendency. Beyond the established names, there were "hip-poppers" capturing a mainstream audience's attention, like the once-battle rapper Professor Green, Example, grime MCs Chip and Tinchy Styder whose mawkish R&B-EDM experiments resulted in festival hits, the enfant terribles N Dubz who graduated from Channel U to chart stardom.

There was also Plan B, who took Eminem's angry white rapper blueprint and turned it into a franchise with the release of music (including a Kray Twins-era soul-singing alias), various film roles—which included writing and directing the brutal *Ill Manors,* starring Riz Ahmed, another rapper turned actor—and cider commercials.

At this point, BBC Radio stopped trying to lead trends and followed the conversation with a comprehensive market research system in place, polling 400 twelve to thirty-year-olds about the stations' playlist choices weekly. Austin Daboh, the music manager at 1Xtra, described 2010 "as the year of urban," adding, "Before, on the Radio 1 playlist, it used to be almost a one-in-one-out policy in terms of urban records… now there are six, seven, eight records on the playlist." Daboh reasoned that the mainstream embrace was partly due to "More senior people in British society who are Black, or Asian, or mixed race or are from a council estate background, and it's not a token gesture anymore."[5]

In an unremarkable meeting room, we spent almost two hours geeking out about the current crop of UK music makers that had resulted in a "cross-pollination of styles"—from dubstep producers like Mala, who made "music on a deep, almost spiritual level," according to Benji, through to new music by Skream, "the only way I could describe it as 'future garage,'" exclaimed Jam—and how they were influencing rap music. The characters were different— grime, dubstep, 'future garage'—but in many ways it was the same story from twenty years earlier, when Britcore, reggae, soul, and rave intersected as they did on nights at The Africa Centre led by Jazzie B. Except in the early 2010s it was Benji B's Deviation or FWD, or other genre-bending club nights which orbited around the hallowed Plastic People nightclub in London's Old Street.

Perhaps even more than other forms of art, music has a cyclical nature, borrowing from and building upon the sound pioneers of the past, but the influential factors were different this time. At the beginning of the decade, music streaming was still in its infancy; the £320 million spent on digital music in 2010—inclusive of services such as Spotify and Pandora, as well as downloads from Apple's iTunes store—accounted for just over a quarter of annual consumer spending on music in the UK.[6] Five years later, it was more than half, and by the end of the decade, nearly 77% of the annual £1.9 billion spent on music was digital.

Yet Giggs and Blade Brown's road rap wasn't going anywhere, and their music certainly wasn't appearing in the Radio 1 playlist. Youngs Teflon, Nines, and Potter Payper all self-released their debut mixtapes between 2010 and 2013, slowly building up an audience from the ground up. If anything, road rap was becoming more popular.

Here's why: Behind the changing tastes and increase in digital dimes spent, there was a healthy music ecosystem in the early 2010s. Numerous blogs covered the progressive "cross-pollination" of rap and electronic music, with multiple daily posts in the UK, such as *FACT, Dummy*, and hip-hop and grime-focused freestyle websites like *GRM Daily* and *SBTV*. And there were specialist print music magazines and papers such as the wonderfully snarky *The Stool Pigeon, Shook* (a short-lived sequel to *Straight No Chaser)*, and *Bonafide,* where we aimed to write about hip-hop and grime with the sort of reverence usually reserved for rock music journalism. Outside of radio, magazines, and blogs, there were all sorts of YouTube shows popping up to celebrate the music and culture that had grown around UK rap in a very organic way–be it *Grime Report TV* and its proto-meme series *Five Pound Munch*, or *Tim and Barry TV*, with their trippy visuals and brilliant chaotic live sets, that was a precursor to *Boiler Room* when it was a subsection of something called *Platform*. In short, there were lots of channels for healthy discourse about music.

The early 2010s were arguably the last time in modern music history when there was still an overground and underground to music. Artists like Giggs and Tinie Tempah could exist and, very broadly speaking, be making the same type of music, but they have nothing in common with each other and have entirely different fanbases. In a few short years, social media would blitz through the publishing industry, draining newspapers and magazines of advertising revenue like a vampiric, Patagonia-clad tech-bro, endlessly preaching of "scale" while making big job-devouring bets with his venture capitalist buddies. As a result, music journalism—an industry not known for its job security at the best of times—suffered immeasurably, and most of the titles mentioned above shuttered within a few years or significantly reduced their staff, freelance rates, and editorial output.

Facebook had 24 million daily active users in 2012. By the end of the decade, there were 45.5[7] million active users (including Meta-owned Instagram and WhatsApp), more than two-thirds of the UK. Twitter went from 8.6 million users in 2012 to more than double by 2020. What was once the innocuous Tom, his friends and a few low-res audio streams on Myspace morphed into a marketing monster for the music industry. And it eventually meant that musicians and labels could control their narrative without the potentially difficult questions of a pesky music journalist.

Parallel to this was the increasing ubiquity of music streaming platforms. Spotify was joined by major players like TIDAL (2014), the revamped Apple Music, and YouTube Music (both 2015), together with dozens of others. Although the propositions and libraries may have subtle differences, the commonality seems to be streaming platforms that see music as 'content' rather than art. (The notable exception is Bandcamp, which allows artists and labels to set their own price for music sales in a community-centric model that includes *Bandcamp Daily*, an active editorial platform dedicated to niche styles and underground communities, Although the acquisition of Bandcamp by Epic Games and a relatively quick sale to Songtradr, the B2B music licensing service, in 2023, and the subsequent cutting of staff by 50%, makes for an ominous future.)

But, inevitably, it's not all bad. When the floodgates of social media blew open at the start of the decade, followed by the neocapitalist fantasy of music streaming, it was a chaotic marriage that allowed the entrepreneurial spirit of homegrown rap music to flourish. The cross-pollination between rap and other musical styles began to accelerate, resulting in unexpected and occasionally beautiful musical collaborations, such as "Chapter 7" between the jazz quintet Ezra Collective and Ty, the unlikely but excellent jazz-grime-funk fusion of "Quest for Coin II " featuring Ezra Collective, JME and genre-bending producer Swindle, and later, Headie One and electronic producer FredAgain surprisingly subtle blend of EDM and UK drill that resulted in the *GANG* mixtape.

Whether or not these collaborations would have taken place so vividly and frequently without the convenience of cherry-picking musical tastes that a generation of listeners has grown accustomed to, we'll never know.

Lowkey and the Art of Protest Rap

In 2011, MTV Base, a vestige of old media, desperately attempted to cling to relevancy and tap into the success of "urban" music in the country by airing a list of the top 10 rappers in the UK. Putting aside the hackneyed debate on turning art into lists (Tinie Tempah sat on top, which is pretty much all you need to know), there was the equal placement of Chip (or Chipmunk as he was then known) and Lowkey at number 10. With the former backed by Sony Music, having moved on from his grime roots and began making music aimed at the dancefloor, and the latter being an unsigned artist known for his lyrical craft and making politically charged protest music, it was a fairly transparent attempt to position commercial artists against an underground MC, and perhaps to a lesser extent, grime versus hip-hop.

Missing from the list altogether was Ghetts, who took umbrage at the snub and released a diss track taking aim at the industry panellists and several MCs from the list, including D Double E, Professor Green, and a throwaway comment aimed at Lowkey: "I like Pro Green, but when I paid for his album, two words: daylight robbery / Lowkey must have had someone on the inside. Yeah that's it, obviously." The reference to Lowkey didn't make much sense beyond the way it rhymed with "daylight robbery," but rap can be a competitive sport, the pugilism of poets, and Lowkey responded a week later over Ghetts' "Top 3 Selected" beat.

The track's focus is Lowkey's role in the UK rap scene and how he has built up a following independently, without any media support, and, of course, he aims Ghetts:

"Never would I side with Lockheed Martin… I don't make tracks for David Cameron."

The line was a reference to Ghetts's "Invisible" song, encouraging ethnic minorities to fill in the 2011 census. Lockheed Martin is America's largest arms manufacturer, and, as *The Guardian* reported in 2011, "The company, which makes Trident nuclear missiles, cluster bombs and F-16 fighter jets, won the £150m contract to run the census on behalf of the Office for National Statistics (ONS)."[8]

It's somewhat speculatory, but looking back at the video for "Invisible," there is also an accompanying behind-the-scenes "making of" video and both are published on a YouTube channel belonging to a shadowy Linstock Communications (from a production perspective, the usual Channel U alumni were involved). Linstock Communications isn't a music PR firm, or a video production agency, but a communications consultancy that describes itself as "help(ing) people manage sensitive issues and crises." Was this a nefarious attempt to coerce Britain's ethnic minorities to give away their data via a popular grime MC? I tried contacting Linstock Communications to learn more about who they are and how they came to be associated with the making of "Invisible" but at the time of publishing, the publicly listed phone number is out of service, and I still haven't received a response to my emails.

Lowkey finished "Top 3 Selected" with a conciliatory tone towards Ghetts, and makes his point strongly: "Don't get it twisted, I didn't make this track to prove Ghetts wrong, 'cos he was right–he is one of the best MCs that this country has ever seen. But I did this track to prove myself, 'cos so am I." He calls out MTV for tying him with Chipmunk "for one reason: friction" and tells them never to "mention my name again. I don't need your support." Ending with the familiar refrain of "Existence is resistance."

Chip responded to the Viacom-assisted "beef," but a rapper whose biggest hits include "Oopsy Daisy" probably wasn't going to cause Lowkey many sleepless nights, and he pulled the plug on him with the diss track, "The Warning." Chip and Ghetts mocked Lowkey for his interests in Palestine, and for the second time in the space of a few years, the rift caused a pseudo-cultural war between grime and (UK) hip-hop fans with unsavoury exchanges across Twitter and YouTube comments.

This could have played out differently; the rappers involved could have united the scenes and responded to MTV for its part in conducting the riff, but rap beefs are often good publicity for all involved. Yet Ghetts didn't respond with a new track and years later went on record to say he spoke with Lowkey and acknowledged "My Lowkey situation came from an ignorant place on my behalf."[9]

The bigger story here was the often-overlooked role of protest rap in the UK, of which Lowkey is a key player. In October 2011, he released his second and most successful studio album, *Soundtrack to the Struggle*, which entered the album charts at number 57. His reference to Lockheed Martin in "Top 3 Selected" is fairly typical of Lowkey's approach to making music, which can sometimes feel more like that of an investigative reporter or a fiery socialist academic, who also happens to enjoy the taste of a word salad. That's not to say Lowkey can't drop cold, hard bars—he is responsible for two of the most memorable "Fire In The Booth" freestyle sessions, where he rapped lyrics in order of the alphabet forward and backwards—but with a particular focus on a "broader disenchantment with political orthodoxy."[10]

Born to an Iraqi mother and an English father, Lowkey, real name Kareem Dennis, cut his teeth as a member of the Poisonous Poets in the mid-'00s on the freestyle circuit. He's part of the same UK hip-hop lineage as someone like Braintax, sharing an anti-imperialist worldview. Still, unlike the (former) Low Life boss, there is self-deprecation, empathy, and nuance, like in "Long Live Palestine," where he targets Coca-Cola and Starbucks, brands that reportedly support the Zionist lobby, as well as virtuous poseurs who appear to share his politics only at a surface level: "Before you talk learn the meaning of that scarf on your neck." In the track, Lowkey also notes that there is "Nothing more anti-Semitic than Zionism...I know there's plenty of Rabbis that agree with me" over Eastern strings and a boom-bap beat from Nutty P.

Aside from "Free Palestine," a title which would always capture attention even if it was five minutes of static, significant tracks from *Soundtrack to the Struggle* include "Cradle of Civilisation," a homage to Lowkey's mother's home city of Baghdad. It's a song that strikes the right balance between sermon and storytelling, with Mai Khalil's tender voice on the hook. It's a sensory overload, with Lowkey longing for the "fragrances he never smelt" as well blood, flesh and bones and suffering while Khalil's hook, sung in melancholic Arabic, transports the listener together with Quincy Tones' sped-up chipmunk soul melody. Lowkey is grateful yet conflicted not to have been there, disturbed by watching the news "Because I look at the victims and see the same face in the mirror." It could be a clumsy mix in a lesser-skilled MC's hands, but not Lowkey, who merges the personal with the historical, charting the troubled late-20th century history faced by the Iraqi people, from Saddam Hussein to the American occupation and his own experience of duality, calling himself an "immigrant Englishman amongst Arabs and an / Arab amongst Englishmen."

Guest appearances come from Klashnekoff, M1 from Dead Prez, the rapper/weed activist Black the Ripper, Immortal Technique, the singer Mai Khalil, and Shadia Mansour, who has been described as "the first lady of Arabic hip-hop." Alongside a few typically ferocious bars from Klashnekoff on "Blood, Sweat and Tears," the standout collaboration track is "Obama Nation (Part 2)," featuring M1 and Black the Ripper.

Barack Obama receives criticism throughout the record; he is essentially seen as a puppet for American imperialism, but on "Obama Nation (Part 2)," the intensity of M1 and Black the Ripper's rage and Lowkey's controlled fury dials the anger up to 11. Referencing everything from the war in Afghanistan, the sickening use of uranium weapons by US and UK military, Wikileaks, backtracking on previously held views on Israel and Palestine, and Obama's rumoured connection to working for the CIA, the song is provocative and conspiratorial, but it also challenges the listener to reconsider the status quo. This is important, even if you don't necessarily agree with everything Lowkey is saying.

Soundtrack to the Struggle maintains a very hip-hop tradition of including multiple skits on an album fused with Lowkey's singular worldview—Pastor Jeremiah Wright, Norman Finkelstein (America's most divisive Israel-Palestine professor), Ben Affleck, and the former presidential candidate John McCain, who makes a bumbling defence of Barack Obama at a debate when an audience member states she "can't trust Obama" and has read that "he's an Arab." "No, ma'am, he's a decent family man."

At twenty-six tracks spanning 95 minutes, *Soundtrack to the Struggle* is a long album. It's also a dense listen, tackling everything from American imperialism, protest, riots, cuts and corruption to personal matters like Lowkey's brother's suicide in the song "Haunted." Even some of *SttS's* brightest listeners might need access to the *Encyclopedia Britannica* or Google (both sources, I'm certain, would be ripe for a Lowkey takedown) to decode some of the references to 16th-century colonialism. But that is probably the point: Lowkey is making music for the mind, even if that comes at the cost of connecting with listeners on a deeper emotional level.

The timing of the album's release could not have been much better, because the London riots took place only two months earlier, sparked by the death of 29-year-old Mark Duggan, who was shot dead by police in Tottenham on 4 August 2011. Duggan was falsely reported to have had a gun when police murdered him, and within the space of a few days, a peaceful protest became violent. London was on fire, quite literally, with double-decker buses set alight and shops being looted across the capital. I was living in Hackney at the time, and it was surreal to poke my head out the window and hear the same aeroplanes and sirens that were appearing on the news, with masked men running around the streets below. It felt like I was living on the periphery of a dystopian nightmare, an unsuspecting extra in the film *V for Vendetta.*

By the following week, the carnage had spread nationwide, from Wood Green to Wolverhampton. The riot lasted five days and was the biggest in modern English history.

One hundred families were made homeless as a result of the unrest, and five people died. David Cameron, prime minister at the time, and Boris Johnson, the then London mayor and future prime minister, were on holiday, eventually returning to the country. Johnson was criticised for not returning soon enough.

Ten years later, David Lammy, the Labour MP for Tottenham, wrote in *The Guardian* that during the years since, "instead of acting to strengthen the fabric of society's fire blanket to reduce the risk of riots," conservative prime ministers have "decimated police forces, youth services and local authority budgets." He adds, "I say this with deep regret: by failing to implement the measures designed to tackle society's dissatisfaction, alienation and fragmentation, Johnson risks letting a spark set fire to the fuel all over again."[11]

Lowkey addressed the riots on "Dear England," probably one of the last songs recorded for the *Soundtrack to the Struggle.*

He points out that the cause for the unrest is "way bigger than Mark Duggan/Bigger than Smiley (Culture)," and juxtaposes it with "bankers lounging," a "government that can't govern," and "assumptions surrounding the looting of London /But this is a system consumed by consumption."

We look to art during dark times for guidance, and though Lowkey had his fanbase, perhaps not enough people outside of that were listening because later that year, he decided to stop making music and turn his attention to studying (gaining qualifications as a personal trainer and a masters in Near and Middle Eastern Studies at SOAS) and focused on his activism work. Lowkey eventually released a follow-up album, *Soundtrack to the Struggle 2,* in 2019, eight years later.

There's an irony in hip-hop. Whereas the most pejorative term the media can label its protagonists is "gangster rapper," within the music, it is the "conscious rapper," a title that fans and artists are often quick to resist. It's probably why we don't hear too much about Swiss when there's talk of So Solid Crew. Yet even the least likely of rappers can make music that fuels social protest—just look at how Lethal Bizzle's "Pow!" was the soundtrack to the student protests in Parliament Square following an increase in tuition fees in December 2010. As Dan Hancox put it, "Like punk at its best, Pow! is a breathless three-minute assault of sheer adrenaline."[12]

Be it Giggs, Ghetts, or Lowkey, all of these voices are important in showing how far UK rap music has come and where it could go. I'll leave the last word in this chapter to Benji B: "There's nothing more hip-hop than that than doing your own thing…it's about identity, and I think now that British identity really zings out."

DISCOGRAPHY

Chapter 10: Terrorist?

This chapter is named after the song by Lowkey.

Albums, E.P.s & Mixtapes
Clipse - *Hell Hath No Fury*
Giggs and Blade Brown - *Hollow Man Meetz Blade*
Krept & Konan - *Redrum*
Lowkey - *Soundtrack to the Struggle*
Lowkey - *Soundtrack to the Struggle 2*
Headie One and Fred Again - *GANG*

Singles
Giggs and Blade Brown - "Sink a Boat"
Giggs and Blade Brown - "Sorry for the Fiends"
Giggs and Blade Brown - "Freestyle"
Giggs and Blade Brown - "Pecknarm Freestyle"
Dizzee Rascal - "Bonkers"
Wiley - "Wearing My Rolex"
Tinie Tempah - "Pass Out"
Ghetts - "Invisible"
Ghetts - "Top 3 Selected"
Lowkey - "Free Palestine"
Lowkey - "Cradle of Civilisation"
Lowkey Ft. Klashnekoff - "Blood, Sweat and Tears"
Lowkey Ft. M1 and Black the Ripper "Obama Nation (Part 2)"
Lowkey - "Haunted"
Lowkey - "Dear England"

Ezra Collective Ft. Ty - “Chapter 7”
Ezra Collective x JME x Swindle - “Quest for Coin II “

Chapter 11

Venom

In early 2024, I saw CASISDEAD perform at a small club called Bitterzoet in central Amsterdam. Typical of the area, it wasn't far from the Red Light District and the weed coffee shops that attract gangs of stag and hen parties all year round but also nestled among the bougie bars and restaurants that appealed to well-heeled locals.

From the outside, with its stained glass windows and red velvet exterior, it didn't look like the type of venue a grimy rapper like Cas would play, but the fuzzy synths and brain freeze-inducing bass from "All Hallows" were unmistakable once we approached the entrance and went downstairs; passing the grotty yellowing walls covered in hundreds of stickers and graffiti tags, and crossed the sticky red floor, through the busy crowd and towards the stage. Bitterzoet, which translates into English as bittersweet, is an appropriate name for the location.

Don't You Know, CASISDEAD?

I've lived in the city for four years, but the first two were written off thanks to COVID-19. I arrived with my family in a new country, with a new job (which I soon hated), all set for new beginnings. Instead, time stood still. So I wanted to make up some ground and watch a rapper who had resisted time by being around for more than a dozen years but had only just released his first album. Surprisingly for a rap show, CASISDEAD started his performance in Bitterzoet not on schedule, but early. I stumbled around looking for a time machine. The sign said that the future was none of my business, but I found the present for the first time in a while.

Aside from a joke about gripping his mic so hard he'll end up with "hands like [the England and Everton goalkeeper] Jordan Pickford" and vague talk of being nominated for a BRIT Award that weekend, there was very little banter from Cas. It could have been down to impatience, nervousness, or the fact that CASISDEAD quite simply does not give a fuck. Still, together with his DJ—and surrounded by his mates, or the "Dead Team" as they're known, passing round joints on the small stage—they played banger after banger of hard, funny, nihilistic rap over an eclectic combination of trap beats, Giorgio Moroder-inspired synths and a 2-step-style song I haven't heard before, Cas credits the new school garage producer "big up Conducta for this one."

It was the final show of a short European tour supporting his new album, *Famous Last Words,* and a near sell-out crowd was lapping up the newest, old hero of UK rap. This meant a few old favourites like "All Hallows," a wicked wordplay of Britishness, where Cas raps about celebrity chefs (he holds a long-running fixation for Nigella Lawson), alongside newbies like "Venom" and "Traction Control," continuing the record's synth-heavy '80s sci-fi futurism aesthetic. "I just jumped out the morgue, ain't nobody fresher / Only MC on my level, M.C. Escher," Cas spits, acknowledging the Dutch graphic artist known for his mind-bending optical illusions and mathematically inspired art, paintings of dizzying landscapes of impossible staircases.

Cas makes intensely visual music. Look through some of his music videos, which he is closely involved in creating, and his eerie vision of retro-futurism will soon coerce you. Yet it's Hieronymus Bosch, another Dutch artist, that Cas' music reminds me of, which Walter Gibson describes as, "A world of dreams [and] nightmares in which forms seem to flicker and change before our eyes."[1] Cas is the drug-addicted dealer, the "psychologist's wet dream" who falls in love with the prostitute, pacing pavements, stomping the dirty, seedy streets of North London sometime between night and day, after the after party, wraps in his back pocket, the coke drip stinging the back of your throat, "Bowie banging in the tape."

It's all a powerful act of make-believe.

After the show had finished, hanging around outside, my friend bummed a cigarette off a couple of young lads who had travelled all the way from Dover for the show. They were boisterous Cas stans, still buzzing about his recent performance at London's Koko, where regular collaborator Giggs joined him on stage for a surprise performance. "It was sick, mate!" "Cas is a legend," said another with eyes as red as the sinking sun.

It's not just fans who worship Cas, but musicians too. Producer and Daupe! label boss The Purist, who has collaborated with Action Bronson, Danny Brown, Westside Gunn, and Loyle Carner, among others, is unequivocal when we speak: "I've worked with some of the best, but he is the best rapper I've ever worked with. Other people aren't even close."[2]

Although MF DOOM, the masked villain of rap and another one of The Purist's collaborators, is the closest comparison I've seen in terms of a cult following for a rapper from the UK (DOOM may have been born here, but he left the country as a baby). There are noticeable differences: DOOM was prolific, releasing dozens of albums and singles through various character aliases before his untimely passing on Halloween in 2020. Cas works at a more prosaic pace. And DOOM's rap style was (is!) denser, a hyper-imagist with intricate rhyme schemes and—similarly to Cas—layered with double and even triple entendre, sprinkled with humour and unexpected references. (When I interviewed DOOM in 2011, speaking on the comedic influences in his music, he confessed, "I love Benny Hill. His shit is retarded." They were different times).

These unexpected references extend to sample choices, with DOOM foraging elements from the Brazilian jazz-funk of Azymuth, classic '90s boom bap, recorded poetry by Charles Bukowski, Scooby-Doo cartoon samples, and everything in between, together with Stendhal syndrome-inducing rhymes. Cas' sonic tastes are focused on sleazy '80s electro, R&B, and new wave–like the inventive flip of The Go-Go's founder Jane Wieldin's schmalzy "Whatever It Takes" into the '80s slow-groove yuppie anthem "Matte Grey Wrap." Cas seems to relish taking the most asinine sample and alchemising it into a brutal coke rap. As The Purist explains, when they first started working together, "it was left-field stuff. We sampled things like New Kids On The Block and flipped them. So we had 'You Got It (The Right Stuff)' and made a track called 'The White Stuff.'"

The closest similarity is the breadcrumbs both artists leave in their songs, like hieroglyphs to a larger supervillain origin story that drives fans to a frenzy, trying to find out more.

Then there are the stylistic affectations: both employ all caps in their rap aliases (and good luck finding out Cas' real name) and use of a mask to protect their identity.

Both are guardians of the rap avant-garde.

For the uninitiated, CASISDEAD was once known as the grime MC Castro Saint. He has repped Tottenham since day one, and though details are more than vague, he may have released as many as a dozen singles in the mid-noughties, the best-known of which is "Chemist," which appeared on JME's *Boy Better Know Vol. 3.* The voice and drug dealing subject matter is familiar, but Castro is in grime mode, faster and more aggressive in his cadence. The tempo for "Chemist" floats around 140 BPM, but, in a sign of things to come, the subtle synth pads have a scent of faded '80s glamour to them, like a budget Tony Montana and Elvie ducking into the toilet cubicles of The Nags Head bopping to Duran Duran on a rainy Friday night in North London. However, before listeners could become fans, Castro Saint was gone.

The reasons for Castro's disappearance from music vary, from jail sentences to a severe motorcycle accident and cancer diagnosis. Still, Castro reemerged as the masked CASISDEAD (or, CASisDead as he was stylised at the time) in the early 2010s, and any trail to Castro practically vanished. Cas' rebirth was completed with *The Number 23* mixtape, released in late December 2013. The title was a likely nod to the "23 enigma," a term coined by the experimental writer William S. Burroughs and further developed in Robert Anton Wilson's *Cosmic Trigger*, the preeminent book on counterculture beliefs of the 20th century. The 23 enigma is a slightly kooky belief that the number 23 has a special significance in our lives, popping up in the most curious and often inexplicable ways.

Most mixtapes act as a calling card, a taster of an artist's potential or a way to maintain momentum between full releases, but *The Number 23* came out fully formed—a dystopian universe haunted by and simultaneously haunting CASISDEAD. Production comes from grime producers JME, Faze Miyaki, the future garage of Rosco and the more hip-hop-leaning work of The Purist and Skywlkr, the tour DJ and regular producer for Detroit maverick Danny Brown, who is responsible for the monstrous "All Hails." After boasting about being the "necro negro" on "T.R.O.N.," Cas lets rip that he has a "Flow so cold when I let go, adagio or allegro / Hear my life as an echo, over grime and electro. It's nothing like you've heard or seen/ You know what I mean?"

Adagio and Allegro are tempo markings that refer to the speed or BPM of music. Adagio is slow and almost ceremonious, at about 55-65 BPM. At nearly double the speed Allegro is described as "fast and bright." Make no mistake, for all the over-the-top narco-dealing horrorcore stylings of *The Number 23,* it becomes early evidence that CASISDEAD is an accomplished songwriter and a sound scholar. He's someone whose musical antecedents explore the niches of UK rap and club culture, as in the Wiley-esc eski-beat style signatures on "Baraka", while simultaneously professing his love for '80s pop royalty Kate Bush—the beginning of Cas' video for "Pat Earrings" includes a drone camera shot across an uncanny forest and has more than a hint of Bush's "Wuthering Heights Version 2" video while the sample, Clint Mansell's "Waves", sounds like an off-key piano melody of the same song— and having the Pet Shop Boys' Neil Tennat appear on his long-awaited debut album.

The most memorable song from *The Number 23* is "Drugs Don't Work". Produced by the experimental bass producer MssingNo, the Verve-sampling track, supplemented by the harrowing music video released the summer before, was an immediate jaw-dropper: a full-born confessional so convincing, it had listeners wondering if Cas' drug-addled lines of character-work were true to life. As the protagonist sinks into depths of inexplicable darkness, Cas' pen game reaches new heights, as if it's been possessed by the spirit of Prodigy of Mobb Deep and Irvine Welsh, with Wildean flourishes like, "Spent most of my life in the dark / Chasing the light like a moth."

Before the release of *Famous Last Words,* Cas only gave three confusing interviews in ten years—perhaps most tellingly, he described himself "as much a director as an artist"[3]—but listen closely enough to *The Number 23* and you'll find some clues to the man behind the mask. Among the scant information we do have on Cas, we know he was born in 1986, his dad left home when he was a kid, and he is mixed race. But really, any attempt to find out who or why Cas is who he is is futile—the grey area of performance versus belief. There is just no point with Cas.

In the culture writer Hua Hsu's excellent memoir *Stay True,* he talks about the Canadian philosopher Charles Taylor and how, in the mid-1990s, he began his life's work thinking about how people throughout history had dealt with the question: "What does it mean to truly be yourself?" Hsu considers the emergence of "new possibilities of economic and social mobility" and how this caused people to wonder about an "innate essence that might be discovered by peeling away layers of our surface."[4] For some, this manifests as endless drifting, while others find the possibility of claiming one's identity empowering. But we were all in search for the same thing, the quality that made you yourself. "Taylor calls this authenticity, and it became the unreachable horizon for modern life."

And this got me thinking: what if it's not a mask but a mirror?

"We sympathise with both the hero and the anti-hero; and we dream of a world in which one could be in the same act both,"[5] writes Charles Taylor in *Sources of the Self: The Making of Modern Identity.*

Identity can hang around like a familiar smell, comforting or chaotic, something to fall back on or learn to leave behind. Shred your identity, and you can be anything, anyone.

Is it part of Cas' appeal that with his mask of anonymity and clandestine backstory, amongst the outlandish behaviour, we're able to project our own version of Cas: The cheeky cockney gangster, the dystopian bounty hunter, even the lovelorn loser, and in a very fantastical way free of responsibility, ourselves?

Two artists emerged around the same time in 2013 and have been described as making grime, hip-hop, drill, and even R&B music at various times. But really, what they make is steeped in a singular identity: they make CASISDEAD and Little Simz music.

Universe Building with Little Simz

A girl wearing a denim jacket and straw hat sat unevenly on a head of wavy curls, bouncing around the stage and gripping a microphone. Bashful she looks barely old enough to attend the festival, let alone perform on stage. Accompanied by a backing band, she breathlessly raps her lyrics, "See, I'm so fabulous…I'm only 18."

At one point, in a confident display of musicality, she ducks onto a piano and performs a soulful hip-hop track before she breaks away from emceeing to sing, "It's time wake up, it's time to live your dream…" the sort of overly earnest lyrics that are excusable from someone so young. It's the summer of 2012 and a couple of dozen people are watching the performance on the BBC Introducing stage at the Hackney Weekend festival. Little did they know they had witnessed the first tentative steps of a generational talent: Simbiatu "Simbi" Abisola Abiola Ajikawo, a.k.a. Little Simz.

To be fair, I certainly didn't. Having briefly stopped to watch the young "female rapper" from nearby Islington who had been causing a bit of buzz, a blip on my radar when I received upwards of 100 press releases a day trying to run an independent hip-hop magazine alongside my day job. I wasn't the only one sleeping on Simz.

Simz already had some buzz thanks to her acting credits on the children's show *Spirit Warriors* and the E4 comedy *Youngers*, which might explain some of the initial scepticism she encountered in music. As we saw with the Cookie Crew in the late '80s and later with Shystie in Chapter 9, be it hip-hop or grime, the UK rap scene hasn't always been welcoming for female artists. Little Simz is a big reason for that change.

Born in 1994 to Nigerian parents who split up when she was young, Simz, or Simbi as she was then known, grew up with her mother and three older siblings—two sisters and one brother. Later in life, her mother became a foster carer when numerous children came to live in what must have been a busy North London household. Music was a constant, from Bob Marley to Little Wayne, Ciara and Kano.

Simz's school, St Mary's, a Church of England primary, had an out-of-hours youth club at the church on Upper Street, Islington (a stone's throw from the Highbury estates of Task Force and Skinnyman). There, she made friends with Inflo, the producer who would become a long-term collaborator. It's where Simz learned to perform–acting, dancing, singing, and rapping.

At 16, Simz bought her first microphone with the money earned from a Saturday job in a gallery. She soon released her first mixtape, *Stratosphere*, which played on national radio but has since been lost to the digital ether. She was barely halfway through her teens, but Simz had already envisioned a singular artistic vision. Simz was convinced that *Stratosphere* would be her big break, the calling card to a major label deal to transport her music beyond the youth club walls of Islington, the opportunity to live out her dreams, saying, "I definitely thought I was going to win hella awards off of it. I just believed in it so much."[6] Except, it didn't work out that way. No record label would touch her, and the rejection fueled her fire.

Blank Canvas, released in late September 2013, was somewhere between a mixtape and her debut album. Musically, Simz wears her influences on her sleeve, sampling Earl Sweatshirt's "Hive" released earlier that year, dancehall icon Shabba Ranks' "Ting-A-Ling" on "The Bells," and the DJ Premier-produced "Mathematics" from Mos Def's acclaimed debut album *Black on Both Sides* (1998) for "Subject Matters."

"Mathematics" takes an almost numerological approach to highlighting the differences between white and African-American citizens of the US. Mos urges young African-Americans to "do their maths" so they can avoid falling fail to some of the degrading statistics he raps about. "Subject Matters" isn't nearly as direct or intricate, but Simz, who is practically half a lifetime younger than Mos, gently urges the question, " How do you, as a person, as an individual in fact / Distinguish yourself from others?" Probing further, "Does your morals and your values / Suggest you have no right to an opinion?"

It's a reimagining of sorts, an update on an indy hip-hop classic, where Simz raps, "They just want us all to play the game like a DS / Trying to insert lies up in my brain, pressing eject." The DS refers to the Nintendo DS games console, a contemporary response to Mos' "Young bloods can't spell, but they could rock you at PlayStation" lyric.

But it goes deeper. When Simz raps, "By the grace of God they'll see, I just say inshallah." Inshallah is Arabic for "if God wills" or "God willing." She grew up in a strict Muslim household but had rejected religion by her late teens (Simz was just 19 when *Blank Canvas* was released). Of course, Mos Def, who changed his name to Yasiin Bey in 2011, went the reverse, having converted to Islam at 19.

Relatedly, on "Mathematics," there's the "I revolve around science" in the hook, sampled from Ghostface Killah's vocal on Raekwon's "Criminology" single. Both Ghost and Rae are noted Five Percenters of the Afro-American Nationalist movement influenced by Islam, with the belief that "the science of Supreme Mathematics is the key to understanding man's relationship to the universe." And though Simz doesn't explicitly mention science or mathematics, she does finish the song by casually telling us, "Alright guys, that's class done for today…I promise next lesson won't be as deep," but let's not forget, there's also her lyric: "By the way I kill flows and then bury 'em / It's that new God flow but no Mary's son." The way she draws out her pronunciation of the vowel in "son" to rhyme with the previous lines last word of "bury em" and the following line's last words of "I'm the chosen one," and in between all that there does seem to be an audible volume increase around "God flow." You can't mention DJ Premier without talking about Nas, who released the album *God's Son* around the time Simz began her musical calling at St Mary's Youth Club.

In "Subject Matters," Little Simz shows us that she can rap and knows about rap music.

Even at a young age, Simz's signature vulnerability is there, as in the clever wordplay from "The Bells": "I pray I never have my father's aim, but my mother's name" when she raps about her missing father. Like signs on a map, it's clear where Simz was heading: inward for inspiration. Listening back to her early work, songs like "The Bells" are like fragments of memory caught on BetaCam tape, an introspection on Simz's absent father that would eventually grow to panoramic IMAX proportions on "I Love You, I Hate You" over Info's epic string arrangements from *Sometimes I Might Be Introvert.*

Simz quickly followed up on *Blank Canvas* with *AGE 101: DROP 1* in August 2014. Released via her own label, AGE 101, it was the first of a sporadic ongoing E.P. release series that continues to this day. Simz treated the 101 Drops like a creative sandbox, experimenting with sounds, subject matter, and her rhyme style. It was almost like a startup, but instead of developing an app or website, Simz developed her artistry, quickly iterating and improving upon the last version in a very public—for those paying attention to this determined 20-year-old MC—and prolific way. By the end of the year,

Simz had released *DROP 3|000*. In less than six months, her sound had taken a soulful, almost mournful turn, with "No Introduction" and "Frozen" produced by IAMNOBODI, the German DJ/ Producer and Soulection affiliate, being particular highlights. In "Frozen," IAMNOBOI's syrupy g-funk oozes with faded sophistication, with Simz playing the part of a once great R&B singer performing cover versions to a half-empty highway bar.

At the time, Simz commented, "I'm not a person to talk about my feelings much to people. Music is the only outlet I can do so with, and you listen to my frustration, my stories, and my journey. I appreciate that." Adding that "these drops are my diary. I tried to sum up my sound on this drop, and as it so happens... I don't have a sound. What would you call it? I have no idea."[7] Fans were getting impatient for an album among all the mixtapes and live shows. Yet, for an artist as ambitious and demanding of her craft as Simz, producing an album is serious business. And as an independent artist releasing music from her own label, it may have been a case of champagne tastes with a lemonade budget.

"She was rejected from meeting after meeting [with record label executives],"[8] explained Rob Swerdlow, her former manager. "They just couldn't find a way to make the marriage work on her terms. And she was very particular about how she would want to present herself. She would never just allow a marketing team to come up with a proprietary set of tools like, 'here's your artwork, here's your video.'"

Fortunately, Simz found an unlikely solution in Red Bull studio, a fully equipped 24-hour studio with an onsite engineer based in Covent Garden, where she recorded her debut album, *A Curious Tale of Trials + Persons*, for free.

Collaborations between brands and artists aren't necessarily new. Vox amplifiers had a significant relationship with The Beatles beginning in the 1960s, a congruous partnership that not only boosted the brand's visibility but also contributed to the iconic sound of The Beatles, making Vox a preferred choice among musicians during that era. In 1984, Michael Jackson was paid $5 million for an endorsement by Pepsi, including a series of high-profile TV commercials featuring Jackson and his music. The partnership helped solidify Pepsi's image as a youthful, energetic brand. However, it also infamously led to Jackson suffering burns during the filming of one of the commercials due to a pyrotechnics accident.

Outside of the superstars, brand sponsorship money has trickled down to most corners of the music industry and beyond, the most spectacular example being Apple's acquisition of Dr Dre's headphone and speakers brand Beats for $3 billion in 2014. The alliances can be perceived with scepticism, but they have ultimately reshaped the industry and, in recent years, provided an alternative revenue stream for artists when recording contracts are shrinking and millions of streams amount to little more than digital dimes. In the case of Simz and Red Bull, the exchange was a modern one: Simz appeared in the brand's social media and website content. There was no mention of the brand on album artwork, nor was Simz featured in any advertising. Red Bull is far from perfect, but it's a pity the brand shut its eleven studios worldwide in 2020, including the one in London, not long after closing down the revered Red Bull Music Academy.

A Curious Tale of Trials + Persons was released in September 2015, and its timing could not have been much better as earlier that summer Kendrick Lamar—who was riding a triumphant wave of hype thanks to the recent release of *To Pimp a Butterfly*—was interviewed by Mista Jam on 1Xtra and in a co-sign of epic proportions anointed Simz as one of "the illest doing it right now." Yet, according to Rob, its impact was overstated and failed to translate into album sales.

A Curious Tale of Trials + Persons is a good but not a great record. *Pitchfork* describes it as an "album [that] feels radically personal: Simz is her own primary subject, and as a result is necessarily exposed. But the soul of the album is abstracted."[9] Despite a largely glowing report, the reviewer lamented the absence of secondary characters, reference to physical spaces, and a general lack of set decoration on the record, concluding: "It's just curtains pulling back on a spotlight and Simz wrestling with her ambitions like Jacob with the angel, reaching no conclusions but activating something deep."

Finally, Simz had her first album out. But rather than be the conclusion of five years worth of hard work, it was only the start of a new chapter. Simz followed up with *Stillness in Wonderland* in 2016, a conceptual record lightly based on *Alice in Wonderland*. With guest features from Syd, Chronixx, Chip, and Ghetts, Simz grapples with uncertainty, escapism, and how to stay authentic in a tragic world full of phonies. Knotty and serious, it's a record displaying symptoms that can be associated with "difficult second album" syndrome.

The tension to succeed, traverse heights that mere mortals can only dream of while retaining street credibility as a rapper—someone whose music is listened to in barbershops, played on Rinse, and debated in GOAT lists—is limited to just a few UK MCs.

By the time of her third release, *Grey Area,* in 2019, Simz had reached those heights and has stayed there ever since. *Grey Area* was the first record to be entirely produced by Inflo, the enigmatic producer who has worked on albums by Adele, Michael Kiwanuka, and SAULT. Inflo's operatic fusion of hip-hop and soul provides the perfect backdrop for Little Simz's audio auteurism, and it has proven to be one of modern music's most fruitful creative partnerships. On the making of *Grey Area*, "They were brave enough to challenge each other, fighting for ideas and ideologies. The magic was made by scrapping with each other," recalls Rob Swerdlow.

This tension plays out to a revelatory effect. Simz's self-belief had never been in doubt, but with lyrics like "I'm Jay-Z on a bad day, Shakespeare on my worst days," the rest of the world would start believing in that confidence, too. She has berated the "female rapper" tag, but gender politics has proven fertile ground for Simz, spectacularly so on "Venom", where she tears into industry doubters with lines like, "It's a woman's world, so to speak. Pussy, you sour / Never givin' credit where it's due 'cause you don't like pussy in power."

Musically, there are classic hip-hop influences, like the Dust Brothers' distorted drums from Beastie Boys *Paul's Boutique* on "Boss," and lyrical nods to *College Dropout*-era Kanye, alongside homegrown sounds like the sinogrime on "101 FM," a style of grime that incorporates elements of East Asian motifs. These influences, combined with Inflo's epic live strings, contribute to an organic and more varied sound. Over a tightly packed ten-track album, Simz sounds looser, enjoying herself like an Olympian limbered up and expectant at the starting line, focused and ready to crush her personal best.

Simz's self-assurance was becoming infectious; the actor (and one-time rapper) Tom Hardy was a fan and handpicked the track "Venom" for a film he was co-producing and starring in.

Venom: Let There Be Carnage wasn't keeping the Oscar judges up at night, but it expanded the Little Simz universe—she also appeared as herself in the film—while she was wooing audiences back home playing the stoic Shelly in the Drake-assisted reboot of *Top Boy*. The song "Venom" later enjoyed a second life as a trending audio on TikTok, as something of a feminist anthem, with *Harper's Bazaar* describing it "as a diatribe built to combat ages of oppression and frustration."[10]

Rob Swerdlow talked to me about "confidence building in the music and entertainment industry," a "zeitgeist moment" with industry gatekeepers "reading the mood and the atmosphere of the universe." He was referring to a broader cultural shift. The accusations against film producer Harvey Weinstein in 2017 accelerated the #MeToo movement, spurring conversations about consent, power dynamics, and gender equality.

In an industry where awards are usually handed out like lollipops to children on a hot day, it seems odd it took Simz so long to receive one. Eyebrows were raised when she won The Breakthrough Artist at The Brits Awards in 2022, but Simz received her flowers because of one thing: Little Simz. As Charles Taylor notes: "Our identity is what allows us to define what is important to us and what is not."[11]

Little Simz is a bonafide superstar who has a legitimate claim to being the "best rapper" in the UK—because, let's face it, rap is a competitive art form—but most intriguing is the journey it took her to get to the summit. If you look at her back catalogue, there's no dodgy electro-pop "Wearing

My Rolex"-style-cash in, don't watch for any made-for-social media dances, and you won't find a contrived collaboration with Rita Ora or Ed Sheeran. Through the warm and messy intimacy of personal experience, Simz has been able to tell universal stories on faith, modern womanhood and humanity.

DISCOGRAPHY

Chapter 11: Venom

This chapter is titled after songs by both CASISDEAD and Little Simz.

Albums, E.P.s & Mixtapes

Beastie Boys - *Paul's Boutique*
Mos Def - *Black on Both Sides*
Nas - *God's Son*
Kanye West - *College Dropout*
JME - *Boy Better Know Vol. 3.*
CASISDEAD - *The Number 23*
Little Simz - *Blank Canvas*
Little Simz - *AGE 101: DROP 1*
Little Simz - *A Curious Tale of Trials + Persons*
Kendrick Lamar - *To Pimp a Butterfly*
Little Simz - *Stillness in Wonderland*
Little Simz - *Grey Area*
CASISDEAD - *Famous Last Words*
Little Simz - *Sometimes I Might Be Introver*

Singles

Kate Bush - "Wuthering Heights Version 2"
Jane Wiedlin - "Whatever It Takes"
New Kids On The Block - "You Got It (The Right Stuff)"
Shabba Ranks - "Ting-A-Ling"
Raekwon - "Criminology"
Mos Def - "Mathematics"
Castro Saint - "Chemist"
Little Simz - "The Bells"
Little Simz - "Subject Matters"
CASISDEAD - "Drugs Don't Work"
CASISDEAD - "T.R.O.N."
Little Simz - "No Introduction"
Little Simz - "Frozen"
Clint Mansell - "Waves"
Little Simz - "Venom"
Little Simz - "101 FM"
Little Simz - "Boss"
CASISDEAD - "All Hallows"
CASISDEAD - "Venom"
CASISDEAD -"Traction Control"
CASISDEAD -"Matte Grey Wrap"

Chapter 12

Question Time

2015 was a good year for UK rap fans. Not long after CASISDEAD was reborn and Little Simz released her first album, a vital new strain of the road rap sound began to harvest, and several genre-defining artists went on to record and release music.

Skepta, Stormzy, Novelist and the Ghosts of 2004: Grime's Don't Call It A Comeback, Comeback

But first, almost like clockwork, a renaissance was taking place. Grime had reached its teenage years, and some pioneers were finding new creative capacities and a surge in popularity. Skepta was, of course, at the forefront of the movement. Singles like "That's Not Me" and "Shutdown" were a throwback to the origins of the sound. In "That's Not Me," the track's juicy synth line with its eski-beat feel sounds like it had been excavated from a lake frozen in time since 2004. It sounds familiar because it is; Skepta used the Plugsound preset 'Bagoo,' a signature grime synth first used by DJ Wonder in the 2003 track "What" and later immortalised by Wiley in "Morgue."

It was a case of addition by subtraction. Skep used to "wear Gucci / I put it all in the bin 'cause that's not me" by stripping away the electro schlock gloss and excess of recent years and going back to grime's roots. "That's Not Me" was a celebration of nostalgia and innovation just when the world needed to hear it. Alongside fellow 2014 tracks like Meridian Dan's "German Whip" and Lethal Bizzle's "Rari Workout," "That's Not Me"—followed by Skepta's 2015 follow-up "Shutdown"—helped catapult a proud but peripheral UK scene onto TV screens, car radios, and smartphones across the country.

All three singles released in 2014 landed in the top 20 charts and clocked up millions of video views on YouTube. The video for "That's Not Me," so lo-fi it could be described as vertical, features DJ Maximum on the decks and Skepta on the mic, later joined by JME, as an entire green screen wall behind them is filled with the projection of a very young Skepta and JME outside Meridian Estate emceeing into the camera, in a *Lord of the Mics*-era visual. Given the likely viewing context for the video on smartphones, it felt like a rare instance of the 'real world' catching up and colliding with the hectic pace of social media: avatar meets analogue. The effect is both disorientating and captivating. Infamously, the video cost just £80 to make, directed by scene stalwarts Tim and Barry, and won the Award for Best Video at the 2014 MOBO Awards.

Lessons had been learned from the failed grime gold rush by the majors of the mid-late '00s, and the back-to-the-basics approach was working for the scene. Grime MCs were suddenly en vogue again. On the industry's fickle nature, Logan Sama recalls, "Skepta showing me a review of 'Doin' It Again' [released in 2007] in the *NME,* and they said, 'Oh, you know, we miss the records Skepta used to make. This is clearly designed for the mainstream.' And Skep said, 'It's not like the records that I used to make back in the day that you ever reviewed anyway.' Do you know what I mean?"

By 2015, Skepta had long stopped pandering to the industry and forged ahead on his own path, and others were taking notice. Echos of grime's past continued to resurface in new and unexpected ways. The same year, Stormzy filmed "Shut Up" in a park, reusing "Functions On The Low"—a white-label produced by XTC, an associate of east London grime crew Ruff Sqwad, way back in 2004—its wood pipe melancholy contrasting memorably with Stormzy's brash emceeing. And there was AJ Tracey's "Wifey Riddim," where the West London MC evokes the short-lived R&G (Rhythm & Grime) subgenre's most notable song, Tinie Tempah's "Wifey," first released in 2004. AJ's version, with its sped-up chipmunk vocal sample and two-step stylings, recalls summers of lovers past, but his lyrics show a cheeky reverence for females and was very much of the moment. The Ladbroke Grove star calls for national unity by "shouting to the girls round the UK, peng" and namechecking various wifeys from Birmingham, Brighton, and Tottenham. As Rahel Aklilu wrote in her blog, "In the internet age where the phrase 'toxic masculinity' is being thrown around like a hot potato, it's clear that although grime's bravado and pace created a perfect breeding ground for toxic masculinity, wifey riddims provide a reprieve of sorts for gentler self-expression and emotional vulnerability."[1]

Alongside Stomzy and AJ Tracey, another young MC helped pioneer the grime 2.0 movement. Novelist may not have the profile of those mentioned above, but he deserves his flowers. The Brockley-born artist was part of a new urgent generation of South London MCs, brought up on grime and road rap, yet 'big Nov' stood out for a progressive approach to making music. He is just as likely to tap into Detroit techno as he is to reference Alchemist-style hip-hop productions while being undeniably grime.

Novelist, whose real name is Kwadwo Quentin Kankam, had been gaining traction for a couple of years, collaborating with the experimental producer Mumdance, where they released music via Rinse Recordings, but "Endz" was Nov's calling card. The two met through Tim and Barry's *Just Jam* broadcast; Mumdance recalls someone "super young with an old-school grime energy that felt refreshing at the time, drawing parallels to what we were doing within the "Boxed" scene—twisting up instrumental grime and taking it to unusual places."[2]

"Endz" was part of the 2015 vintage, where Novelist spits about everyday, relatable matters—chasing the gyal dem (Jamaican creole for 'girls'), New Era caps, and putting soundboys (another term of Jamaican origin, meaning a junior selector who has much to learn) in the trash—messing around with his mates in the ends over staccato synths and minimalist drum patterns. "Endz" is also produced by Novelist; it's a throwback to the days of Channel U, emphasised by the grainy music video with its 'Text Novelist…' graphic and images of a pitbull pulling on a lead reminiscent of photographer Simon Wheatley's iconic photography of Crazy Titch holding back a ferocious looking dog at a park in Stratford in 2004. "Endz" could have been released in the same year, but this isn't just a nostalgia trip. This is grime at its most authentic, made by one of its most genuine and interesting stars. There are also subtle signs in the music video that Nov isn't one to play by the rules; riding a skateboard and, to a lesser extent, tagging estate walls with graffiti aren't signatures of grime music.

Later that year, Novelist reunited with Mumdance on the *1 Sec E.P.*, released on XL Recordings. The producer told me it was a sound inspired by "Musique Concrète, a style of music that often takes sounds from the real world and uses various studio techniques to abstract them into really crazy, unrecognisable sounds. I was really enamoured by the concept and wanted to see if I could use it to make something darker and more grime-oriented."

Nov was the first British rapper to sign a deal with the iconic label since Giggs. A European tour supporting Diplo's Major Lazer alias followed, and he was the first guest to feature on Skepta's Mercury Prize-winning album *Konnichiwa* the following year. "Lyrics" references some of the genre's rich history of diss tracks and war dubs, from Wiley's clash with Heartless Crew to Skepta and Devil Man's iconic clash.

Unfortunately, XL dropped Novelist, but that didn't deter him. He set up his own label, MMMYEH Recordings, where he challenged the possibilities within grime by releasing gospel and G-funk-inspired music. Yet just as important as the music, Novelist had a message. He explained to *The Guardian*, "I am not really interested in money. I feel like I could be as rich as I want, but the problem is people understanding what it's like to be rich inside. I'd like to get that message across to people."[3] He was just 19 at the time, and as a younger teen, Novelist had been elected deputy young mayor of his London borough of Lewisham.

By 2016 grime had been officially classified as its own genre on iTunes, and Skepta followed up the success of *Konnichiwa* by appearing on the Billboard-topping *More Life* album by

Drake, which also included a feature by Giggs. Meanwhile, Stormzy's *Gang Signs & Prayer* became the first grime album to reach UK number one in early 2017, selling 70,000 copies in its first week. Just as grime had reemerged as a cultural and commercial force, a thunderous dissonance had taken shape in the nation's consciousness in the form of Brexit.

'Youthquakes' and Grime4Corbyn. When Politics and Music Mix.

Twenty-sixteen was a year for big story spoilers, from Leicester City's unlikely Premier League success to Donald Trump winning the US election in November, characterised by an overload of information, sensational headlines, and continuous coverage. And sandwiched between those events was the UK's fateful EU referendum. The Conservative Prime Minister David Cameron let hubris get the better of him, gambled with the country's future, and lost everything, including his job.

In my mind, we seemed to be entering a moment of maximalism: big events and immense divide. This sense of size was even reflected in the way we dressed: baggy oversized hoodies and heavily branded streetwear, a visceral reminder of this excessive abundance came a year later when Supreme collaborated with Louis Vuitton. Indeed, in another sign of grime and UK rap's growing influence, brands were queuing up to sponsor its biggest stars—from Ghetts advertising Clarks shoes to Stormzy's work with adidas, which saw him collaborate with Manchester United to announce the world record transfer signing of Paul Pogba for £89 million, and Skepta, who worked with Levi's, the luxury fashion store Selfridges, and most notably Nike, where he was the first ever non-athlete in the UK to have his own silhouette, the Nike SKAir.

Yet pigs must have taken flight, and hell is a frozen tundra, because a major political party was now aligning itself with grime music. It started as many things did in the mid-2010s: with a tweet. During the attempted coup against the leadership of veteran socialist MP Jeremy Corbyn, Novelist shared his support on Twitter. "Don't resign," he said, "the mandem need you." Days later, he would join the Labour Party. The social media-appropriate moniker #Grime4Corbyn was born (hashtag was optional). Despite the newfound recognition, grime's leading figures hadn't forgotten its struggle.

Novelist was the first in a series of grime MCs, including Stormzy, AJ Tracey, P Money, and Akala, who, despite being politically active for years, would only be voting for the first time in the 2017 election "For the first time in my adult life, and perhaps for the first time in British history, someone I would consider to be a fundamentally decent human being has a chance of being elected." Adding that Corbyn's lack of deference to Britain's imperial past helps, being "someone who approaches politics without the assumption that Britain has inherent moral superiority over the rest of the world," although Akala concedes he is an "imperfect leader" who "was abysmal during the Brexit campaign."[4]

JME would take the support one step further, appearing on Jeremy Corbyn's Snapchat to encourage voters and interviewing him in a cafe in Islington for *i-D magazine's* YouTube channel, where the pair discussed social cleansing, why people vote for the Conservatives, and the Labour leader's divisive following. Corbyn explained, "Political change doesn't always come from politicians, does it? It comes from everybody else."[5] In little over a decade, grime had gone from a niche concern to an appendage of cultural credibility in British politics. Even Matt Hancock, then Secretary of State for Digital, Culture, Media and Sport, and a peculiar squirm of a man, praised Skepta's 2016 Mercury win. "He tells a story of his background," Hancock said, "But the thing that excites me is that he can break through. I don't like to wallow in poverty... Grime represents modern Britain, the entrepreneurial, go-getting nature." Although Hancock wasn't wrong, grime has come to represent modern Britain, but, when pressed on the matter, he was unable to name a single grime song. However, neither has Corbyn.

Yet, statistics for voter turnout among the young were telling. Turnout among 18-24-year-olds rose to more than 60 per cent from just 43 per cent at the 2015 general election, and the 2017 elections saw the highest share of 18-24 voters since 1992; some 64 per cent of registered voters went to the ballot box with the vast majority backing Labour.[6]

Jeremy Corbyn may have been right; political change doesn't always come from politicians, but it's their responsibility to deliver on public policy. Despite Labour doing better in the polls than expected, Corbyn didn't get the opportunity to deliver on his policies, and by the snap election of 2019, things had unravelled spectacularly. Internal divisions marked Corbyn's leadership over issues like Brexit and allegations of antisemitism within the party, and the election was Labour's worst performance in terms of seats since 1935.

He stepped down as leader shortly after, but it wasn't soon enough for several grime MCs, including Lethal Bizzle, who tweeted, "I can not see us getting back into power any time soon...let someone else have a go" and Skepta, who, with a touch of libertarianism, explained, “Everyone was tellin’ everyone, all the youth to ‘vote for my man’. I’m not watchin’ them, I’m laughin’ at them, bruv…If they’re [young people] in a place where they really feel like at the mercy of the system and the government, then they should vote.” Outlining his vision for the U.K., Skepta added, “I think some things that are better for me are not good for other people, innit,” concluding, “They need to run their self. Everybody should run their self.”[7]

The danger with a movement like Grime4Corbyn is that it can obscure a diversity of opinions that artists and fans may have had for the Labour Party and Jeremy Corbyn—not to mention other political parties, considering Skepta later stated a preference for the Green Party. By the end of 2017, the Grime4Corbyn movement had all but fizzled out, and the pseudo-campaign website grime4corbyn.com now carries just a single post on the impact of blockchain technology on the music industry. But for a brief period, it was a glorious reminder of the power of music to inspire and motivate people to make a difference.

Perhaps the era’s most significant political legacy for UK rap came from tragedy. On 14th June 2017, a high-rise fire broke out in the 24-storey Grenfell Tower block of flats in North Kensington, West London. Seventy-two people died at the scene, while 600 people, including 100 children, were referred for specialist mental health assessments, and a whole community lost its home in the wake of the disaster. It was the deadliest fire in Britain for more than a century. A fridge exploding on the fourth floor caused the fire to spread around the building due to cheap flammable cladding banned in many countries and used only because it was inexpensive to install. It was a tragic failure of manufacturers, sub-contractors, and other local politicians involved in the refurbishment of Grenfell Tower that unsettled the country and exposed harsh inequalities in one of London's wealthiest neighbourhoods. The Prime Minister, Theresa May, flanked by security guards, police, and aides, arrived at the site the following day and spoke only with the firefighters and those in charge of the response. She did not meet with any survivors, unlike Jeremy Corbyn, who was pictured comforting victims at a community centre on the same day.

May later admitted her initial response was not good enough, writing in the *Evening Standard* that she would "always regret"[8] not meeting survivors of the blaze when she first visited the site. Instead, the burden of responsibility and an outpouring of empathy was led by rappers: local MCs and cousins AJ Tracey and Big Zuu, who lost friends in the disaster, were quick to record tributes, help out on the ground, and raise money in support. Lowkey released "Ghosts of Grenfell," featuring survivors and footage of the fire in a powerful visual tribute to victims. With typical polemic, Lowkey spoke of how "Grenfell is an example of how neoliberalism kills people."[9] Yet it was Stormzy who became a totemic figure of justice, using his increasing profile to expose and call out the government for its failings and urging them to release payments to the victims of Grenfell sooner, first during his double-award winning performance at the Brits—"Yo, Theresa May where's that money for Grenfell? What you thought we just forgot about Grenfell?" and again during his 2019 headline set at Glastonbury, to which we'll return.

DISCOGRAPHY

Chapter 12: Question Time

This chapter is titled after the song by Dave.

Albums, E.P.s & Mixtapes

Novelist - *1 Sec* E.P.
Skepta - *Konnichiwa*
Drake - *More Life*

Singles

DJ Wonder - "What"
XTC - "Functions On The Low"
Tinie Tempah's "Wifey"
Wiley - "Morgue"
Skepta - "Doin' It Again"
Meridian Dan - "German Whip"
Lethal Bizzle - "Rari Workout"
Skepta - "That's Not Me"
Stormzy - "Shut Up"
AJ Tracey's "Wifey Riddim"
Skepta - "Shutdown"
Novelist - "Endz"
Skepta Ft. Novelist - "Lyrics"
Lowkey - "Ghosts of Grenfell"

Chapter 13

AJ Tracey

AJ Tracey is among the rarest of MCs. The charismatic West Londoner is as comfortable jumping on a garage beat, like the iconic "Ladbroke Grove," as he is lacing a drill crossover track, like "Ain't It Different" alongside Headie One and Stormzy, or spraying furiously intense bars over a drum & bass set. Although he came up in the mid-2010s among a new generation of grime MCs, AJ has never been defined by genre: "There isn't a particular genre or sound I always go for. I just like good music," he explains. As one TikTok user commented: "Aj Tracey can just destroy every beat you put in front of him."

His real name is Ché Wolton Grant, born to a Trinidadian father and a white Welsh mother, who brought him up and named her son after Che Guevara, the Marxist revolutionary.

As I learned during our conversation, AJ's politically engaged mother remains a significant influence in her son's life.

AJ Tracey was one of my last interviews before the book went to print. We spoke a few weeks after Keir Starmer led the Labour Party to an election victory for the first time in fourteen years and just days after violent demonstrations began in cities across the UK. The demonstrations, often involving those from far-right groups, followed a tragic incident where three children were stabbed in Southport, North-West England, after which misinformation was circulated on social media about the suspect's background and motives.

Both topics hung heavily over our conversation. AJ may have started his career by making music fuelled by "testosterone," as he put it, but that belies his interests in politics and community and decoding what it means to be young, successful, mixed-race Black and British.

You're from Ladbroke Grove. There are extremes of wealth disparity in that part of London. What was it like to grow up there?

I'm very grateful for my upbringing. It's a place that taught me a lot of life lessons. Half of the area is extremely deprived. And the other half is, as you know, extremely wealthy. So I think it's about [finding] that balance, teaching people that you can make it to where these people are. You just need to work hard, and that's what it taught me, whereas a few other people that I know were extremely disheartened by the fact that they lived in poverty and alongside extreme opulence. It can go either way, you know, discourage you or encourage you. And for me, it just put batteries in my back because I felt like, "Oh, if you lot can do it, why can't I?"

What legacy do you think #Grime4Corbyn left?

Honestly? Nothing, bro. That was pointless. It seemed like a good idea at the time, but it was just a gimmick to get the Black youth vote. Look, it was good marketing for them.

Yeah, they were smart for doing it. So good for them. No one involved in that campaign benefited from having a relationship with Corbyn or the Labour Party.

I couldn't tell you how many kids contacted me on Snapchat [after I showed support for Corbyn]. Hundreds of kids were snapping me, saying, "I told my mum she has to vote Labour." And my area is like a very affluent area in terms of voting power, bro, so obviously it had some positive effect on Labour. But I just think for people involved in it and those who believed in it, I'm not sure we got anything out of it.

There was a big youth turnout in that vote, but it unravelled.

Yep. And if you're, whatever you want to call it, a celebrity, or just a person of interest, encouraging kids to vote is amazing and something we should always do. But when you tell people who to vote for, I wonder if that's morally correct.

What does Britishness mean to you?

Today is the perfect time to ask that question since there has been much unrest around this topic. I could answer it in two ways.

For me, being British is the very essence of my life. And that sounds very vague, but it is the truth. I wake up [and] I have a cup of tea, and I flipping stick the telly on. And last night, I went down to the pub with my friends, that's British—having pride in winning gold medals at the Olympics, getting upset when the England manager was still there and he should have been fired. All these things are British to me, but also, being British means getting some Caribbean food.

Knowing that my family and people who came before me came to this country via the Windrush, they were welcomed here. They helped build the country and are a staple in Great Britain's community. All of these things, from our healthcare being hailed as one of the best in the world—I know it's falling off a bit right now—were thanks to many Indian, African, and Caribbean people who came and worked these jobs that a lot of people didn't want to work to a high standard as well. So, for me, all of that is being British.

On a personal note, my mother is British. I'm British by blood. It's like when racist people say, "Oh, you should get deported." You can deport me to Cardiff [where my mum's from]. Sorry to get too political, but the powers that be would like us to think that it's a race war, but it's a class war. And at the end of the day, no matter what, people will read or hear this and think, "Oh well, AJ Tracey makes money; why does he care about a class war?" Because, bro, I'm 30 years old, and for the majority of my life, I was poor. I was born poor, and I grew up poor. Only recently have I made money and done well for myself, but I still care about my community and where I come from.

My lifelong goal is to make sure my mum is comfortable but still lives the way she was living before. I've put her in a house, but she refuses. If I try to buy new shoes, she gets annoyed at me. She doesn't want anything fancy.

And I won't sit here and campaign for a government and change that would benefit me financially [because] it will hinder the rest of my family and people like me. So I just wanted to make sure that's on record because many people say, "Why does AJ talk about the community when he's made money or XYZ?" Like, bro, it's bigger than me. What I'm saying is, that regardless of how comfortable I am, I want everyone else to be comfortable. I work with a company called North Kensington Secret Santa every Christmas. We go back to the community, give out food and try to ensure a sense of togetherness, but we don't really publicise it.

Because our area is predominantly Muslim, I go to the mosque and make sure all the food I'm donating is halal. It doesn't matter if you're Black, white, Christian, [or] Muslim; everyone should work together to ensure that the community is doing well. I'll be genuinely happy if more rappers do stuff like that. It's not always about the massive gestures. It's just about making sure that things are running smoothly.

Does fundraising come with the job of being a rapper?

It's not anyone's "job" to do that. I'd be happy if I saw more rappers do that. I'm not saying rappers don't do charity because they do. But I think boots on the ground charity is a bit different from just sending a cheque because when people meet me, they say "Ra. Okay, you lot ain't just spraying bars with a chain on. There's more to it. You stand for something." Sending a check is easy, bro. We're in a privileged position. I think going down, meeting the community, seeing what the issues are and trying to address them is more important.

Given the change of government, do you feel more optimistic about the country's future?

The problem is that it doesn't matter who's in government because the UK has to run a certain way. I'm not a conspiracy theorist at all, [but] the UK has to run by generating money. Caring for people, caring for people's feelings, caring for integrity, and humanity does not make money. So, I don't have too much optimism just because money has to be made when it's all said and done. Same shit, different flies.

My mum is a highly political woman who loves to be in the loop about everything happening. She's very opinionated and taught me the differences between the parties from early on. She hates the Tories, but she doesn't say, "You should hate the Tories because I hate the Tories." She says, "This is why I hate the Tories. You form your own opinion."

As I've grown up, the parties have become increasingly similar. I don't see much difference between Labour and Tories right now. One is blue, and one is red. The political climate right now is merging into one theme, and the theme is not something I'm on board with. I spent a lot of time outside the country this year, like in Korea, Germany, and France. And everywhere I go, they seem to be in a better place than us. It looks bleak right now. When I see people fighting, attacking people, innocent people and places of worship over false information that's been spread. It's like people need to start doing their research. They just wake up [and] get a text message from their mate: "Yo, this is what's going on. There are too many of them on the boats; attack whoever you can." It's nuts.

And they go on X, and they see all that nonsense.

They see Elon Musk pushing the racist agenda as well. I've seen it in my own eyes, and it's just insane. And it's a shame because I'm very proud of this country and love the UK. I love it whenever people say, "Why do you love London so much? London is dangerous, London's this, London's that." I love London; I'm from here, man. It's beautiful. It's an amazing place. But I also think some dire things need to change because it's unsafe for people. And it's easy for me to say, bro; I'm speaking from a position of privilege. I've made money. I'm six-foot-four; I'm not intimidated by these people, though I feel for people. It's worrying.

Let's change track. How would you describe the style of West London? What makes it unique?

I liken it to Harlem. Different parts of New York all have their own unique style. Certain areas are more focused on getting money, while others are more street. And for me, West London has never been about violence. That's not our mantra. It's been about always looking fly. No matter where or whatever you're doing, someone from the West will try and turn up looking fly. No matter what negative vibes are going on, we will stay fly. We grew up in a place that's not too pleasant. You want to make it as pleasant as possible. You want to get some girls, and, bro, you gotta look good. You know what I'm saying? You look good. You feel good, you act good. That's it.

I was looking at your TikTok before, and you had a BAPE Xbox controller. I'm probably too old for it now, but I used to be a bit of a streetwear OG, and I'm interested in unusual pieces like that. What's your biggest grail?

Ha. I've got some serious ones. Some are worth loads of money. But that's not really a grail. My grails are the ones that have a meaning behind it. I think my holiest grails are my Air

Max 90 x Off-Whites because Virgil [Abloh] personally gave them to me, and he wrote "Pasta" on them [*after AJ's song of the same name*]. Virgil was such a great guy; he just went out of his way to help everyone. He was spinning "Thiago Silva" in clubs in Paris and at big fashion events, putting Dave's and my names in spaces we weren't in. Rest in peace, Virgil.

What are your ideal conditions for making music?

Nowadays, I need to be well-fed and caffeinated, and I've got my energy loaded. I've got my bredrins and a fire producer, and I usually like recording at night. I'm in a long-term relationship now, almost six years. Before that, it was very different; as long as there was liquor and bare girls in the studio, I didn't care. A lot of my old songs were fuelled by testosterone.

You've always been quite open with your sound. From garage to grime and melodic trap even. Can you talk about that?

It all stems from my mum's eclectic taste as a DJ. She loves every genre and has records from different sonics. I grew up on that. I used to listen to James Brown, Michael Jackson, N.W.A., Lauryn Hill, Sweet Female With Attitude, Goldie—everything. So, I grew up with a wide range of sounds blasted at me from different directions. There isn't a particular genre or sound I always go for. I just like good music.

How do you see the relationship between football and UK rap music?

Football and UK rap are just entwined because of the high pressure that comes with the job at the top end and the fact that on the low end, it's a means to a better life coming from an impoverished background. It's like when you see [Raheem] Sterling come out on stage at Wireless [joining AJ, Steel Banglez, and MoStack on stage for the performance of "Fashion Week"]. I think UK rap and football crossovers have become so natural now.

How did the song "Thiago Silva" with Dave come about? Can you talk about the process of making that track?

At first, we did [a rap] over "One Take," the beat that Rude Kid made. It was hard.

And then Dave just said to me, "But we're way harder than just making a version of someone else's rhythm. We can just do our own thing."

I agreed. So we went back and forth and thought, "Let's take an iconic beat]'Pied Piper' by Ruff Sqwad] and make a new version of that beat." Then we started going back and forth writing our verses, and we both changed our verses a couple of times. There are versions of "Thiago Silva" with different verses that the world hasn't heard.

There have been rumours of a follow-up single, "Kylian Mbappe." Is that in the vaults?

There are many unreleased songs with Dave. None of them are called "Kylian Mbappe," I'll tell you that. But if you go on TikTok and type in "Dave AJ unreleased," a bag of them will come up because of hackers... I don't know, man, but I hate them.

What makes a good MC, a good MC?

I feel strongly on this one because I think a lot of emcees are shit. You need to have vocal projection. If you're rapping and I don't believe what you're saying, then it's pointless. I don't want to hear it. That's number one: I need to believe what you're saying. Number two, you need to have cadence. You need to learn to use your voice and inflect it into the right tone so that people, again, believe and understand what you're saying.

Another thing is that you need to have a stage presence. If you don't have stage presence, then you're not a mic man. You need to be able to control the crowd. After that, it comes down to beat selection, the ability to change your flow, and good diction, bro. Good diction. You need to have a good vocabulary and an understanding of the English language, or whatever language you emcee in, but obviously, I'm English.

Why haven't you ever signed with a major label?

Because they didn't have enough money to sign me, that's the realest. I'm not against working with a major label. Just the deal just has to be right. If you know the ins and outs of being an independent artist, as long as you're willing to bet on yourself, the house always wins, bro. So I'm good. But I'm not against any major label deals. I've always been an independent guy just because it made sense. And I was just willing to do the extra work everyone else didn't want to do. That's all it is.

It's like the saying, "99% perspiration, 1% inspiration."?

That's a fact. People sleep on that. I know loads of good rappers. I know good rappers from the ends that you've never heard of that are better than most of these super-lit rappers. It's not about how good you are as a rapper; it's about how hard you're willing to work and how much you want it. There are a lot of footballers right now who are stealing a living. Not because they might not be that good but because they're working harder than everyone else.

DISCOGRAPHY

Essentials

AJ Tracey - "Wifey Riddim"
AJ Tracey - "Ladbroke Grove"
AJ Tracey - "Buster Cannon"
Dave and AJ Tracey - "Thiago Silva"
Headie One. Ft. AJ Tracey and Stormzy - "Ain't It Different"
Steel Banglez Ft. AJ Tracey and MoStack - "Fashion Week"

Deep Cuts

AJ Tracey - "Packages"
AJ Tracey Ft. Digga D - "Bringing It Back"

Chapter 14

Attempted 1.0

If grime was now playing in primetime—sweeping up awards, topping charts, and receiving co-signs by global pop superstars and political leaders—then what would fill the vacuum left in what is most conveniently described as the rap 'underground'?

UK Drill and the Curious Case of the Section Boyz

While AJ Tracey, Stormzy, and Novelist provided fresh impetus for grime, a menacing sound had crystallised in the new heartland of UK rap. Street hits like "No Rules" and "Delete My Number" from the *Sectionly* mixtape in 2014 helped establish the Section Boyz as part of a burgeoning South London rap and drill scene that included acts like the group 67, Krept & Konan, Youngs Teflon, and early collaborator Stormzy.

Their sound combined the lyricism of road rap with trap elements and the drill music that had originated in Chicago in the early 2010s through pioneers like Chief Keef and King Louie—a sound as raw and unfiltered as the cold whipping off Lake Michigan. A brutal, unadorned reportage from the front lines of inner-city life, drill has a language and semiotics unique to its own that's almost impenetrable to outsiders. It is a truly 21st-century phenomenon—a fast dissemination of sounds and images with YouTube being the dominant distributor.

With "Lock Arf" from the *Don't Panic* mixtape, Section Boyz had created a UK drill anthem. It's clear from the opening moments that this was a reimagining, a rhythmic and cultural gear shift from its Chicagoan cousin. Menacing and minimal, producer Producer Nyge's sliding 808s and intricate drums provide ample space for Section Boyz—Deepee, Littlez, Knine, Sleeks, Inch, and Swift—to drop bars in patois and patter straight from the Big Smoke, with

hooks as sticky and memorable as anything to ever chart. The group won Best Newcomer at the MOBO Awards later that year.

Chicago drill tends to operate around 120-140 BPM, while UK drill is usually faster, around 130-145 BPM and uses sliding 808 basslines, a hallmark of the anglicised sound, giving the beats a distinctive wobble and adding a layer of unpredictability. The use of British slang, intricate flows, and social commentary—as opposed to the hyper-aggressive stream of conscious lyrics of Chief Keef, etc.—further differentiates it from Chicago and, later, Brooklyn drill, a sub-genre it would go on to heavily influence. There are also stark aesthetic differences, as the Brixton-based rapper Skengdo explained: "The Chicago lot had True Religion jeans, Timberlands, they were all swagger. But coming up as 15-16-year-olds in the ends, not everyone can afford expensive brands. So [we're wearing] Nike tracksuits and Tech hoodies in the video."

UK drill is both intensely territorialised and yet a sound "porously penetrable by external influences, the opposite of insular," writes Simon Reynolds.[1] Curiously, in an age of oversharing, there is also an absence of individualism in the music for the most part. "67, my brothers. Spare no one for my bredrins," raps LD beneath a distorted Phantom of the Opera style mask on "Let's Lurk." The collective is all important.

Where Chicago drill is all about the immediate, visceral impact, UK drill invites you to get lost in its labyrinth, to feel the chill of its haunted streets, and to be drawn to the delirium of digitally processed voices from mysterious balaclava-clad figures. It's a transatlantic dialogue of defiance and despair, each with its own accent and rhythm.

By 2016, the UK drill sound had unfathomably begun to cross over, and Section Boyz was at its heart. Performing at London's Village Underground the same night as the BRIT Awards, the group were joined on stage by a myriad of musicians and rappers connecting the UK scene: the ascendant singer Bakar, the controversial rapper Milkavelli who connected the dots to the revitalised UK hip-hop scene, Boy Better Know's Frisco, Shorty, and, bursting through a sea of Trapstar baseball caps and Section Boyz hoodies, Skepta, soon followed by Drake dressed head to toe in a white tracksuit and gold trim. The Canadian superstar tore into "Jumpman"—his recent Metro Boomin-produced hit alongside Future—Section Boyz and Boy Better Know all join in on the high-energy track. In a frenzy of movement and joy, bodies fly off and onto the stage. Drake and Skepta had shunned various BRIT Award after-parties, knowing full well where the real excitement was in British music. It was a Damascus moment for UK rap and the beginning of the end for Section Boyz.

Soon after, the Croydon collective supported Drake at the O2 and Beyoncé at Wembley and recorded with Chris Brown.

The six members moved to a mansion in the countryside, complete with a home recording studio, and got to work on more music. However, as Section Boyz's profile grew, so too did click-bait articles appearing in right-wing tabloid newspapers demonising the nascent UK drill sound and drawing connections to gang-related activities. But worse was to come for the group as a legal storm brewed in the background.

The group had registered the Section Boyz name as a trademark, but someone else owned the intellectual property rights—a broader category that includes various types of legal rights in UK law—and they weren't prepared to give them up. Rumours circulated that it was a frustrated former manager, but the group never confirmed this, only that it was "someone kinda close to us," according to Sleeks.[2] Despite regularly playing shows and recording, the litigation prevented the group from releasing new music, and by 2018, the group was forced into a name change, becoming the Smoke Boys. In echoes of the London Posse from 30 years earlier, the group didn't release any new music for nearly three years, which may as well be a decade in the social media era. As the UK rap scene accelerated around them, a seemingly minor issue became a major hurdle, and momentum had stalled for the group.

Don't Panic 2 was released in late 2018, featuring the new stars of UK drill and grime, including AJ Tracey, Headie One, D-Block Europe, and LD. Yet the group seemed to adapt their sound to what was hot rather than vice versa, and the mixtape failed to shift the dial with fans. The group called it a day with *All The Smoke* two years later. Yet Section Boyz's impact on the modern UK rap scene cannot be underestimated. Using little more than YouTube and entrepreneurial street smarts, the group reached an audience of millions without the support of a major label or the media. Songs like "Lock Arf," "Trapping Ain't Dead," and "Section Anthem" are absolute belters that helped create a blueprint for what was to follow.

As Stormzy said to *VICE*, "They birthed an entire generation and sound that many people don't know originated from Section," adding, "From the lingo to the production, to the flows and cadences. Legends of UK rap, undeniably."[3]

Skengdo x AM: Censorship, Sensationalism and Folk Devil Scares

"Drill is here to stay, bro,"[4] AM tells me down the wire of a Google Meet calling from his new home in West London because "things got a bit too hectic in the South." We're speaking a little more than five years since he and Skengdo, usually stylised as Skengdo x AM, went from being at the epicentre of UK drill to making UK legal history. If the Section Boyz name change was a legal blip in UK rap history, a probable case of avariciousness from a jealous former associate, Skengdo and AM's legal concerns were a blimp that prevented them from making or performing music together, talking to various friends, or even stepping foot into their native South London for two years—not to mention being issued a nine-month suspended sentence. What was the nature of their breach? Performing their song "Attempted 1.0" at a concert in London in December 2019.

Drill might be the new sound, but this was a case of the same old police treatment and media censorship. The suppression of Black music predates the grime, road rap and garage detailed in these pages and goes back a century. Before jazz became acceptable in polite society, as Ian McQuaid reports, "Leyton council (unsuccessfully) attempted to shut down any venues hosting jazz dances, the outraged council – fuelled by a racist, hysterical right-wing press." (Sound familiar?) Yet there was always a new sound, a rebel klaxon call to take its place. Next up was rock 'n' roll. In a 1956 editorial, the *Daily Mail* declared, "It has something of the African tom-tom and voodoo dance [about it]. It is deplorable. It is tribal…We sometimes wonder whether it is the negro's revenge."[5] Punk and anti-rave laws followed. Usually, these obstacles turn out to be an inverse positive, a sign of an artist or a scene's influence.

AM, joined minutes later on the call by Skengdo, is confident that drill, if not quite joining jazz in the ranks of polite society, is here to stay. And given chart-topping singles by Tion Wayne and Russ Millions and number-one albums by Digga D, Headie One and Central Cee, whose success has gone transatlantic with the viral monster "Doja" (currently at 174 million views on YouTube), it's hard to argue otherwise. "Central Cee is opening doors for everyone else to go to America and network," declares Skengdo.

Yet Skengdo and AM ran the hard yards so others could follow. The friends grew up together in Brixton. At first, they rapped for fun recording themselves on their phones, influenced by gangster rap and the "Chicago drill type beats we heard on YouTube," explains Skengdo, before graduating to a bedroom studio setup with GarageBand.

It's been a long time since the days of Cookie Crew, Outkast, Mobb Deep, and even Clipse. Save for a few notable exceptions—the evergreen Run The Jewels, Krept and Konan, and trappers D-Block Europe—rap duos are increasingly rare, especially in the UK. While Skengdo and AM, the standout double-act from group 410, aren't quite in the same bracket as some of those mentioned, they do have a sound of their own; the perennially sunglass-wearing Skengdo's juddering higher-pitch bars complement AM's menacing baritone, which sounds like blocks of cinder dropped into an endless furnace. The latter, never seen without a balaclava covering his face, is also capable of imaginative wordplay and distinctive adlibs, dropping bars in French and even Morse code. AM puts it down to a background in education and having a foot on the road, "I'm going to put a message in there. And those who get it, get it."

"One of my things is to get the attention of [YouTube] reactors that would break lyrics down," AM puts it, explaining these "gimmicks, my unique little selling points," including the time he rapped in binary code on Charlie Sloth's *Fire in the Booth* on Radio 1. It meant the duo caught the attention of an increasingly influential cadre of YouTube creators like Walkz and LeeToTheVi that passionately dissect the minutiae of the latest drill and UK rap tracks–finding "talking points in my bars rather than just spitting."

Inevitably, Skengdo and AM's big break came via YouTube, first via their "Mad About Bars" freestyle on Mixtape Madness, hosted by Kenny Allstar in 2017. "It came at an integral time for UK drill," Kenny explained via voice notes left on WhatsApp during a busy summer touring schedule. "This was before the TikTok boom. They found a sweet spot for delivering something with so much virality. It's seven years old, and you can still play it at any event because of those easy-to-recite lyrics, 'Bally on when I step, left, right.' It's a cult classic."

The video currently has 37 million views on YouTube. And the following year, in a statement of their and UK drill's growing stature globally, Skendgo x AM dropped the video for "Pitbulls" in collaboration with genre trailblazer Chief Keef. Filmed in Chicago, Skengdo lurks menacingly with a pair of pit bulls, alongside AM and a physically imposing Keef, "You don't wanna see my dargs when they risen," a likely double entendre to a shotgun, it's enough to put the chills in Chuck Norris.

A slew of mixtapes and singles followed, including "Attempted 1.0." Released in 2018, the offending track plays it close to the bone, describing alleged historic violent clashes with several members of rival crews Moscow17 and Harlem Spartans from nearby Walworth and Kennington. Technically, in a song by AM, the rapper name-checks several foes, mixing supposedly real anecdotes with exaggerated, cartoonish scenes of violence delivered through a vocoder over JB Made It's beat.

"Attempted 1.0" was released barely a year after three south London MCs had been killed: 22-year-old Tuggzy, 17-year-old Mdot, and 16-year-old Showkey. The latter two tragedies were affiliated with gang tensions across New Cross and Lewisham, in the south-east.

Even now, you can scroll through the comments written beneath drill videos on YouTube to study the cartography of how the scene has grown beyond its spiritual home of South London and how it is intertwined with gang warfare.

I asked Skengdo and AM if art imitates life or if life imitates art. "I feel like they go hand in hand. It's like the chicken and the egg," explains AM. The authorities soon started hitting drill rappers and their labels (often self-run) where it hurt—by removing their videos from YouTube, which, aside from the promotional benefits, also resulted in financial loss to the artists affected.

The Met had been pursuing drill rappers since 2015 under the Orwellian title Operation Domain, but as of 2018, they began working directly with YouTube. According to data from the Freedom of Information (FOI) laws, the London-based force referred 510 music videos to be taken down from YouTube in 2021. In 96.7 percent of cases, the clips were removed. In 2020, 125 referrals were made, resulting in 124 removals; a year before that, 110 videos were referred and 107 were removed. The 2021 figures mark a year-on-year increase of almost 300 percent.[6]

I spoke with Post, the CEO and founder of *GRM Daily*—with nearly 7 million subscribers it is one of the most-watched music channels in the world—about Operation Domain, whose business has been directly impacted by the Met operation. He told me that *GRM* would be contacted directly by their partners at YouTube and occasionally by the Metropolitan Police, who pull videos without reason. He also said, "Some videos that don't need to get taken down might get taken down." But he concedes that "there's some shocking things that don't deserve a platform or need to be heard."[7]

"Attempted 1.0" was considered one such video, and though the lyrics could be regarded as provocative to the rival crew members AM is calling out, it could also be part of a long lineage of rap diss tracks. The video content is almost benign compared to the violence of computer games like *Grand Theft Auto* or *Squid Games* on Netflix. Yet in January 2019, the pair were found guilty of breaching a gang injunction issued to them in August of the previous year after they performed the song at London's KOKO and *Link Up TV* uploaded the performance to YouTube.

The Met decided to classify 410 as a gang (the duo denied being part of a gang), with the injunction declaring that 410's activities, "including but not limited to the production of drill music videos ... have amounted to gang-related violence." Confusingly, the case did not go to criminal but to civil court. "I think it works with people knowing the law and running rings around it to suit an agenda," sighs AM.

Yet the rappers' management team point out that incitement to violence is a crime in itself, for which no charge has been brought—and that neither of the rappers has ever been convicted of a violent crime. Although the case was a first in British legal history, it's not a unique instance of police using rap lyrics as evidence of gang-related crime. Even with a number-one album, the drill rapper Digga D must notify the police within 24 hours of releasing new music and provide them with the lyrics. If a court finds that his words incite violence, he can be sent back to prison.

As AM puts it of the police, if "what we say incites violence, and it's so bad in our area, why is it okay for us to live there? [Yet] we can't speak about it." He doesn't believe enough is being done to "improve the communities and the situations we live in," adding that "violence could happen every day if nobody knew about it." But once the newspapers started reporting on it—"Drill the 'demonic' [quotation the paper's own] music linked to rise in youth murders" ran a headline from *The Times* in 2018—the police became scrutinised.

"So they have to do something. And say, 'Well, we've banned this music, which is responsible for [the violence] that's going on.' So that's their attempt to make it look like they're doing their job," rations AM. Of course, drill music isn't entirely blameless. There are cases of drill music being associated with violent responses, but it's difficult to isolate and define the connection.

According to a joint study—Compound Injustice: A Review of Cases Involving Rap Music Evidence in England and Wales—led by the University of Manchester in association with the Centre on the Dynamics of Ethnicity (CoDE), rap lyrics are rarely used as "direct evidence of intention or confession [to commit crime]...Instead, rap tends to be used as indirect or 'bad character' evidence to suggest violent mindset, intention to commit serious harm, or gang membership."[8]

Any "evidence" is often tied up in Joint Enterprise, "The highly controversial legal doctrine that enables prosecutors to charge multiple people with a single crime, gives the state power to charge parties who are not suspected of having carried out the principal offence (often with little or no forensic evidence associated with them) to be tried for the principal offence under Secondary Liability rules on the basis that they have intentionally 'assisted or encouraged' it." In other words, if you happen to be in the vicinity, friends or even acquaintances with someone who has been suspected of committing a crime, that can be enough to get you on the dock and incriminated of "gang-related violence."

The report, made up of media and academic articles as well as legal data, included several key findings that revealed age, ethnicity and even regional biases when it came to cases involving rap music. Among the most striking statistics, "Children and young people made up 54% of defendants in the CPS (Crown Prosecution Service) Joint Enterprise study of all Joint Enterprise cases; this compares to 87% in our equivalent rap-enabled Joint Enterprise cases."

The report concludes that the UK judicial system "Paints a picture of compound injustice, with rap music being used as a procedural tool that can sweep young Black men and boys into group prosecutions for crimes they had no significant role in committing."

If anything, Skengdo and AM appeared to be guilty of a crime of optics, and 65 signatories, from human rights organisations to musicians, lawyers, and academics, signed a petition urging the Metropolitan Police to stop using these injunctions against the pair and musicians in general to reduce gang violence. The Labour MP Diane Abbott invited the pair to speak about their experience at the Houses of Parliament. AM reflects that the support was "Unexpected, but (we were) grateful because now we don't seem like we're going crazy."

For the first time during our hour-long conversation, there is a pause, an uncomfortable silence, and the strain of the memory is audible in both of their voices. Fans appreciated their "outlandish" songs, and the duo had to find creative ways to make music, omitting any lyrics that police might deem provocative. They couldn't see or speak to one another even though they shared a business account. It was a "difficult time," Skengdo admits.

A pair of underground drill rappers suddenly became the poster boys for art and censorship in the UK when all they wanted to be known for was making music. A collaboration with the conceptual Russian artist Andrei Molodkin—titled *Political Drills (The Media),* vinyl artwork that "comments directly on racial profiling and authoritarian methods of repressing the music genre"—soon followed. Channel 4 news ran a report on them where AM spoke of "a root problem" in the estate where he lived, adding that "nobody cares." Five years on, has anything changed?

AM isn't optimistic, pointing to a broken education system: "There's no opportunity for kids. They're being told in school, 'If you fail this exam, you won't get a job.' [But] no one is tapping into their creativity or finding their strengths." The roots of austerity: "Some kids are from single-parent homes. They might have problems at home and are labelled as a bad child. They need money, and their parents don't have any money. He ain't got nothing better to do. He's going to be out on the roads." And finally, "drugs are being dealt left, right and centre. Not everybody has their choice."

He paints a bleak picture, but music provides a way out, a safe haven, and an outlet for expression—"the beauty of music and art" is how Skengdo describes it. Censoring it could only push young people in the wrong direction.

"A modern form of the blues"

Lest there be any doubt, 2015 was a very good year for UK rap fans. Aside from the grime renaissance, the Section Boyz and 67 ushering in a dynamic new sound, there was J Hus' "Lean & Bop."

The Afrobeats—not to be confused with Afrobeat, originally popularised by Fela Kuti—sound led by Mista Silva, Kwamz, and Fuse ODG had been bubbling away for a while. Second and third-generation children of the African diaspora born in the UK experimented with traditional African rhythms fused with UK sounds, including grime, garage, hip-hop, and R&B. This sonic bouillabaisse laid the foundation for Afrobeats.

And J Hus was arguably the genre's breakout star. The wiry East Londoner of Gambian descent came with the snake hips, an infectious grin and 'that' dance. "Oi mate, if you're out here getting this wonga, then this one's for you," announces DoccyDocs, the fictional radio DJ introducing the world to J Hus in the music video to "Lean & Bop." It's not a complicated dance, "If you're feeling the vibe, make your woolly hat lean to the side." A granny joins Hus for a spin, *SBTV*'s Jamal Edwards shows us how it's done, and so too do groups of beaming school kids outside Stratford shopping centre.

Kenny Allstar was in the "Lean & Bop" video and saw it as an essential song and a reminder of "how UK rap could be fun," explaining, "Of course, there are hard-hitting stories that resonate with people who tend to have not much of a voice, but we can also make songs your family can vibe to. If you don't have 'Lean & Bop,' do you have 'Gun Lean,' the drill dances? Probably not. Hus understood the power of bringing in people with a positive message."

For all the hardships J Hus would experience in his life—he was stabbed five times in 2015, causing PTSD, and was later convicted twice of possessing an offensive weapon—this was the start of a genuinely joyous music adventure anyone can get down to. J Hus came with a style and swagger all of his own, and alongside his trusted producer, JAE5, the pair pushed the dial on rap UK once more with the release of *Common Sense* in spring 2017.

Much was made of the album's disparate influences—Afrobeat, dancehall, 2000s-era hip-hop, tinges of grime, and even garage—but this was a sound sui generis to J Hus and JAE5, resulting in the sometimes label of "Afroswing," alongside peers and collaborators Kojo Funds, Mostack, and Not3s.

Yet there was more to the music than exhilarating alchemy. Even amongst the grit, *Common Sense* has an effervescent shine thanks to celebratory bashment rap fusion on album openers "Common Sense" and "Bouff Daddy," JAE5's surprising trumpet solos and sparkling piano chords ("Closed Doors"), and the gorgeous timpani on "Did You See."

There's so much going on that it probably shouldn't work, but it does, and J Hus carries it all with style and grace. From the contemplative to the gregarious ladies man, and street tales "Still on tings if you're wondering" ("Plottin"), flitting between pidgin English, patois and even cockney.

Common Sense pulses with the push and pull between the untouchable persona Hus often puts on wax and the introspective, vulnerable side of someone barely out of their teenage years trying to figure it all out. This Jungian quality extends to Hus' superpower: his vocal range. "Find out who you are by the company you keep/ As kids we saw things that no man should see," he croons on vocoder-assisted "Who You Are." Hus recognised an opportunity between the UK Afrobeats scene and road rap and grime that soundtracked his adolescence, "Even though I had no experience of singing—I always used to rap—I thought I would start adding melodies. A lot of rappers have a road image. They don't want to sing. They're scared it'll mess with their image." Hus had no such concerns and was among the first and most effective to merge the sounds to "create something brand new."[9] It's probably because of his unique versatility and vocal range that he's the only artist to feature on albums from Dave, Skepta, and Stormzy.

Dave is another member of the 2015 alumni—a generational talent in the making who was still in high school when he recorded his breakout freestyle for *BL@CKBOX*, the YouTube channel dedicated to new rappers. Currently sitting at 15 million plus views, Dave's freestyle video remains the most watched on the channel. The babyface belied the emotional depth of his story, a biographical rap about his brothers who were imprisoned due to Joint Enterprise. Dave eschewed the Afrobeats, grime, and drill sound in vogue to rap over a minimal piano loop with a storytelling approach synonymous with hip-hop (a title that had slowly fallen out of favour, at least in the UK).

The world would soon discover Dave's talent extends beyond rapping to playing the piano.

And it would soon become apparent: music isn't just what Satan Dave does. It's who he is. He breathes in soundwaves with purity and lets them course through his bloodstream. The act of creation drives him. In J Hus, he found a natural collaborator; the pair recorded "Samantha" together in 2017—a holy missive that straddles two worlds with a hook that stings, a mix of "gentleman with gangster." Directed by Dir. Lx, the music video pops, the track is produced by JAE5 (who else?), Dave and Hus head to toe in Stone Island and then, their Sunday best, outside the council estate and inside the church by the stained glass windows of Christ. They are two young men on the cusp of greatness, Hus the preacher and Dave the singer, rapper, and piano player. High art and Tetley tea. You don't have to be a believer to know this was the new sound of Britain.

Yet something special was happening at a nearby junction, the intersection between Afrobeats and UK drill. It would have been unthinkable only five years earlier, but UK rap music influenced hip-hop to such an extent that it helped birth a new sound in the Big Apple, their home ground no less! "An artefact of the New York summer," gushed NPR, "a hypnotic study in tone," declared *GQ*; these publications and many more were hyperbolic in their praise of Pop Smoke and his Brooklyn Drill anthem "Welcome to the Party," a hardy crossover track that took the sound global, except, the sound was made by 808Melo, a producer from Ilford, East London. 808Melo was joined by AXL Beats in connecting the London sound with the kids of Brooklyn, who gravitated to its melodic force and in-your-face drumwork.

Despite being barely out of their teens, they were already icons of the movement, leading a wave of restless young producers like MK The Plug and M1 On the Beat. Even those far beyond the capital were drawn in, pushing drill further away from its American origins—and way beyond road rap. "The drums are fast, the bass is sliding everywhere, the kicks hit hard, the melody is always dark. You can't really avoid it," says young Welsh producer Chris Rich Beats. "It surrounds you."[10] Rich may be based on the rural outskirts of Cardiff, but it hasn't stopped him from making tracks for Central Cee, Stormzy, Unknown T, and MCs as far a field as Australia and Ghana.

In some ways, it is a phenomenon reminiscent of the desi music mini-boom of the late '00s, where Timbaland reportedly shut down ABC Music, a well-known desi music shop in Southall, to hunt for samples with local bhangra legend Juggy D. The resulting stash would further fuel Timbaland's habit of using Hindi sampling material to make era-defining hip-hop that came to fruit with the tabla drums he used on Missy Elliott's ubiquitous "Get Ur Freak On." Thus, South Asian music was broadcast to the world via the margins of West London suburbia.

But, respectfully to desi music—for further exploration, I recommend Ciaran Tharpar's excellent article "How Britsh Asians Impacted UK Rap (And Beyond)" for *TRENCH*—UK drill has been a mega-boom in terms of exportability. Because alongside the music, there is the language. As *The Economist*, of all publications, explained, "Crucial to UK drill's success is multicultural London English (MLE), a dialect that combines Jamaican patois with Cockney, American and African slang, as well as other influences from London's melting-pot."[11]

The article goes on to describe the spread of UK drill throughout Europe: "Dutch crew 73 De Pijp mix in words like 'mandem'...and 'oppboys' (a London neologism for a rival gang). Spanish crew 970BLOCK use MLE lingo like 'you get me' and 'gally' and break into English to compare themselves to Headie One, a London MC: 'I'm the one like Headie.'"

And even beyond Europe, Australian drillers like OneFour use words like "bruddas" (brothers) and "shh," a term popularised by Headie One and Skengdo x AM to self-censor potentially incriminating lyrics.

Yet the international appeal works both ways. I don't believe a generation in UK rap history has been so open to integrating non-English languages into its music. Skengdo x AM even released *EU Drillers*. Skengdo described it as "a chance to branch out and connect with different artists." A mixtape featuring MCs from Ireland, Sweden, Germany, and the Netherlands—proof of drill's unifying qualities.

It's a very long way from Hijack rapping with an American accent, but, strangely, not so far from what Malcolm McLaren and the troupe of musicians involved in the making of *Duck Rock* attempted—a global dialogue through music, but there can be few accusations of cultural appropriation when it comes to creators like JAE5, J Hus, Dave and 808Melo.

This is all the more pertinent when you factor in the big-ticket Afrobeat and UK rap collaborations between Burna Boy and Dave, Wizz Kid and Skepta, Davido and Tion Wayne.

I spoke with Ian McQuaid, the writer and co-founder/owner of MOVE Recordings, a label at the intersection of UK drill, which he calls "a modern form of the blues," and Afrobeats—having released music by Skengdo x AM and "Drogba (Joanna)" by Afro B, which topped the US Billboard R&B/Hip-Hop chart, among others—to better understand some of the patterns behind the success.

"The British public has a complex relationship with Black British culture, obsessing over it and emulating it whilst also having blatant racism within our society. When Black British kids started building their own music industry infrastructure around 2012 - 2015, it was only a matter of time til the wider public was ready to start accepting the music" Ian explains, and a changing demographic makeup from a predominantly Caribbean to African British identity, led to an influx of "young African diasporic kids going to university. Where they began putting on raves from the early 2010s. Shows from Wiz, early Burna Boy, Davido." Superstars today, playing small shows across the UK back then.

Ian continues: "At the same time, you're getting Afro B and Tion Wayne making bangers together. An underground network happened. And over the course of nearly ten years now, it's inside the mainstream. And I don't think we can underestimate the power of Britain as a sort of a tastemaker, especially in Black music." The university connection—perhaps as a result of Labours expansion of education opportunities under

Tony Blair and the £3,000 annual fees cap set until 2010—is apparent during the making of this book as many of the rappers I spoke with, from Jehst to AM, Tion Wayne through to Loyle Carner, completed some form of higher education.

* * *

Songs like "Samantha", "Lean & Bop," "Lock Arf," and Skengdo x AM's "Mad About Bars" are modern pop masterpieces straight out of the mud. And now, not only does the rest of the world know it, they're imitating it too.

DISCOGRAPHY

Chapter 14: Attempted 1.0

This chapter is titled after the song by AM.

Albums, E.P.s & Mixtapes
Section Boyz - *Sectionly 2104*
Section Boyz - *Don't Panic*
J Hus - *Common Sense*
Smoke Boys - *All The Smoke*
Skengdo x AM - *EU Drillers*

Singles
Missy Elliott - "Get Ur Freak On"
Section Boyz - "No Rules"
Section Boyz - "Delete My Number"

J Hus - "Lean & Bop"
Section Boyz - "Lock Arf"
Section Boyz - "Trapping Ain't Dead"
Section Boyz - "Section Anthem"
67 Ft. Giggs - "Let's Lurk"
Skengdo x AM - "Mad About Bars"
Dave and J Hus - "Samantha"
Skengdo x AM -"Pitbulls"
J Hus - "Common Sense"
J Hus - "Bouff Daddy"
J Hus - "Did You See"
J Hus - "Plottin"
AM - "Attempted 1.0"
Pop Smoke - "Welcome to the Party"
Central Cee - "Doja"

Chapter 15

Loyle Carner

Loyle Carner has been steadily carving a lane since the mid-2010s with his trademark confessional and clever lyricism over jazzy boom-bap beats. The Lambeth-born MC is further evidence of the rich kaleidoscope UK rap had become by the end of the decade—an alternative artist with mass appeal.

Softly-spoken and doe-eyed, Loyle, real name Ben Coyle-Larner, joins me for a call over Zoom from his baby's bedroom at his home in Hackney. We spoke ahead of the release of his third album, *Hugo*. Beyond the book's conceptual timeline, it's well worthy of mention and follows on from the critically acclaimed *Yesterday's Gone* (2017) and *Not Waving, But Drowning* (2019). On *Hugo,* Carner has created his most accomplished and complex music yet, venturing deeper inward for inspiration, exploring his British-Guyanese roots, a dysfunctional relationship with his biological father, and what it means to become a recent dad himself.

Born in 1994, Carner grew up in the grime generation, inspired by MCs like Kano and Ghetts alongside J Dilla, Native Tongues, and his hero MF DOOM. Yet his rap style has more in common with the UK hip-hop lineage of Jehst and Rodney P, and as Carner sees it, "All I ever wanted to be was a link in the chain, to kind of take it from where it was at before and allow another generation to love it as much as me."

Yet, in many ways, he's also very different, willing to be more honest and vulnerable in a way that is—undoubtedly better than worse—supposedly typical of his generation, particularly around personal relationships and mental health. Some might describe Carner's sound as jazz rap or alt. rap, but to these ageing ears, it sounds like a new take on good old hip-hop, and there's nothing wrong with that.

What's your earliest musical memory?

I [haven't] thought about that for so long. My mum and dad used to play the guitar, so my earliest memory is the image of being on the sofa and watching them playing. And I wish I had learnt to play. I leant more into the piano when I was growing up, probably as a tiny rebellion within music, but I've fallen back in love with [the guitar] recently.

You attended the BRIT School (the prestigious performing arts and creative school in South London, where previous alumni include Adele and Amy Winehouse). What was that experience like?

Yeah, I enjoyed it. It was brilliant to have a place where you could fail behind closed doors. Especially now, with mobile phones and [how] everything is broadcasted and shared, you can't start out without everyone already seeing your shit and thinking that is wack. [And] you know, all of my early shit was wack, so it was just nice to be in a place where you could just fail over and over again, and there was no judgement.

I studied theatre because I wanted to write plays, and I just loved it for that. It was a weird place, like any school, especially one focusing on the arts, but I took from it what I could, and I enjoyed how we were treated like adults.

You just touched on your theatre aspirations. How does that inform your approach to writing and performing rap?

I just love storytelling. That's why I fell in love with [rap]. And I still appreciate a whole body of work: an album, an E.P., or a live show. I don't see them as individual pieces. If you zoom out, there's a bigger picture. It made me focus a bit more on the narrative.

The red thread in your music is this sort of transparency and vulnerability, which is refreshing. You've spoken about having ADHD in the past; obviously, you wouldn't know any different, but I was wondering how you feel that's influenced your music.

I think it helps me take risks without realising it, because talking about yourself and making yourself vulnerable is risky and doesn't always pay off. And it hasn't always paid off for me. And it's hurt my life in some ways, hurt my family in other ways, you know. But it's also given me my deepest moments of joy, mainly in the creative process. I can't write about anything else. I've tried to be more hedonistic because I love music, which makes me feel like, "Yeah, I could take over the world, and I've got £1,000,000 in my pocket." Even when I don't. I'm sensitive and can be moved easily; that comes across in my music. So, yeah, it's a blessing and a curse. I think it is the same way that ADHD is a blessing and a curse.

Are there any examples of the hedonistic music you like?

Yeah, loads. I mean, essentially, half of the rappers out right now. And Red Hot Chili Peppers, who I've been listening to a lot recently. They have a kind of hedonistic mysticism.

I got heavy into Anthony Kiedis over the lockdown because I was looking for inspiration that wasn't necessarily within my field. And I know that from listening to him when I was younger, he's inspired by rap music. I love the way that he writes so freely. So I read his autobiography, listened to the music, and wondered, "How can I say more with less and make it a bit more abstract?"

Californication **is an amazing album, and had they been born or started the band ten years later, it would encompass more rap, right?**

Yeah, because you can hear it in the book. He says the first time he started to write was when he was listening to Grandmaster Flash and realised he could be a part of this band even if he weren't musical. He was witty and intelligent and wanted to express himself creatively.

And that's a big thing for a lot of people, myself included, that you know your musical in some way, but you can't sit on the guitar or hit that high note. So rap gave a voice to me and a lot of my friends.

You grew up when grime was starting to emerge, but your music isn't like that. Early on in your career, you collaborated with Jehst. In some ways, I see your music as part of the UK hip-hop lineage. How do you see it?

And what do you think is the current state of the union for British rap?

I mean, there's unity for sure. But I've always felt like an outsider, in a nice way. And that's given me maybe a more honest perspective and more of an open perspective.

But there is a togetherness. I've been struck by the love that I even get, you know, on the fringes of this rap thing from guys that I grew up [with] being massive fans of guys like Kano and Ghetts and whatever. And on the other side, [rappers] like Rodney P, Jehst, and Klashnekoff. All I ever wanted to be was a link in the chain, to kind of take it from where it was before and allow another generation to love it as much as me.

It changed my life not just by making money from it but also by meeting all the people I know. All the people I love are connected to this thing of ours. And I feel lucky to be a part of it and don't care where I get put as long as I'm in the conversation.

On your last album, *Not Waving, But Drowning,* there's the Stevie Smith poem recited in the title track. We British seem to do nostalgia well. What's your take on that?

Yeah. I guess there's an arrogance missing from British culture, which is a good thing in many ways for personal relationships. But, in art, I think there needs to be a newfound confidence, which I think is being seen in guys like Skepta, etc., who can go, "Fuck that, I don't care." That's kind of the African influence; a lot of my Nigerian friends have what they would call arrogance, but I just think it's this beautiful self-confidence: "I'm better than you think I am."

When I look back, the album is funny because when I made it, I was having a good time and a bad time for different reasons. The idea was that the songs would sound super happy, but there's a guy in there who's struggling, and I think I did a good enough job of hiding that it was lost on people, which complements the themes.

Now that I'm a father, I look back on my childhood and feel nostalgia for the stuff I listened to. That's why I would always struggle to hate Kanye West [*the interview took place not long after West's infamous "I'm going death con 3 on Jewish people" tweet, Carner briefly mentioned;* "I'm not saying I agree with what's gone on..."], When I was growing up, that guy was blowing my mind. He opened my eyes to homophobia in the Black community, supported loving your mum, and being okay to be different or nerdy or whatever. But yeah, [in] the UK, we just need to step away from the humbleness a bit because it's not rude not to be showing [pride in yourself].

Not Waving, But Drowning **got to number three in the charts. That's mad because—for want of a more elegant word—it's a weird album, right? And to achieve that level of popularity, how does that feel?**

Yeah, it's funny because within the world I was in, it was something I'd never dreamed of even happening because it doesn't happen to my genre of music. But then, on the other side, the industry side, when you see those people, they talk about it like a failure. "Oh, you didn't touch number one or number two?" I mean, it's not meant to be in the top ten. It doesn't exist in this world, you know? But I was very proud of myself, if I do say so myself.

And it reinforced my opinion of how powerful and open people are. People don't just [want to listen to] bullshit about nothing, you know? I would never blow my trumpet too much because I'm one of those British guys who doesn't want to do that. But the one thing I would say is music means something deeply to me. And to put that into a place where it finds some success it's a testament to the fact that many people also want to talk about meaningful things.

Let's talk about some of the themes in the new record, *Hugo*. When did you first become aware of the particularity of your identity?

I think I was probably in primary school, going in and seeing my friend's parents and being like, "What? Why are they not all different?" You know, my white friends had white parents, and my Black friends had Black parents. And I was confused because I just kind of thought you just came out, however.

That was probably the first time, but it wasn't really talked about. I internalised it a lot. You don't realise it when you're young until you look back. But I was treated like a bad kid and all this stuff just because I was darker skinned than some of my counterparts. But then I also kind of didn't. It's complicated.

That's what this album is about. Some of it is specific to my lived experience. But the whole album is about many things: forgiveness, fatherhood, and not fitting in is the big thing. And everybody feels that, you know. I became close with [someone] transitioning to a woman when we were young, like 14 or 15. And it was very confusing for them. And they didn't have many people who wanted to talk to them about it. But I was so interested because I felt an affinity with my friends in those spaces. When you're in those little gaps in the middle, that's where the most beauty can arrive. And anyone can find themselves in those gaps in between.

Just be slightly different.

Right? You don't have to be mixed race or gay, just a bit wonky.

The album also explores your relationship with your biological father on "Polyfilla" and touches on your experience of becoming a dad. That must have been quite exposing; how did you get into that headspace and out of it?

The beautiful thing about working like this is that it's exhausting, but it's real life. So, it wrote itself. I was having a child, and I finally found some inspiration I've been looking for for a long time. I started writing again, and I was reconnecting with my father. I had to reconnect with him for my son to see his Black lineage, his ancestry, and his family.

So on this journey, I began to dig up shit that maybe I had buried with my father. And I hated him, and I was angry with him. And he taught me to drive over the lockdown in his car. So we had a really beautiful space to air this out. And so the whole album is just the process of learning how to forgive not only my father but myself, too.

In hip-hop, it's a tried and tested formula; I'm a kid. I made money for my mum, fuck my dad. And then the story ends. But that's not the end. Because I've done that. I've made peas [money], sorted my mum a house, you know, a success to her. But still, there's a feeling of dissatisfaction, of emptiness. The next step was like, "Where else can I look?" Because it's not the bank, and it's not the car, or whatever.

The whole idea before is that rap music [required] thinking [that was] outside the box and now it's become pop music. So now that's the box. And outside of that box is the next bit. And it's trying to find some perspective and help guide the next generation of people on this journey to set themselves free. Because by forgiving my father it unshackled me from pain, grief and heaviness. It wasn't even about him, you know.

This reminds me of a point EL-P made when I interviewed him for the twentieth anniversary of his first album, *Fantastic Damage*. He used that record to exorcise the demons of his abusive stepfather. He talked about how the writing process allowed him to heal, and it was something he became addicted to, even though he didn't necessarily see himself as a solo artist or an MC.

I love El-P, legend. I think that's the point, though. It's beautiful to hear that because I'd never thought about it like that. Because this shit caused me a lot of fucking pain then, putting the shit out to the world and letting people judge my life sucks.

Like the blessing and the curse?

Precisely. Because I'm in the process and [the album is] about to come out, I'm excited because I'm proud of it. But I'm nervous, as I'm giving people a space to have an opinion on my shit. But I always find myself in this situation because I cannot stop working through my life like this. This is the only way I know how to do it.

And what a gift to have a space to get paid and to do my own therapy. And I understand exactly where he's coming from because you achieve something. "Okay, I've worked through this," and then you go, "Cool, I don't need to rap anymore." And then something pops up, and you go, "I'm back again." And that's what it is for me. This is the thing I love, but when it pops up, it's usually because I have to figure something out.

So, considering what you mentioned about theatre, are there other art forms you'd like to use to express yourself?

Yeah, definitely. The possibilities are endless. Why can't I make films or be in films? I would love to write a film or a play. [I would] never stop rapping, but look at Childish Gambino. That's a guy who isn't confined by this shit… "Oh, you have to be a certain way, dress a certain way, or do a certain thing." At first, everyone clowned on him. But now people know, and they want to be in *Atlanta*. My dream is to be creative forever, no matter what that is. It's the only thing that keeps me going sometimes.

"Blood on my Nikes" is about knife crime. Threats to kill involving a knife or sharp instrument have increased by almost 350 percent between 2011 and 2021. This is alongside twelve years of austerity measures led by the Conservative government. This is quite open-ended, but how does that make you feel?

Now, I'm a father, and I think that's why I finally made that song. And I think people are surprised by it. People forget just because I don't talk about [violence] doesn't mean I don't open my door and see [knife crime]. Like, I didn't go to school and see it, or I didn't know people who sadly are gone or went to jail.

It upsets me because now I'm a father, I'm thinking about

it further than [myself]. I spoke about it because my mum is a teacher, my girlfriend is a teacher, and my auntie teaches. [And] the lack of funding and support because these people are on the front line. These are the caretakers of our children.

And the arts, the after-school clubs, the sports clubs, in a city don't get any love. Youth club was one of the things that saved my life and allowed me to love theatre, music, and dance instead of just love making money. Because you need guidance, kids grow up with no parents around. And even if their parents are brilliant, they're working fucking hard just to keep them afloat. If mum's out until 11 because she's working nights, what is the little boy to do?

I feel passionately about it, but the best thing you can do is listen. So I think the best thing for even my generation, but definitely for the Tories, is to just shut up and listen.

DISCOGRAPHY

Essentials
Loyle Carner - "The Isle of Arran"
Loyle Carner - "Damselfly"
Loyle Carner Ft. Jordan Rakei - "Ottolenghi"
Loyle Carner - "Speed of Plight"
Loyle Carner Ft. John Agard - "Georgetown"
Unknown T Ft. Loyle Carner - "Hocus Pocus"

Deep Cuts
Loyle Carner - "Tierney Terrace"
Kae Tempest & Loyle Carner - "Guts"

Chapter 16

Karma

"My parents are Nigerian, so African music is a big part of my heritage. Like Fela [Kuti], he's our Bob Marley,"[1] Tion Wayne explains to me from the plush cream leather back seats of his vast BMW Hummer, driven by his friend, as we slowly snake through the rush hour traffic between Wapping and Peckham during a piercing cold winter's evening in 2019.

"Everyone should always chase their dream."

In the weeks leading up to our interview, Wayne, whose real name is Dennis Junior Odunwo, had released the track "Keisha & Becky (Remix)" alongside Russ Millions, featuring a slew of rappers including JAY1, Sav'O, rapper turned professional boxer Swarmz, and cheeky-chappy Mancunian Aitch. "When Russ and I made the song, we knew it was a hit when we were in the studio together. When making the hook, we didn't want to limit it to certain people," he explains. "We knew we wanted to make something for people to dance to and attract females who don't necessarily like drill." The production features the skittering drum pattern and sharp hi-hats that had become increasingly typical of UK drill, while the lyrics, rich with adolescent lust, counter the usual aggressive subject matter. Between producer Gotcha, alongside Wayne and Russ Millions, the trio had essentially landed on a winning formula that smoothes out drill's harsh edges.

I later described it as a "menacingly funny, drill pop earworm" in the cover interview for *Notion,* a small but well-produced music magazine. Wayne explained, "Before you had to make pop songs, now you can just make a song that happens to become popular." After nearly ten years of hard graft, Tion Wayne had become that. Months earlier, he headlined a sold-out performance at the O2, and by the end of the year "Keisha & Becky (Remix)" had 25 million views on YouTube and sold 400,000 copies, making it the highest-charting UK drill song at the time. Eighteen months later Wayne released "Body," also with Russ Millions, the first UK drill song to reach number one in the singles chart.

Wayne's early music sat at the intersection of Afrobeats and UK drill, or more accurately, road rap with a sprinkling of melodic trap elements and R&B vocals. Songs like "Streetz Dem," alongside Brandz, and "I'm On," with its bright Pokémon-style synth and Kojo Funds catchy hook, highlight this amorphous sound where the pursuit of girls seems to be the constant.

Growing up in Enfield, in Edmonton, North London, Tion Wayne was inspired by local grime MCs like Scorcher and Terminator, describing his hometown as "a small area with a huge cultural mix—very lively" and crediting it as a big influence on his music: "Environments are so important to your own sound, your own special sauce." Wayne completed a university degree in Birmingham, "Commuting back and forth for three years, but kept releasing music. My main goal on one side was 'Yo, I gotta make it out the ends and make it in music,'" earning himself a 2.1 (the second highest mark) in business and accountancy, but he also found trouble. In 2017, he was charged with affray after being involved in a brawl outside a Bristol nightclub. He was filmed on CCTV kicking the victim in the head and given a 16-month sentence.

He was one of 14 co-defendants involved in the fracas, but the only person to be arrested, the "headline" as he described it, and was treated as such by the tabloid press who incorrectly labelled him a "grime music star" (*The Mirror*). When the subject comes up, his voice lowers with remorse, although he echoes AM's message of police wanting rappers, burgeoning young Black men like him in jail. "[Police] don't want us to win. They want us to go to jail," he continues, meaning people from his background. "That's why they want the rapper so much; we're the platform to the people they don't like."[2]

Prison didn't deter him, and after he got out, he knuckled down on music, defining his sound.

"I could have been stuck in jail or dead, but I feel like this is supposed to happen. Everyone should always chase their dream." Wayne had only just turned 26, but his focus was notable, and he was a polite, understandably guarded interviewee. Looking ahead to 2020, he said, "My goal now is getting myself comfortable, and I feel I'm ninety percent there. I want to inspire others and help people where I can. I can help people coming up; I can show them there's always a way." We eventually pulled up near my flat in Peckham. We wish each other the best for the future, what will soon be the first of many cover features, and joke about Wayne's "wingman role" for his driver, who's going on a date later that night.

Similar to J Hus, Tion Wayne's knack for melody sets him apart—those punchy, staccato rhythms and sing-song delivery blend effortlessly with the drill hi-hats—and his success was further evidence that UK rap music had taken over pop music.

Commercially and critically, 2019 was a watershed year for UK rap music. There were landmark albums by Little Simz, with *Grey Area*, and a then-21-year-old Dave, with *Psychodrama*, whose words are bold, bright and moving. Private and very rare to give interviews, I knew better than to try to speak to Dave for this book, although I did talk with Fraser T Smith, who executive produced *Psychodrama*, a day before the album won the BRIT Award. The affable Smith spoke of Dave's "obvious musicality," attention to detail, and commitment to craft: "Dave will write one line down 100 times."[3]

On the surface, Fraser T Smith—a white, 49-year-old dad from rural Buckinghamshire who got his start touring with progressive rock savant Rick Wakeman—is an unlikely collaborator for rappers like Kano, Stormzy, and Dave. Yet the songwriter and producer has worked on some of those artists' biggest and best moments, executive producing both Dave and Stormzy's debut albums.

A Grammy Award winner to boot, he has an impressive list of songwriting and production credits, including Adele and Sam Smith. Yet his eyes seem to light up when speaking about the Streatham-born MC: "I remember sitting at the Mercury Awards next to Dave's mum, who has been through a very tough time. She came to this country with five pounds in her pocket. Her husband died, two of her children are in prison, and, to be fair to Dave, it probably looked like he would go through the same thing or at least be in a gang, but he's come through. To see the joy from Dave's mum [when *Psychodrama* won the Mercury Award] was greater than most things in life."

Psychodrama proved a lodestar album for British rap music. A concept record structured around a fictional therapy session, musically, there are elements of hip-hop and Afrobeats fused together with Smith's melancholic piano work. Bar the song "Location," featuring Burna Boy, there are no obvious radio hits, yet it is a singular body of work capable of leaving fans and critics' ears in celestial awe. The following night after we spoke, Smith performed on the piano alongside Dave for the song "Black" at the BRIT Awards, a complex, intelligent examination of racial identity that questions the use of the word "Black" as a monolith. Sombre and powerful, it might just be the saddest victory dance you've ever seen.

* * *

Outside of the top two, 2019 was also blessed by *Hoodies All Summer*, a potential career-best album from Kano, Slowthai's debut *Nothing Great About Britain*, a gut punch of a record timed to perfection for a country badly divided by Brexit, and Headie One's *Music X Road*, technically a mixtape, which kick-started the dubious trend of UK drill songs sampling Eurodance hits, as he did via Ultra Nate's "Free" on "Both."

Both Dave and Stormzy released number-one albums (the latter with *Heavy Is the Head*). Yet, multiple UK rappers enjoyed Top 10 album success in 2019, including AJ Tracey (with his self-titled full-length debut, which reached No.3), D-Block Europe (two Top 10 albums), Skepta, Mostack, Loyle Carner, Fredo, Slowthai, Kano, and Krept & Konan. And in the singles market, more than 21 percent of all consumption was homegrown rap music, according to data from the BPI (British Phonographic Industry).

After a lifetime spent in the margins of culture and years spent harassed by politicians and the police, British rap had gone mainstream. Asher D, once the bastion of British tabloid rage while part of So Solid Crew, was beamed on the family-friendly everyman viewing of Sky One, playing—oh, the delicious irony—a middle-class police officer in the show *Bulletproof.*

Asher D also starred alongside Kano as the now iconic pairing of Dushane and the perma-grimacing Sully in the triumphant return of *Top Boy* after six years away from our screens. The show was brought back via Netflix thanks to a pitch fronted by Drake alongside Ronan Bennett, the show's writer and creator. Credited as an executive producer for the show, the Anglophile's role on *Top Boy* isn't entirely clear. Ultimately, it's arguable that the show gave Drake more credibility than vice versa.

Surely, all this success can only have been a good thing, can't it?

As the year drew to a close, the seeds of this story began to grow in my mind, although there were two conflicting thoughts to contend with first. The landscape for British rap music had never been so vast, varied, and, at times, exciting, a sprawling labyrinth made up of scenes and micro scenes that simultaneously overlapped and operated in complete isolation. However, there were also so many songs with lyrics centred around violence, misogyny, and materialism. For every thoughtful *Psychodrama,* there was a D-Block Europe tearing up the charts. Not only is it music void of substance, it is style without style—a meandering vocoder-driven opulent nothingness.

More hip-hop, grime, and UK drill seemed to be coming out of the country than ever before, an algorithm-feeding frenzy that left fans—both diehard and the increasing cabal of casual, gun finger-toting, know the big AJ/Skepta/Stormzy-festival-hits—wanting more. More likes, more tweets, more streaming, and less filtering. More of more.

But if it's difficult to know exactly where it all started—from Newtrament, McLaren, or The Mexicano to Smiley, Britcore, and Dizzee and Wiley—it's relatively straightforward to define when UK rap went stratospheric.

From Worthy Farm to the World

"How can I create a culture around this whole thing?" Jay-Z asks rhetorically. He's speaking to Stormzy, standing at 6.5 feet with a grin a mile wide, and the producer Fred Again, crouching at a table secretly filming the conversation while at a studio in Johannesburg.

"Culture moves the world," Jay-Z continues. "When you step on that stage, you're going to see it because they are ready for it." From there, Stormzy struts onstage as flamethrowers and fireworks fill the sky above Glastonbury Festival 2019, jumping into an incendiary version of "Know Me From."

The video marked the introduction of Stormzy's headline performance. Fred Again later wrote of the iPhone recording, "I'm also totally at peace wit [sic] the fact that the best thing I've done in music is have my lil mugshot in his intro vid."[4] It's easy to overestimate the symbolism of the opening. Jay-Z, the first rapper to headline Glastonbury back in 2008—click-baiting a hip-hop is "wrong" for the festival Noel Gallagher with his rendition of "Wonderwall"—hands the baton on to the young MC from Croydon, the first Black British solo artist to headline the festival and the second youngest artist since David Bowie in 1971.

It's easy because Stormzy made it so. It was an explosive performance that contained both BMX bikers and a powerful collaboration with Ballet Black that showcased new pointe shoes specifically designed to match Black and mixed-race skin tones—something previously unavailable for dancers of colour. There were also the British sign language interpreters who specialise in grime and, just in case another B was needed, there were chants of "fuck the government, fuck Boris" from "Vossi Bop."

Three songs in, Stormzy flashed crime statistics on the video screens while sampling a speech by Labour MP David Lammy on racial disproportionality in the criminal justice system. The message was as potent as the volume was loud. Use hearing protection.

Whether you like Stormzy's music or not, it doesn't matter. Everyone from Adele to Wiley and Jeremy Corbyn lavished the performance with praise. This was UK rap's Woodstock moment. The culture had entered a new world where it would remain: the realm of superstardom and commerce. But to Big Mike's credit, his performance was as much about everyone else—the legends of UK rap he thanked and, more importantly, those who lost loved ones after the Grenfell disaster—as himself.

* * *

Our current culture encourages us to look back at previous times with a nostalgic gaze. Especially on the internet, people romanticise eras that preceded ours, when life, parties, and culture appeared freer, more enjoyable, and devoid of social media to document them. Perhaps in twenty, thirty, or fifty years, a new generation will be floating in their pods, drifting through a megacity, scrolling through dreamscapes projected directly into their vision, and they'll stumble across a grainy 1080p video of Glastonbury 2019. It will evoke a similar yearning for a time when life seemed visceral and more real.

DISCOGRAPHY

Chapter 16: Karma

This chapter is titled after the song by Headie One.

Albums, E.P.s & Mixtapes
Little Simz - *Grey Area*
Dave - *Psychodrama*
Slowthai - *Nothing Great About Britain*
Kano - *Hoodies All Summer*
Headie One - *Music X Road*
Stormzy - *Heavy Is the Head*

Singles
Ultra Nate - "Free"
Tion Wayne Ft. Brandz - "Streetz Dem"
Stormzy - "Know Me From"
Tion Wayne Ft. Kojo Funds - "I'm On"
Dave - "Black"

Dave Ft. Burna Boy - "Location"
Stormzy - "Vossi Bop"
Headie One - "Both"
Russ Millions and Tion Wayne Ft. Aitch, JAY1, Sav'O, Swarmz - "Keisha & Becky (Remix)"
Tion Wayne and Russ Millions - "Body"

Epilogue

Fast forward two years later, and the mood of the country—and the wider world—was very different. It had been almost twenty months since the first recorded case of COVID-19 in the UK, and summer had offered a respite from lockdown.

Going Back to Manny

It was late July, a few days after the so-called "Freedom Day," where most legal restrictions, including mask mandates and social distancing, were lifted. I was back in Manchester to interview a local rapper for a newspaper, but for reasons beyond my control, the interview was cancelled at the last minute. I sat in a small dingy room at the Best Western Hotel in Wilmslow Road, pondering what to do, staring at the beige wallpaper, followed by my notepad, phone, mask, and hand gel, scattered across the desk like remnants of a time capsule most would prefer to forget. The interview was supposed to be the catalyst for starting this book, but now it felt like I was left in limbo—a false start.

Later that night, I met up with old university friends and explained the rough outline for what would become this book. One of them put me in touch with Keith, who organised open mic cyphers at a small community centre in Levenshulme, South Manchester. The next day was the first in a long time that I had been hungover, and I closed my eyes tightly on the train to Levenshulme, trying to shut out the dull thud oscillating in my head.

After leaving the station, I walked along the rows of redbrick terrace housing, exchanging a pass or two with the kids playing football in the street. Even though I hadn't visited the city in years, it felt familiar and warm as the late afternoon sun shone down before finally arriving at the community centre. It was an innocuous-looking building from the outside, a blue facade that had faded with time and chipped window frames and handwritten "Clap the NHS" and "Keep Smiling MCR" signs sat lopsided in the main window, obscuring dimly lit rooms.

Manchester has a musical heritage that rivals any in the UK. From the pioneering post-punk of Joy Division to the carefree energy of the Happy Mondays' "Madchester" era, the city has also fostered a rave scene that gave us acts like 808 State, A Guy Called Gerald, and the Chemical Brothers—not to mention the Britpop-induced anaemia of Oasis. Despite this impressive history, Manchester's contribution to British rap culture often goes overlooked.

Yet, typical of the city, it's always had a tight-knit loyal community of hip-hop "heads" and its intersection with grime being more affable than it is in the capital. I experienced this firsthand when I studied there. I worked part-time at Hussains Shoe Parlour, a tiny little shop barely selling any limited edition trainers on Tib Street, in the Northern Quarter, home to various independent boutiques, record shops and Afflecks Palace, a labyrinth of vintage bric-a-brac aimed at parting students with their loan money.

Various musicians and artists would stop by Hussains, perusing the rows of adidas Samba, Nike Air Force, and SBs *de rigueur* at the time time, telling me about their life story, latest art project, album or club night (in the early '00s everyone seemed to be putting on a club night in Manchester). Among the regulars were Virus Syndicate, a local grime collective, and in particular, their producer MRK1, who spoke proudly of local hip-hop crews like pioneers Krispy Three, Broke 'N' English, who would later find a soulful renaissance as Children of Zeus, and the rapper Fallacy, originally from London but a fixture in the city for years, connecting the dots between garage, UK hip-hop, and grime.

I'm told the scene has become less coherent recently, but MCs like Aitch, Bugzy Malone, and Meekz have elevated the city nationally and helped shake off any cobwebs of nostalgia.

As can be the way in big cities, it's in the margins, the outskirts, where culture tends to bloom, and here I was in Levenshulme, hopeful more than expectant.

I ring the buzzer and a short, stout man with a 5 o'clock shadow answers the door. He introduces himself as Keith, and we have the obligatory small talk about the weather. "Amsterdam?" he says. "Must be nice this time of year." Followed by the compulsory reference to COVID-19: "Such a relief; hopefully, we're over the worst of it now," he says with uncertainty. "Alright, you better come meet the lads." He takes me through a short corridor and opens the door into a backroom where we're greeted with a blast of trap music from the speakers, mastered by a baby-faced DJ behind the decks, head to toe in black Nike Tech apparel, focusing intently on his mix.

Nearby, a group of teenagers, mostly boys and a couple of girls, furiously take turns to grab at a microphone being passed around the cypher. Keith looks on with fatherly pride and nods to the group, alerting them of my presence. One or two come towards me, "You should write about me," grins one lad. "Follow me on 'Gram," says another, pushing his phone towards me, and then, PLOW, PFFF, PLOW. The amp has blown. The baby-faced DJ goes beetroot, frantically looking around under the mixing deck for a solution while the cypher disperses to loud groans.

The group gravitates towards me. While some younger MCs hang back, others are more rambunctious and keen to show off their freestyle skills. Up first is a tall, skinny boy wearing a Trapstar cap; he swings his arms energetically and begins his rap confidently, yet there's an undeniable London influence, the dun-dun-dun cadence popularised by Central Cee and the crowd soon dismisses him. Someone shouts, "Come on man, we got our own sound. Manny [a nickname for Manchester] sound, get off that London 'ting." Then a short girl with braids steps forward; her rap style is aggressive with funny lyrics. She rhymes, "I hit the Trafford Centre, bagged a new sweater / Popped into Greggs, 'cause you know there's nowt better." The group laughs and raw with approval, and we take turns to fist bump the girl.

I ask the group who their favourite local MC is: "Me!" "Black Josh!" "Chunky's got bars!" and a volley of names that I'm not familiar with. The group begins to part, looking referentially towards a tall, thoughtful-looking, light-skinned teenager on the cusp of manhood trying to help fix the broken amplifier. Let's call him Tyler.

He speaks with a command facility that I hadn't expected and explains that he grew up surrounded by the Manchester hip-hop and grime scene. He offers to take me back to his house and play “important records.” On the short walk back to Tyler’s, he tells me about his brother, a local DJ who played all the clubs, made beats, and once supported 50 Cent when he performed in the city. He beams with pride, but I sense some sadness when he speaks of him, and he reveals that he is currently serving time in prison.

We arrive at Tyler’s house and, carefully unlocking the key, enter into a small garage space.

A pair of Technics SL-1210 decks are the centrepiece. The walls are covered in flyers for raves, open mic cyphers, and tours: Skepta at The Warehouse Project, Wu-Tang Clan at The Apollo, and in the centre of one wall appears an unlikely image—it’s a poster from local design legend Peter Saville, known as *The Factory* or *Use Hearing Protection,* created for the infamous Hacienda nightclub. The striking yellow and black colour scheme is reminiscent of a warning sign, while the minimalist illustration of a man covering his ears is almost hypnotic in its repetition of lines and, in some ways, offers a romanticised view of Britain’s industrial past.

Tyler wouldn’t be born for several decades when it was first made, and he doesn’t strike me as a post-punk fan. I ask if it’s his brothers’ poster, “Na, it’s mine.” I ask, “What do you like about it?” wondering if his attraction is more based in aesthetics or hometown pride. “It’s a bit different, innit?”

Endnotes

CHAPTER 1

1. Quote attributed to Malcolm McLaren, from an article on 40 years of Duck Rock, for *The Guardian* https://www.theguardian.com/music/2023/may/30/duck-rock-at-50-malcolm-mclaren-seminal-album-with-a-queasy-underside
2. Quote attributed to Keith Haring, *Ibid.*
3. Trevor Horn interview with *The Guardian* https://www.theguardian.com/music/2022/oct/24/grace-jones-trevor-horn-mega-hits-frankie-goes-to-hollywood-abc-tatu
4. Quote attributed to Rodney P, from an article on 10 records that helped British hip-hop find its own voice, for Vinyl Factory https://thevinylfactory.com/features/the-10-records-that-helped-british-hip-hop-find-its-own-voice/
5. Colin Brock, *The Caribbean in Europe: Aspects of the West Indian Experience in Britain, France and the Netherlands.* (1986). pp. 62–84.
6. Paul Gilroy, *There Ain't No Black In The Union Jack* (1987). pp. 49-51.
7. All quotes from Jazzie B are taken from a first-person interview in 2023.
8. Quote from an article by the journalist Amelia Hill for *The Guardian https://www.theguardian.com/uk/2011/nov/29/smiley-culture-death-no-charges?INTCMP=SRCH*

9. Paul Rambali 'Electro: The Beat That Won't be Beaten' for *The Face* magazine in 1984.
10. Morgan Khan interview with the *NME* - https://www.street-sounds.co.uk/assets/images/nme3of3-2000x2826.jpg
11. Arush Quereshi *Flip the Script: How Women Came to Rule Hip Hop (2021). p.17*
12. *Ibid.*
13. Susie Q interview with Britts Across the Pond - http://www.britsacrossthepond.com/cookie-pryce.html
14. All quotes are from a Hijack interview with *Rock the Bells* https://www.rockthebells.com/blogs/articles/hijack-rap-group
15. First-person interview with Squarepusher for *Wax Poetics,* 2021.
16. Liam Howlett of The Prodigy, quoted from https://theprodigy.info/history/
17. Bionic quoted from the *Bad Meaning Good* documentary, YouTube https://youtu.be/r0ykYAAqLxc?t=1432
18. All quotes from Rodney P come from an interview with RBMA https://daily.redbullmusicacademy.com/2013/06/london-posse-rodney-p-interview
19. Statistic from https://www.ethnicity-facts-figures.service.gov.uk/crime-justice-and-the-law/policing/stop-and-search/latest

CHAPTER 2

1. Quote from a first-person interview with Trevor Jackson, 2023.
2. Tricky interview with The Guardian - https://www.theguardian.com/music/2019/oct/14/tricky-interview
3. Daddy G interview with The Observer - https://www.theguardian.com/music/2012/oct/28/massive-attack-blue-lines-remaster#:~:text=For%20the%20recording%20of%20Blue,co%2D-writing%20on%20three%20songs. via The Observer, 2004

4. Tricky interview with Simon Reynolds for SPIN, September 1999.
5. Mark Fisher, *Ghosts of my Life: Writings on Depression, Hauntology + Lost Futures, (2014). P.40*
6. Tricky interview with *The Wire*, Issue 294, August 2018.
7. Tricky interview with David Bowie for Q, January 1995.
8. Quote by the poet Byron Vincent from the BBC, https://www.bbc.co.uk/news/magazine-26254706
9. Blak Twang interview with Bonafide magazine http://www.bonafidemag.com/blak-twang-interview/
10. All quotes from Will Ashon are taken from a first-person interview in 2021 (unless stated otherwise)
11. William J Samarin, *Tongues of men and angels: the religious language of Pentecostalism* (1972). p.126.
12. Roots Manuva interview with the *Independent* https://www.independent.co.uk/arts-entertainment/music/features/roots-manuva-interview-why-britain-s-greatest-rapper-swapped-tottenham-leafy-surrey-10234556.html
13. Roots Manuva interview with RBMA https://www.redbullmusicacademy.com/lectures/roots-manuva-son-of-a-preacher-man
14. All quotes from an email interview with producer, DJ, and MC Wayne "Lotek" Bennett from 2021.
15. *Pitchfork* review of *Brand New Second Hand* by Roots Manuva - https://pitchfork.com/reviews/albums/5099-brand-new-secondhand/ , 1999.
16. Stevie Chick, *20 Years of Beats & Pieces: Ninja Tune* (2010), quote from Roots Manuva pp.116.
17. Stevie Chick, 20 Years of Beats & Pieces: Ninja Tune (2010), quote from Roots Manuva pp.116.
18. All quotes throughout are taken from a first person interview with rapper and producer Juice Aleem in 2021.
19. Ty interview with Channel 4 News https://www.channel4.com/news/the-west-african-children-brought-up-by-white-foster-families-in-the-english-countryside.

20. Unless stated, all quotes throughout are taken from a first-person interview with Ty 2011.
21. All quotes on this page are from Ty's interview with *The Independent* in 2008.

CHAPTER 3

1. Statistic taken from an article by Daniel Boffey and Phillip Inman for *The Guardian https://www.theguardian.com/cities/2016/nov/19/brain-drain-southward-310000-graduates-left-north-ten-years*
2. All quotes in this chapter are taken from a Lewis Parker interview with UKHH (unless stated otherwise) https://ukhh.com/lewis-parker-exclusive-interview-with-ukhh-com/
3. All quotes are from a person interview with Will Shields, aka MC and producer Jehst, from 2021.
4. Farma G interview with BritishHipHop.co.uk - https://old.britishhiphop.co.uk/ukhiphop/artists/task_force.htm
5. *Lotek fondly recalled to me the time he saw Juice Aleem beat Angel Face Terror in the final of Cream of the Crop, Juice 'Managed to fit 'bovine spongiform encephalopathy' into a freestyle. Weirdly, the final was only one round each so Angel Face Terror was not given a chance to reply to Juice having gone first. I would love that to have gone to (a) second round, I don't think the outcome would have been the same. Angel Face Terror, changed his name to Chester P Hackenbush not long after that battle.' Juice chuckled and did not recall the event when I put the tongue twister to him.*
6. Quote by the writer Simon Reynolds, Perfect Sound Forever - http://www.furious.com/perfect/simonreynolds31.html
7. A phrase I've happily pillaged from Scott Plagenhoef's review of *A Grand Don't Come For Free* for *Pitchfork* https://pitchfork.com/reviews/albums/7533-a-grand-dont-come-for-free/

8. Mike Skinner interview with the BBC http://news.bbc.co.uk/2/hi/entertainment/2262033.stm
9. All data from https://bestsellingalbums.org/artist/13229

CHAPTER 4

1. Dingwalls is a live music venue, and bar in Camden, North London.
2. Although the source for the quote is unclear, this is a reference to the conspiracy theory that Nostradamus, the fifteenth-century French apothecary turned writer, predicted the 9/11 attacks based on writing that included '*Two steel birds will fall from the sky on the Metropolis*', although the provenance of this text is highly contentions as steel suitable for aeroplanes wasn't invented until 1854, nearly 200 years after Nostradamus died.
3. The Jazz Cafe is an iconic live music venue, also based in Camden, North London.
4. Marcus Rashford is a professional footballer for England and a small team from Manchester. In 2019, he led a campaign for a Free School Meals campaign, ultimately leading to the UK Government contributing £400m over 12 months to support poorer families with the cost of food and household bills during the COVID-19 pandemic.
5. This statistic is based on an All-Party Parliamentary Group (APPG) analysis on Knife Crime. More information can be found here - http://www.preventknifecrime.co.uk/wp-content/uploads/2020/03/Securing-a-brighter-future-the-role-of-youth-services-in-tackling-knife-crime-v.2.pdf
6. This is a reference *to the company CoreCivic, formerly Corrections Corporation of America (CCA), that in 2012 contacted 48 states, offering to buy prisons from them in exchange for a 20-year management contract with a guaranteed occupancy*

rate of 90%. Two of the largest shareholders in CoreCivic are the investment management companies Vanguard Group Incorporated and BlackRock, who also have significant shares in Warner Music, Sony Music, and media giants Viacom. Full disclosure: I once worked for Viacom, somewhat uneasily in this context.

CHAPTER 5

1. All quotes are from a first-person interview with Sarah Love, December 2021
2. All quotes by Vincent Olutayo, from a feature on Deal Real for *Bonafide magazine*, issue 10, 2015
3. Quote by Doc Brown, from a feature on Deal Real for *FACT* - https://www.factmag.com/2015/04/04/deal-real/
4. *Ibid.*
5. *Ibid.*
6. Klashnekoff quote from a feature on Terra Firma for *UKHH* - https://ukhh.com/terra-firma-interview/
7. Reference from filmtheory.org, author unknown - https://www.filmtheory.org/body-horror/
8. Ms. Dynamite interview with *The Guardian* - https://www.theguardian.com/music/2011/may/22/ms-dynamite-interview-neva-soft 2011
9. Quote by Maxwell D from a feature on garage fashion for *RBMA* - https://daily.redbullmusicacademy.com/2019/02/uk-garage-fashion
10. DJ Target interview with *i.D.* - https://i-d.vice.com/en_uk/article/a3vbk5/danny-weed-and-dj-target-discuss-the-history-of-grime
11. Megaman interview with *Vlad TV* https://youtu.be/7f8WCZd-kVrQ
12. Mc Harvey interview with *The Independent* newspaper

13. Quote from Ms Dynamite. From an article on gun culture for *The Guardian* https://www.theguardian.com/uk/2003/jan/06/ukguns.immigrationpolicy1 2003
14. Simon Reynolds for *The Wire* https://web.archive.org/web/20190925150047/https://www.thewire.co.uk/in-writing/essays/p=14844

CHAPTER 6

1. Napster: The Black Market that Publicly Dominated the Music Industry, academic essay by Elliott Obermaier for Indiana University https://iu.pressbooks.pub/perspectives3/chapter/napster-the-black-market-that-publicly-dominated-the-mu-sic-industry/#:~:text=Without%20the%20legal%20rights%20to,was%20fueled%20by%20its%20popularity.
2. JME interview with *VICE* https://www.vice.com/en/article/6ad-mdg/youneedtohearthis-jme-talks-technology *2013*
3. Unpacking new labour's 'Urban Renaissance' agenda: Towards a socially sustainable reurbanization of British cities? Academic paper by Claire Colomb https://www.tandfonline.com/doi/full/10.1080/02697450701455249
4. Dr. Joy White, *Terraformed: Young Black Lives in the Inner City. (2020).* pp.24
5. First-person interview with Elijah, 2021
6. First-person interview with DJ Target (together with Benji B and DJ Target for a '1xtra round table') for Bonafide magazine, 2010
7. First-person interview with Logan Sama, 2023
8. All quotes from a first person interview with Martin Clark, 2021
9. Dizzee Rascal interview with *DJ Mag* - Dizzee Rascal interview - https://www.youtube.com/watch?v=Juvpr1tV7f0&ab_chan-nel=DJMag
10. *Ibid.*

11. Richard Russell quote from the documentary *Together We Rise* - https://youtu.be/VrcfJBSvyH0?t=405
12. A title he has been forced to relinquish after being cancelled for a bizarre and sprawling antisemitic tirade on social media in Summer 2020.
13. Wiley interview with Time Out - https://www.timeout.com/music/wiley-you-want-to-know-the-truth-im-gonna-tell-you-the-truth
14. Son Raw for Complex UK, *Treddin On Thin Ice* revisited - https://www.complex.com/music/2016/04/wiley-treddin-on-thin-ice-revisited
15. First person interview with with Bruza for *ukhh.com*, 2005
16. First person interview with Juice Aleem, 2021

CHAPTER 7

1. Rodney P quote from Huck - https://www.huckmag.com/art-and-culture/music-2/how-hip-hop-magazines-shaped-uk-rap-as-we-know-it/
2. In-person interview with Andy Cowan (2021)
3. Dan Hancox, *Inner City Pressure: The Story of Grime* (2018). p.81.
4. All quotes from a first-person interview with DJ Excalibah (2022)
5. Quote from Ian Parkinson for *The Guardian* - https://www.theguardian.com/media/2002/aug/19/bbc.race
6. Quote from Jammer from *Home Invasion: The Story of Channel U* (Documentary) | Link Up TV Originals - https://youtu.be/8_TboeIWh_o
7. Quote from *Home Invasion: The Story of Channel U* (Documentary) | Link Up TV Originals - https://youtu.be/8_TboeIWh_o
8. First-person interview with Lethal Bizzle for UKHH.com (2006)

9. Both Cat, Stuart, and all artists quotes on this page are from *Home Invasion: The Story of Channel U* (Documentary) | Link Up TV Originals - https://youtu.be/8_TboeIWh_o

CHAPTER 8

1. Alex Petridis review of *Home Sweet Home* by Kano, for The Guardian https://www.theguardian.com/music/2005/jun/17/popandrock.shopping5
2. First person interview with DJ Target, 2010.
3. Grime is dead. Didn't you know? Article for RWD Magazine, May 2007.
4. All quotes throughout the chapter come from a first-person interview that took place with Logan Sama in 2023.
5. Dan Hancox for *The Guardian* - https://www.theguardian.com/culture/2009/jan/21/police-form-696-garage-music
6. *Ibid.*
7. *Inner City Pressure*, Dan Hancox. P.173
8. Andrew Orlowski for *The Register* - https://www.theregister.com/2008/11/11/met_police_live_music_terror_trawl/
9. *Inner City Pressure*, Dan Hancox. P.176
10. P Money quote from the BBC article -
11. Giggs interview with Lilly Allen for i.D. https://i-d.vice.com/en/article/d3x3xw/why-giggs-is-brilliant-by-lily-allen
12. Leroy Logan for Tortoise Media - https://www.tortoisemedia.com/2020/09/02/200902-police-and-music/
13. Statistic borrowed from *Rolling Stone* magazine https://www.rollingstone.com/pro/news/music-is-finally-making-more-money-than-it-was-in-2007-816480/
14. Sway interview with GRM Daily - https://youtu.be/erBH-3VMTgzs
15. London Gang Culture. Ep. 14 - https://youtu.be/Uza-JIzYix-k?t=126

16. Skepta & JME interview at *Krispy Kreme*, 2005 - https://youtu.be/0XdGiVDMgvk?t=26
17. JME Alumni profile - https://alumni.gre.ac.uk/yourstories/jamie-adenuga/
18. Boy Better Know company accounts, 2021 - https://find-and-update.company-information.service.gov.uk/company/06775928/filing-history
19. Skepta interview with Red Bull Music Academy, 2008 - https://www.youtube.com/watch?v=k_45NF8uJvo&ab_channel=RedBullMusicAcademy
20. *Ibid.*
21. Interview from The Evolution of Ghetts: Chapter 1 - https://youtu.be/ffX6cnd00eM?t=287
22. *Ibid.* Chapter 3 - https://youtu.be/S0FngoNOz9o?t=292
23. *Ibid.* https://youtu.be/S0FngoNOz9o?t=260
24. Akala interview with Revolt TV - https://www.revolt.tv/article/2016-12-21/22730/ten-years-of-akala-how-the-uk-artist-has-maintained-his-independence/
25. Orwell, George (1949). *Nineteen Eighty-Four.* Martin Secker & Warburg Ltd, London, part 1, chapter 3, pp 32
26. Lil Simz interview with *VICE* - https://www.vice.com/en/article/little-simz-interview-2016/

CHAPTER 9

1. Data courtesy of a 2021 UK Music Diversity Taskforce report
2. p.40 *Flip the Script*, by Arusa Qureshi (2019)
3. Genius Cru was the late '90s/early '00s garage collective that experienced chart success with the singles 'I Say It's Time For Action' and 'Course Bruv', reaching number 12 and 39 in the singles chart
4. The 'golden hour' refers to the last hour before sunset and the first hour after sunrise, often coveted by film directors, photographers, and media professional poseurs.

CHAPTER 10

1. Data courtesy of The Office for National Statistics (ONS)
2. J. L. Mackie, *Ethics: Inventing Right and Wrong*. Pp. 48 (1977).
3. Richard Garner, "Abolishing Morality". *A World Without Values*. pp. 217–233 (2009).
4. All quotes from Benji B, DJ Target and Mista Jam are from a first person interview in 2010
5. As told to Dan Hancox, *Inner City Pressure*. Pp. 203 (2018).
6. Data provided by Statista - https://www.statista.com/statistics/325479/consumer-spending-on-music-in-the-uk-by-format/
7. Data provided by Statista - https://www.statista.com/statistics/1012080/uk-monthly-numbers-facebook-users/
8. Report on Lockheed Martin, from *The Guardian*, 2011 - https://www.theguardian.com/uk/2011/feb/19/census-boycott-lockheed-martin
9. Ghetts interview with GlobalFaction YouTube https://youtu.be/iNz7d8TyX4A?feature=shared&t=486
10. Lowkey interview with Vice https://www.vice.com/en/article/597mdn/lowkey-return-interview-uk-rap-2019
11. David Lammy article for *The Guardian* - https://www.theguardian.com/commentisfree/2021/jul/30/tottenham-social-alienation-riots-tory-governments-family-youth-police
12. Dan Hancox article for *The Guardian* - https://www.theguardian.com/music/2011/feb/03/pow-forward-lethal-bizzle-protests

CHAPTER 11

1. Quote from art historian Walter S. Gibson taken from the biography of Hieronymous Bosch - https://www.hieronymus-bosch.org/biography

2. First person interview with The Purist 2022
3. https://web.archive.org/web/20130622103712/http://sbtv.co.uk:80/2013/06/sb-tv-exclusive-interview-cas/
4. Hua Hsu, Stay True (2022). p.81
5. Charles Taylor, *Sources of the Self: The Making of Modern Identity* (1989). P.32
6. Little Simz quote from an interview with The Gentle Woman - https://thegentlewoman.co.uk/library/little-simz
7. Little Simz writing on her Bandcamp page https://littlesimz.bandcamp.com/album/age-101-drop-3-000, 2014
8. All quotes with Rob Swerdlow are from a first-person interview, 2024
9. Jia Tolentina review of *A Curious Tale of Trials + Persons* for Pitchfork https://pitchfork.com/reviews/albums/21107-a-curious-tale-of-trials-persons/
10. Quoted from '53 of the Best Feminine Anthems of All Time' from *Harpers Bazaar*- https://www.harpersbazaar.com/culture/art-books-music/a18832473/best-feminist-women-empowerment-songs/
11. Charles Taylor, *Sources of the Self: The Making of Modern Identity* (1989). P.43

CHAPTER 12

1. Quote from Rahel Aklilu from Ode to the Wifey Riddim https://medium.com/@rahellowrites/an-ode-to-the-wifey-riddim-d2276801e9d6
2. All quotes from Mumdance were shared over email 2024
3. Novelist interview with *The Guardian* - https://www.theguardian.com/lifeandstyle/2016/dec/10/mc-novelist-grime-music-interview (2016)
4. Quote from Akala originally posted on his Facebook page, later published on *The Guardian* - https://www.theguardian.com/

commentisfree/2017/may/12/never-voted-before-jeremy-corbyn-changed-mind

5. JME interview with Jeremy Corbyn for *i-D* https://youtu.be/A-rxp_QwjmQ?feature=shared&t=327
6. Statistics from YouGov - How Britain Voted at the 2017 general elections - https://yougov.co.uk/politics/articles/18384-how-britain-voted-2017-general-election
7. Boy Better Know interview with *The Guardian* - https://www.theguardian.com/music/2017/jun/22/boy-better-know-we-should-have-been-playing-big-festivals-six-years-ago
8. Theresa May writing in the *Evening Standard* - https://www.standard.co.uk/comment/comment/i-made-mistakes-but-one-year-on-i-m-going-green-for-grenfell-writes-theresa-may-a3860046.html
9. Lowkey quoted from a panel discussion on lessons from Salvador Allende's Chile, as quoted in *The Canary* https://www.thecanary.co/trending/2019/06/26/grenfell-is-an-example-of-how-neoliberalism-kills-people-says-lowkey/

CHAPTER 14

1. Simon Clark, writing in the preface for Kit Mackintosh's *Neon Dreams: How Drill, Trap and Bashment Made Music New Again*, (2021). P.12
2. Section Boyz interview with the *Independent* - https://inews.co.uk/culture/music/smoke-boys-section-boyz-grime-757922
3. Stormzy quote from a Section Boyz feature for *VICE* - https://www.vice.com/en/article/section-boyz-break-up-reflect-on-legacy/
4. All quotes from Skengdo and AM are from a first person interview in 2024
5. Felicity Martin writing about music and censorship for DMY

https://dmy.co/features/behind-bars-uk-banning-music-censor-drill-alarming-new-ground

6. Data courtesy of Freedom of Information act via a report from Will Pritchard for VICE https://www.vice.com/en/article/met-police-youtube-drill-music-removal/
7. All quotes are from a First person interview with Post in spring 2024
8. All quotes and data are from the study, Compound Injustice: A Review of Cases Involving Rap Music Evidence in England and Wales (2024), by Eithne Quinn, Erica Kane, and Will Pritchard for the University of Manchester. chrome-extension://efaidnbmnnnibpcajpcglclefindmkaj/https://documents.manchester.ac.uk/display.aspx?DocID=72455
9. J Hus interview with VICE https://www.vice.com/en/article/j-hus-interview-2017-common-sense/
10. Quote from Chris Rich Beats from an article for *DJ Mag* - https://djmag.com/longreads/these-are-most-exciting-uk-drill-producers-right-now
11. Quoted from *The Economist* - https://www.economist.com/britain/2021/01/30/grime-and-uk-drill-are-exporting-multicultural-london-english

CHAPTER 16

1. All quotes from a first person interview with Tion Wayne published by Notion in 2020 unless stated.
2. Quote from a Tion Wayne interview with *The Guardian* 2021 https://www.theguardian.com/music/2021/sep/17/rapper-tion-wayne-police-dont-want-us-to-win-they-want-us-in-jail
3. All quotes from a first person interview with Fraser T Smith originally published on Dazed 2021 https://www.dazeddigital.com/music/article/47986/1/fraser-t-smith-producer-songwriter-interview
4. Quote from Fred Again on Instagram, 2019

ACKNOWLEDGEMENTS

Firstly, all thanks to the MCs, DJs, and producers who made the music that inspired several generations of listeners and new creators ready to continue a rich legacy of UK MC culture. Hip-hop, garage, grime, drill, or Afrobeats—it doesn't matter, and it also matters immensely. You all deserve your flowers, and it has been a privilege and an honour to help tell some of your stories. Thanks to the fifty-plus people who kindly gave them time in interviews, plus the many more who helped set them up.

Props to Billy Issac and Paul Kane for reading early drafts of the book. To Andy Cowan and Laurent Fintoni, thank you for the valuable tips on becoming a first-time author, Ben "MC English" Hawkins and Jamie "Groovement" Ernesto for the local insights.

Thanks to Colin Steven at Velocity Press for your faith in my idea; we got there in the end. And to Ryan Pinkard, my editor, who did an incredible job and provided several much-needed pep talks. Big up to Trevor Jackson, who took my chaotic cover design brief and hit the nail square on the head with a sledgehammer.

Finally, and most importantly, family. Thanks to Mum, who, along with Dad, brought me up to have a deep appreciation for music, my kids, in-laws (for looking after our many children over the summer and giving me some much-needed headspace), and, most especially, my wife, who showed incredible patience during the many late nights and early starts spent writing this book.

Special thanks to everyone who pre-ordered the book. Your support means a great deal.

Gleb Albert, Adam Ballantyne, Lee Ballen, Joel Baker, Kieron Barrett, Angus Batey, Louis Bloomberg, Jesse Boyce, Daniel Brooks, Matt Brown, Elliott Carson, Benjamin Cheung, Nick Clark, Robert Clegg, S J Cook, Adam Curtis, Lee Davis, Mike Davis, Richard Denahy, Nilesh Deshmukh, James Egan, Matt Fergusson, Tim Forrester, Matthew Francis, Owen Green, Joe Grundy, Matthew Gyngell, Ian Halliday, David Hannam, Ben Harris, Joel Harris, Lev Harris, Benjamin Hatton, Ben Hawkins, Steve Howard, William Isaac, Adnan Jamil-Mir, Anita Kane, Lee Kane, Simon Kelly, Andrea Lai, Jamie Lang, Adam Levy, Mike Lewis, Barbara Lindgren, Patrik Lindgren, Daniel Luper, Jonathan Lynch, Paul Mann, Gabriel Millet, Charlotte Mitchener, Anna Nathanson, Ida Nordgren, Tega Okor, Joshua Owide, Saul Owide, Terry Paleologos, Gilles Pariente, Clifford Kumar Perianayagam, Lauri Piipponen, Renaud Ploquin, Dean Posthuma, Sarah Ramsey, Chris Rang, Nicolas Rapp, Ariane Sherine, Richard Stacey, Lee Stuart, Daniel Suter, Mik Tanate, David Taylor, Werner Thenmayer, John Trevains, Natalie Williams, Tom Wood